PATERNOSTER BIBLICAL MONOGRAPHS

Praying Lament Psalms

The Psychodynamics of Distress

PATERNOSTER BIBLICAL MONOGRAPHS

Praying Lament Psalms

The Psychodynamics of Distress

David J. Cohen

Copyright © David J. Cohen 2016

First published 2016 by Paternoster

Paternoster is an imprint of Authentic Media Limited
PO Box 6326, Bletchley, Milton Keynes, MK1 9GG
authenticmedia.co.uk

The right of David J. Cohen to be identified as the Author of this Work
has been asserted by him in accordance with the Copyright, Designs
and Patents Act 1988.

All rights reserved. No part of this publication may be reproduced, stored in a retrieval system, or transmitted, in any form or by any means, electronic, mechanical, photocopying, recording or otherwise, without the prior permission of the publisher or a licence permitting restricted copying. In the UK such licences are issued by the Copyright Licensing Agency Ltd, Barnard's Inn, 86 Fetter Lane, London, EC4A 1EN.

British Library Cataloguing in Publication Data
A catalogue record for this book is available from the British Library

ISBN 978-1-84227-844-4
978-1-78078-073-3 (e-book)

Printed and bound by Lightning Source

Series Preface

One of the major objectives of Paternoster is to serve biblical scholarship by providing a channel for the publication of theses and other monographs of high quality at affordable prices. Paternoster stands within the broad evangelical tradition of Christianity. Our authors would describe themselves as Christians who recognize the authority of the Bible, maintain the centrality of the gospel message and assent to the classical creedal statements of Christian belief. There is diversity within the constituency; advances in scholarship are possible only if there is freedom for frank debate on controversial issues and for the publication of new and sometimes provocative proposals. What is offered in this series is the best of writing by committed Christians who are concerned to develop well-founded biblical scholarship in a spirit of loyalty to the historic faith.

Series Editors

I. Howard Marshall	Honorary Research professor of New Testament, University of Aberdeen, Scotland, UK
Richard J. Bauckham	Professor of New Testament Studies and Bishop Wardlaw professor, University of St Andrews, Scotland, UK
Craig Blomberg	Distinguished Professor of New Testament, Denver Seminary, Colorado, USA
Robert P. Gordon	Regius Professor of Hebrew, University of Cambridge, UK
Stanley E. Porter	President and Professor of New Testament, McMaster Divinity College, Hamilton, Ontario, Canada

Contents

Acknowledgements	xi
Abbreviations	xii
Chapter 1: Introduction	3
Background to the study	3
Aim and scope of the study	5
Overview of the study	5
Chapter 2: Signposts in Scholarship	8
Signpost 1- Lament: What's in a name?	8
Two forms	8
Lament	9
Complaint	10
Disorientation	11
Psalms of distress	12
Signpost 2 – Cultic function and ritual	13
Cultic function	13
Ritual	14
Signpost 3 – Discourse and dialectic	24
Narrative	24
Poetry	26
Dialogue or dialectic?	32
Signpost 4 – Form and meaning-making	37
Form	37
Structure	38
Meaning-making	39
Signpost 5 – Speech act and prayer	41
Speech acts	42
Prayer	46
Reflections	49

Chapter 3: The Matrix of Lament: A Model   52
    Expressing constellation   55
    Asserting constellation   60
    Investing constellation   63
    Imagining constellation   67
    The characters within psalms of distress   70
        The 'psychological' relationship   71
        The 'theological' relationship   71
        The 'social' relationship   72

Chapter 4: Lament process in practice   75
    The function of lament process   75
        Who is a lament process for?   76
        What does a lament process provide?   78
        How can a lament process be engaged?   82
    Lament process and meaning-making   86
        The nature of God and psalms of distress   86
        The nature of humankind and psalms of distress   88
        The relationship between God and humankind in psalms of distress   89

Chapter 5: The psychodynamics of distress   92
    Implications for processing lament   93
        Cognition   95
        Affect   97
        Experience   98
    Aspects of psychodynamic change   99
        Levels of distress   99
        Locus of control   100
        Sense of relationship with God   102

Chapter 6: Research design   105
    Research methodology   106
    Method   107
    Research instruments   111
        Personal journal   111
        Selected psalms of distress   112
        Psychometric tests   117
    Selection of participants   119

Chapter 7: Results from action research   120
    Formulation of the group   120

Initial group meeting	120
Individual participant summaries	121
Participant 1 – John	121
Participant 2 – Charles	126
Participant 3 – Anton	130
Participant 4 – Jim	134
Participant 5 – Peter	138
Participant 6 – Samuel	142
Participant 7 – Joan	146
Participant 8 – Sandra	150
Participant 9 – Julie	155
Participant 10 – Tanya	159
Participant 11 – Fran	162
Participant 12 – Donna	166
Final group session	167
Level of distress	168
Locus of control	168
Sense of relationship with God	169
Summary	170
Chapter 8 – Discussion	**173**
Chapter 9 – Conclusions	**203**
Appendix 1 – Matrix of lament	**206**
Appendix 2 – Summary: Matrix of lament with explanation	**207**
Appendix 3 – Ritual and prayer	**209**
Appendix 4 – Coded psalms of distress	**211**
Appendix 5 – One-on-one interview questions	**218**
Appendix 6 – Final group discussion questions	**219**
Appendix 7 – DASS questionnaire	**220**
Appendix 8 – Locus of control questionnaire	**222**
Appendix 9 – Spiritual assessment inventory	**224**
Appendix 10 – DASS and Locus of control results	**227**
Appendix 11 – Spiritual assessment inventory results	**230**

Bibliography	233
Author index	248
Subject index	250

Acknowledgements

Completing this research and its subsequent publication marks the end of a journey which began formally in 2002, even though the 'seed' ideas explored here were planted almost twenty years earlier in the context of pastoral work. Research such as this does not come without the commitment of others who have supported, encouraged, advised and shared the journey at various points, or walked the whole distance with me. I thank my family whose patience and reality often bought me back to earth when I needed it. My wife, Christine, has been an invaluable encouragement as we often discussed and wrestled with the ideas I encountered along the way. Christine's ability to see my research through her own particular lens of expertise and her willingness to share her insights and ideas have been greatly beneficial to my ongoing discoveries. I also thank my two sons, Ashleigh and Jayden, for the patience with me and encouragement of me to complete the task I had set myself.

During the years of research I have been privileged to work with two outstanding academics as my supervisors. Dr. Nancy Ault and Dr. Alex Main have been honest, patient and always encouraging as the have helped me in so many ways to complete this research. Their ability to critique my work fairly and thoroughly has been invaluable and enabled me constantly to refine the research I have completed.

Finally, I wish to thank the Principal and staff of Vose Seminary, where I teach. for their unwavering support and encouragement. Finally, I acknowledge the support of Dr. Michael Parsons, a former colleague and friend, for his proofreading of my work and for keeping on track towards publication.

David J Cohen
Vose Seminary (Australian College of Theology)
August 2015

Abbreviations

CE	Common Era
DASS	Depression, Anxiety and Stress Scale
JSOT	Journal for the Study of the Old Testament
LOC	Locus of Control
NRSV	New Revised Standard Version
Ps.	Psalm
Pss.	Psalms
SAI	Spiritual Assessment Inventory
TNIV	Today's New International Version
Trans.	Translation

CHAPTER 1

Introduction

Background to the study

The Psalter, as a collection of prayers, acts as a window into the nature of humankind, a window into human experience, and even a mirror in which we can see ourselves vividly reflected.[1] Perhaps the psalms which resonate most deeply with our humanity are the lament psalms. These psalms voice a sense of brokenness and vulnerability common to human experience and the strong desire of human beings to reach wholeness. The intentional and systematic use of lament psalms, constituting a major genre within the Psalter, throughout Judeo-Christian history self-evidently reinforces their significance.[2] The nature of the Psalter and its common use prompted John Calvin to conclude:

> I have been accustomed to call this, I think not inappropriately, 'An Anatomy of All Parts of the Soul'; for there is not an emotion of which anyone can be conscious that is not here represented as in a mirror. Or rather, the Holy Spirit has here drawn to the life all the griefs, sorrows, fears, doubt, hopes, cares, perplexities, in short all the distracting emotions with which human minds are wont to be agitated.[3]

The aesthetic qualities of the psalms and the wide gamut of experience expressed within them have provided a substantial resource for articulating deep emotion and thinking about God, self and others. There is a sense of timelessness about the psalms yet those who wrote them, and those who have used them, share in the familiar experiences of life so markedly expressed throughout the Psalter. It is for this reason that the Psalter has always featured prominently in Judeo-Christian history as people have sought to express themselves in authentic ways to God.

---

[1] Thomas Merton, *The Signs of Jonas* (New York: Image, 1956), 248. Merton captures the concept well, stating, 'This is the secret of the Psalms. Our identity is hidden in them. In them we find ourselves, and God. In these fragments He is revealed not only Himself to us but ourselves to Him.'
[2] David J Cohen, 'Usage of the Psalms During the Post-Exilic Period up to 200 CE.' (Murdoch University, 1990). This study explored the issue from an historical perspective.
[3] John Calvin, *A Commentary on the Psalms*, vol. 1, trans. T.H.L. Parker (London: James Clark, 1965), 16.

Over the past hundred years, in particular, scholars have explored and explained the Psalter in many ways, in part attempting to understand why such prominent use has persisted in much of Judeo-Christian history and tradition. Diversity in more recent approaches to researching the psalms could be broadly viewed as three distinct and yet complementary perspectives. First, there are those scholars whose programme has focused on the original *Sitz im Leben* of psalms.[4] Second, some have focused more particularly on the literary content of various types of psalms in terms of language, style and genre.[5] Third, there are those who have explored the practical application of the Psalter within the contexts of pastoral care and worship.[6] Emerging from this rich seedbed of research is a significant conversation about the relevance of lament psalms as a useful pathway for engagement with, and expression of, distress forming a normative feature of both personal and communal devotion.

Considering historical context, literary style and practical use of the Psalter as a whole and viewing these three approaches as complementary in nature provokes an important question: 'What might the efficacy be for individuals in using lament psalms as a pathway for engaging with personal distress?' Responding to this question provides a focus for this study. An extensive literature review, as part of this study, suggests that empirical research into the rôle of lament as a form of prayer and its potential efficacy for people faced with distress has not been previously undertaken.

The challenge to respond to this gap in the research arises for two equally significant reasons. First, the lack of specific action research in the area and, second, the reality that within my particular faith tradition use of the psalms in an intentional or systematic way has diminished and has not been encouraged. This has been acutely evident during the latter part of the twentieth century.[7] Decreasing use is evident within three broad contexts: personal devotion, pastoral care and corporate worship. However, this observation is not to suggest a total absence of the use of psalms. Rather, in my faith tradition, the occasional use in

---

[4] This term is commonly used in the study of the Psalter to indicate the possible original setting in life of particular psalms. Notable scholars employing the phrase are Kraus (1988, 1989) and Weiser (1962).

[5] Cf. Walter Brueggemann, *The Message of the Psalms: A Theological Commentary* (Minneapolis: Augsburg, 1984), Erhard S. Gerstenberger, *Psalms Part I*, vol. 14, The Forms of Old Testament Literature (Grand Rapids: Eerdmans, 1988), Hermann Gunkel, *The Psalms* (Philadelphia: Fortress, 1987).

[6] E.g. Kathleen D. Billman and Daniel L. Migliore, *Rachel's Cry: Prayer of Lament and the Rebirth of Hope* (Cleveland: United Church, 1999).

[7] While it could be argued that both the Baptist and Churches of Christ traditions, with which I have experience, have historically made some use of lectionary readings, including readings from the Psalter, a systematic and intentional employment of the Psalter generally, and lament psalms specifically, as a constituent of personal devotion or corporate worship has diminished in the twentieth century.

any of these settings is normally limited to psalms which fall into the category of praise or thanksgiving. Sadly, psalms of lament have largely been ignored.

Aim and Scope of the Study

Therefore, the aim of this study is to examine the psychodynamic effects on individuals using lament psalms intentionally, in the form of ritual prayer, as a way of engaging with experiences of personal distress.[8] The study focuses only on a particular, defined use and efficacy of what scholars often refer to as the *individual* lament psalms.[9] The nomenclature attached to these psalms rests on Gunkel's seminal work in identifying various *Gattungen* within the Psalter.[10]

The use of selected individual lament psalms in this study is based on a theoretical framework which considers the historical use of these psalms, the literary features of the text itself and the nature of literature as prayer and speech act. Also, the study examines the significance and implications of ritual behaviour as part of a process incorporating lament psalms. The research also necessarily involves an examination of issues regarding the role of ritual, discourse analysis, literary form, speech act theory, prayer and the potential psychodynamic efficacy of such material. While these issues contribute to forming a theoretical model for such a study the action research component seeks ultimately to examine the efficacy of using individual lament psalms.

Overview of the Study

To achieve the aim of the study, chapter two examines five signposts in psalms research relevant to both an understanding and use of lament psalms. The goal of the examination is to highlight the relevant contribution of scholars on a diverse number of fronts, thus forming a foundation for this study. From this foun-

---

[8] The terms psychodynamic, lament and ritual will be defined for the purposes of this study in following chapters.

[9] It is beyond the scope of this study to incorporate an examination of communal psalms of lament in such a way. However, an earlier study of the lament genre demonstrated that the matrix of lament applies to both the individual and communal forms of lament. The study also noted that while a distinction between individual and communal forms is evident in literary terms this does not preclude the usage of individual laments by communities nor communal laments by individuals (David J. Cohen, 'The Potential Function of the Lament Psalms and the Relevance of This to the Practice of Spiritual Direction with Both Individuals and Communities of Faith' (Murdoch University, 1999).

[10] *Gattungen* is the German term coined by Gunkel to identify different genres of psalms—in Gunkel, *The Psalms* (Philadephia: Fortress, 1987). It denotes a wide variety of major and minor types of psalms including individual lament. Although scholars have approached and understood individual lament psalms in a diversity of ways Gunkel's terminology has been retained at this point. Further discussion of the appropriate term for identifying these psalms will be entered into in chapter two where the nature of biblical lament will be more fully explored and defined.

dation a theoretical model is developed to explicate the nature and potential present-day function of the individual lament as prayer within the wider body of the Psalter. As a result, individual lament psalms are shown to be more than a collection of prayers which both record and voice the experience of distress for individuals in the past. They can also be viewed as a rich resource for individuals to engage with distress in daily life.

Chapter three explores, in detail, the theoretical model characterized as a matrix of lament, providing a lens through which the text of individual lament psalms can be viewed for the practical purposes of this study. An exploration of the theoretical model highlights both the literary nature of lament and the potential dynamic of the text as a way of engaging distress and promoting psychodynamic transformation. The four major elements (expressing — asserting — investing — imagining) of the proposed matrix are defined and brought into sharp focus.

Chapter four provides a background survey of ways in which lament, as a process, has been used in practice as a way of engaging with distress. The more recent work of pastoral theologians is considered in particular. The survey includes various perspectives on both specific and generalized distress being faced by individuals and/or communities.

Chapter five explores the nature and direction of three potential psychodynamic changes for individuals engaging with distress through individual lament psalms. These changes are embedded in the matrix of lament presented in chapter three. They are as follows:

- Level of distress
- Locus of control
- Sense of relationship

The first potential psychodynamic change is that of the level of distress being experienced by an individual because of personal distress. The second is the sense of control, or empowerment, the individual experiences. This psychodynamic change is characterized as locus of control. The third is the sense of well-being in the individual's relationship with self, God and others and the potential for movement from isolation to intimacy.

Chapter six presents the action research design which connects the matrix of lament, as the theoretical framework, with the research on the role of ritual, discourse analysis, literary form, speech act theory and prayer discussed in previous chapters. The goal of the research design is to produce a method for action research, which can then be utilized to examine the efficacy of viewing the individual psalms of lament through the lens of the matrix of lament. In addition, the research design will also seek to evaluate the efficacy of the ritual employed and any indications of change in the three specific psychodynamics identified above. Although these psychodynamics are specifically targeted, the method developed is open-ended, providing opportunities for an examination of any other issues which may emerge.

Introduction

Therefore, the resulting method will introduce a process whereby a group of participants can engage with selected individual lament psalms both practically and reflectively. Various modes of examination employed to explore the usefulness of the selected lament psalms for engaging with distress are both introduced and explicated in chapter six. The modes include a ritual to be followed, an intentional journal reflection process, an interview procedure and a series of psychometric tests. Chapter six will also include a rationale for various aspects of the method including the selection of the designated psalms and the participants for the study.

Chapter seven offers an analysis of the results from the action research. Responses from the interviews, journal reflections, psychometric testing and final group discussion included in the analysis to show exactly what they do or do not demonstrate about the experience of those involved in the research. The analysis focuses initially on the specific experience of each individual participant followed by a general analysis of themes which emerge from discrete groups of participants and/or the cohort as a whole.

Following the in-depth analysis, chapter eight provides a detailed discussion of the results. The final chapter then presents conclusions based on the results from and discussion of the action research. A summary of strengths in this study, any weaknesses identified in the process employed, and areas of further study are subsequently highlighted.

Having charted the general course for this study we now turn to examine, in detail, the most prominent signposts in previous psalm's research. They mark our beginning point and illuminate a pathway for this research to take.

CHAPTER 2

Signposts in Scholarship

The following survey highlights five significant signposts in various areas of scholarship which provide both the background to, and a basis for, understanding the nature and function of lament psalms. In different ways each signpost can also be viewed as contributing to an understanding of the matrix of lament, which will be introduced in chapter three, and the need for action research based on such a model.

Signpost 1	-	Lament: What's in a name?
Signpost 2	-	Cultic function and ritual
Signpost 3	-	Discourse and dialectic
Signpost 4	-	Form and meaning-making
Signpost 5	-	Speech act and prayer

Signpost 1 – Lament: What's in a name?

The first signpost points towards a working definition of lament psalms for this study. In other words, what does the term 'lament' mean, and is there a potentially superior descriptor for this type of psalm encountered in the Psalter?

Two forms

Lament, in the Psalter, exists in two forms. Some laments are distinctly individual while others are communal in nature.[1] As indicated above, the particular lament psalms in focus here will be individual psalms of lament. These psalms provide a context to express views and emotions in response to experiences of distress. They also record an openness and authenticity in expression between the psalmist and God. Claus Westermann argues that while lament may be prayerful in nature it is the context out of which prayer emerges.[2] Walter Brueggemann takes this one step further suggesting the laments act as 'invitation[s] to prayers beyond these words.'[3] His comment highlights the efficacy of the material in being far more than text on a page, or even text that might be a definitive expression of a psalmist's experience. The expression formed in lament psalms may provide a locus of reference as a starting point, for a continuing

---

[1] It has been noted that there are lament psalms that appear to be communal using a collective 'I' as the key identity in the text.

[2] Claus Westermann, *Praise and Lament in the Psalms* (Edinburgh: T&T Clark, 1981), 266.

[3] Walter Brueggemann, *The Psalms in the Life of Faith* (Minneapolis: Fortress, 1995), 33.

and developing articulation of perception and emotion associated with personal distress.

While lament psalms do represent an openness and authenticity to articulate experiences of distress, they rarely provide any clues about their historical context for either the individual or the community. This has caused much discussion among biblical scholars about the psalms' original *Sitz im Leben*. However, the absence of such references in fact strengthens the stereotypical function of these psalms. One result of this is that their continued use in various contexts by people of faith is more easily facilitated. The individual subject, implicit within the lament psalms, is also anonymous. However, as an interesting quirk of history, the later inclusion of attributions to figures such as David, Moses, Solomon and others reinforce a connection between expressing lament and lived experience.

Lament

The most frequently used nomenclature for this genre of psalm is 'lament,' originally identified by Hermann Gunkel. However, while the term is helpful, it can obscure the breadth of expression found in these psalms. For example, 'lament' can suggest the process unfolds more in the form of a soliloquy or monologue. However, it becomes obvious from the content of these psalms, and an understanding of their historical use, that the process is more in the form of a dialectic between the person and themselves, the person and God and the person and their sensed 'enemies.'

In more recent times many scholars have explored the breadth of content in lament. From this several features have been highlighted which are significant in building a more complete picture of both the content, and the function, of these psalms. In the broader scheme Westermann observed the twin themes of praise and lament within the Psalter, as a whole, as counterbalancing each other, suggesting that lament '…has no meaning in and of itself.'[4] He identified a general movement through the Psalter from lament to praise and so, for him, the Psalter culminates in praise. However, it should also be noted that a microcosm of this movement from lament to praise can also be observed *within* most individual lament psalms. Notwithstanding Westermann's perspective it ought not be assumed that the movement through the Psalter, or within individual lament psalms, is uniform or sequential. In fact the Psalter continues to oscillate between the poles of lament and praise from beginning to end.[5] The lament psalms also often reflect the same oscillation between lament and praise internally, perhaps mirroring the chaotic form of expression associated with personal distress. Despite this oscillation there is no question that most of the lament psalms do culminate with an expression of praise directed towards God. These observations, when viewed together, suggest that individual lament psalms reflect the human

---

[4] Westermann, *Praise and Lament in the Psalms*, 266.

[5] Of interest here is the decreasing number of lament psalms and the increasing number of praise psalms present as one moves towards the end of the Psalter.

experience of, and response to, personal distress as an expression of prayer. They also suggest the potential for psychodynamic shifts within the person involved.

Complaint

Gerstenberger prefers to characterize the lament psalms as 'complaints' which were expressed by the psalmist and used as part of a ritual. He concludes that,

> ...individual complaints belonged to the realm of special offices for suffering people whom assisted by their kinsfolk, participated in a service of supplication and curing under the guidance of a ritual expert.[6]

While Gerstenberger's observation is helpful, to limit the use to cultic, ritual occasions, is of course speculative and ignores the possibility of a functional place for these psalms in a broader context. Despite this, Gerstenberger's observations do provide three valuable perspectives. First, he supports expressing complaint as a legitimate form of prayer for members of a faith community. Second, he highlights that such expression was not *improvised* but, rather, an integral part of the ritual of prayer within the community of faith. As a result, these expressions may have promoted movement through critical, distressing, 'threshold' life experiences.[7] A final observation is that 'complaint,' though it may be an expression by an individual of that person's experience, is not disconnected from the community. In fact Gerstenberger's view suggests that lament, by definition, is a process which takes place within the community of faith.

Craig Broyles' position also underlines the 'complaint' nature of lament psalms but also highlights the presence of a definite 'plea.' He correctly points out that it 'pleads a case, so it is an argument.'[8] With the plea in focus it can be noted that lament psalms possess a sense of direction in relationship and resolution of the complaint for the person praying. The psalmist is not content to remain in the place of distress and recognizes the efficacy of expressing their distress to God in the form of a prayer, as a potential pathway towards resolution. Broyles' emphasis on the 'plea,' also reveals something of the fluid nature of the power dynamics within the relationship between the psalmist and themselves, God and others. It also highlights the individual's need to express, to a significant other, the internal turmoil as part of the struggle to progress towards resolving distress. So while the focus on complaint is helpful it is too restrictive to capture the breadth of these psalms.

---

[6] Gerstenberger, *Psalms Part I*, 14.
[7] H.P.V. Renner, 'The Use of Ritual in Pastoral Care,' *Journal of Pastoral Care* 23.3 (1979): 164-74.
[8] Craig C. Broyles, *The Conflict of Faith and Experience in the Psalms: A Form-Critical and Theological Study* (Sheffield: JSOT, 1989), 13.

Disorientation

Brueggemann takes a broader perspective on lament psalms by employing Paul Ricoeur's image of 'disorientation' and describing psalms of lament as 'songs of disorientation.'[9] The term 'disorientation' highlights both the psychological state being portrayed and the relational nature of these psalms. Brueggemann views lament psalms as psalms of disorientation with psalms of praise being psalms of orientation and psalms of thanksgiving being psalms of reorientation. While these three descriptors are helpful in describing features of the various types of psalms it is important to recognize that disorientation, orientation and reorientation are present *within* individual lament psalms. It could also be argued that lament psalms represent a movement from disorientation through reorientation to orientation within themselves. In this process the individual is not simply struggling with distress but also with relational disorientation between themselves, God and others. Viewed in this manner, the terminology 'reorientation' is particularly helpful in suggesting a *process of engagement and change*. Following are examples of each aspect of relationship within the individual psalms of lament selected for this study:

- **Disorientation or dislocation** - Psalm 88:4-5 - 'I am counted among those who go down to the Pit; I am like those who have no help, like those forsaken among the dead, like the slain in the grave, like those who remember no more, for they are cut off from your hand.'
- **Reorientation** – Psalm 35:28 - '… my tongue shall tell of your righteousness and of your praise all day long.'[10]
- **Orientation** - Psalm 10:16 - 'The LORD is king forever and ever…'

The portrayal of disorientation to reorientation is significant both as an expression of experience and as an indicator of process. It is also another way of understanding Westermann's idea of movement from lament to praise, highlighted previously. Here, there is also a movement in the disposition of the psalmist from a place where God is at best distant, or at worst absent, to a point where the psalmist expresses God's presence in a new way.

There is no question that lament psalms can be characterized in all the ways described so far (lament/praise, prayer, complaint or disorientation). However, while each highlights particular features of an individual lament psalm, none on its own describes what lament is in its totality. If we were to characterize lament only as *one* of the descriptions above we could overlook the diversity of ways in which these psalms might potentially function for human beings.

---

[9] Brueggemann, *The Psalms in the Life of Faith*, 8. See this reference for a detailed description of how Brueggemann applies Ricouer's thinking to the characterization of various types of psalms.

[10] These examples have been selected from many similar expressions found both within the lament psalms chosen for this study and others.

Psalms of distress

Based on these preceding observations some general conclusions can now be drawn. Each of the characterizations of lament is clearly expressed as an address to God. While the address' substance ranges from specifics to generalities the circumstances which result in such material can be best described as experiences of distress. These psalms provide a framework, *and* potentially a process, through which experiences of distress can be viewed and expressed to a significant other, reflected on and even possibly resolved. While the resolution alluded to here is not necessarily a restored relationship between the individual and their 'enemies,' or even between the individual and God, lament psalms voice at least an intrapsychic resolution of hope for the future.

The individual is distressed about themselves, God and others and that distress almost demands the presence of a dialectical process. That is, the presence of distress involuntarily results in questions, accusations, complaints, descriptions of the predicament and pleas for help. In a paradoxical way the individual expresses a desire for God's action, *to* God, even in the face of God's felt inaction.

Therefore, a more general descriptor for these psalms encompassing all the aspects discussed above could be 'psalms of distress.' Using 'psalms of distress,' as a descriptor, also allows for the possibility that these psalms may be describing experiences of specific or generalized distress in life. The descriptor is broad enough to incorporate expressions of lament, complaint and disorientation while not limiting the response to any one of these. Distress is also a more familiar term for describing life experiences that would fit well with the biblical genre of lament. Therefore, for this study I employ the description 'psalms of distress' to identify these particular psalms.

Having surveyed the genre of individual lament, and notwithstanding the choice of a particular descriptor, it must be recognized that psalms of distress are complex. Because of their complexity perhaps they can be more fully understood and appreciated by those who use them rather than by those who seek to observe them or analyze them. Westermann highlights the usefulness of psalms of distress suggesting that 'lamentation is the language of suffering....'[11] His observation suggests the need to view psalms of distress *not* as a static structure or form but, rather, as a process by which the depths of human distress can be expressed through a dialectical interaction with a significant other amid lived experience.

Having examined various ways in which psalms of distress can be identified and described, we now turn to their function historically in the cultic practice of ancient Israel. As a result, the positive implications of a connection between these psalms and continuing ritual practice can then be suggested.

---

[11] Claus Westermann, 'The Role of the Lament in the Theology of the Old Testament,' *Interpretation* 28.1 (1974): 27.

Signpost 2 - Cultic function and ritual

Cultic function

The second signpost in exploring psalms of distress is the cult-functional approach as a way of understanding these psalms. Many have pursued the elusive goal of identifying the original *Sitz im Leben* of the Psalms.[12] At least these attempts have undoubtedly brought into focus that psalms in general, and psalms of distress in particular, emerged from the experiences of real people. Their responses to real events subsequently became progressively enshrined in the text of the Psalter and the cult of the ancient Israelite community.

While the people involved and the events described are more often than not too difficult to identify accurately, the authenticity of their experiences could hardly be questioned.[13] Therefore, psalms of distress, as a significant and continuing part of cultic practice, self-evidently support the significance of both the content and the form. They also suggest that their inclusion may have provided a validation of the people's experience of distress.

Of course various attempts have also been made to link psalms to specific events within the liturgy of Israel.[14] Again, despite being largely inconclusive, it does highlight the continuing place of the Psalms as a whole, and psalms of distress specifically, as a way of expressing lived experience through liturgy. The Psalms' importance as a basis for individual and communal expression to God is also reinforced by the later identification of the Psalter as the hymnbook of the Second Temple.[15]

The language of psalms of distress, viewed alongside their inherent nature as an expression of real existential distress, and the consistent use of these psalms in the Judeo-Christian cultic context prompts several further observations. Psalms of distress are unique in quality within biblical literature, as a whole, and the Psalter, specifically.[16] Their uniqueness lies in their grappling with the vicissitudes of human life, particularly with experiences of personal distress. This grappling is expressed through individual psalms of distress as experience which

---

[12] Gunkel, Mowinckel, Weiser, Kraus *et al*. It should also be noted that this approach was in no sense limited to examining just lament. Rather, the scope of this approach included the whole Psalter.

[13] The significance of the presence of titles in some psalms of distress is beyond the scope of this study. However, despite some doubt concerning their authenticity and the accuracy of attribution in the psalms' original form they do suggest an existential origin for the experiences expressed in the literature.

[14] Cf. Hans-Joachim Kraus, Theology of the Psalms (Minneapolis: Augsburg, 1986), Sigmund Mowinckel, *The Psalms in Israel's Worship*, vol. 1 (Oxford: Blackwell, 1962), Artur Weiser, *The Psalms* (London: SCM, 1962).

[15] Cohen, 'Usage of the Psalms.'

[16] While other psalms of distress are present in the Hebrew Bible such as the Jeremianic 'confessions' (cf. Jer. 11-20) these are linked specifically to historical characters and not necessarily utilized as forms of prayer within cultic practice.

fits within the context of a person's relationship with God and does not exist apart from that relationship.[17] The self-evident use of the Psalter in both Jewish and Christian liturgy over the centuries provides a historical precedent for employing these psalms as a continuing, integrated expression of individual devotion and corporate worship. Such use also suggests the efficacy in the continuing spiritual formation of people.

These observations also underline the importance of exploring the potential effect of ritual use with these psalms.[18] Because of this we must now turn to a brief survey of relevant ritual studies which will provide a broader theoretical base for this aspect of this study.

Ritual

Having highlighted the use of the Psalter, as a whole, and psalms of distress, specifically, as a regular and ubiquitous part of Judeo-Christian ritual it is important to address some questions about the *effect* of using psalms of distress as a ritual.[19] To gain further insight we will examine some of the more significant voices in ritual studies to explore their understandings of both the nature and function of ritual.

One of the first questions we must address concerning ritual is a definition. Although ritual appears to have always been a common part of human behaviour it is not simple to define. Here I will use Tom Driver's work as a beginning point because of his focus on the functional nature of ritual. In his extensive work on the subject he argues that ritual has the following major results:

- rituals are often and ideally powerful;
- this power is properly used not to instill conformity to what is old and entrenched but to facilitate various kinds of transformation; and
- the truly ethical kind of transformation is that which results in the increase of freedom.[20]

---

[17] Of course this kind of grappling activity is not limited to psalms of distress found in the Psalter. Distress is freely expressed on a number of occasions by the prophet Jeremiah in chapters 11-20. In contrast to these examples the psalms of distress in the Psalter are not connected directly to historical events or persons, notwithstanding the titles which were added at a later date.

[18] The issue of how a ritual usage might affect a community, while of significance, is beyond the scope of this study.

[19] Of course, within the Christian liturgical context this observation is only valid in certain settings. As highlighted in chapter 1 the setting with which I am most familiar is among the contexts which *do not* view psalms as having a ubiquitous place in the liturgy.

[20] Tom F. Driver, *Liberating Rites: Understanding the Transformative Power of Ritual* (Boulder: Westview, 1998), xi. Of course many others have made attempts at defining ritual. Among them are Herbert Anderson and Edward Foley, Mighty Stories, Dangerous Rituals (San Francisco: Jossey-Bass, 1998), Edward R. Canda, 'Therapeutic Transformation in Ritual, Therapy, and Human Development,' *Journal of Religion and Health*

For Driver the action of ritual is not something one decides to do. He states that, 'The human choice is not *whether* to ritualize but when, how, where and why.'[21] Driver's observation prompts an important question in relation to distress. Perhaps, rather than asking whether distress *ought* to be ritualized the more relevant question is about *how* distress *will* be ritualized. So, if it is accepted as a given that ritual will happen, is it better for the ritual to be spontaneous and ever-changing or planned and structured? Or is it possible to find a middle ground between the two extremes?

The more popular notion of ritual being a static practice is challenged by Driver in two ways. While he argues that ritual implies a revisiting of the same action over and again, the ritualizing can change in the process of engagement. The physical activity itself may not alter but understanding it and experiencing it may evolve. Driver captures this tension by suggesting that, 'As a particular act of ritualizing becomes more and more familiar... it comes to seem less like a pathway and more like a shelter.'[22]

When this observation is applied to ritual involving praying psalms of distress as an engagement with distress it suggests two possibilities. First, that a ritual could provide a process, or pathway, towards something not yet faced and second, that it may increasingly provide a place of safety and security in which the person can repeatedly express and engage with their distress. Thus, such a process might lead to an evolution of understanding and experience.

If this is the case it is also important to ask how these changes might be observed. First, it is significant that ritual can be viewed as something which extends beyond the cognitive processes of the individual and can be more than an expression of emotion. Theodore Jennings notes that ritual 'is primarily corporeal rather than cerebral, primarily active rather than contemplative, primarily transformative rather than speculative.'[23] His description of ritual stresses the wholistic pathway of involvement for those who take part in such activity. However, Jennings also underlines the transformative potential of ritual without lim-

---

27.3 (1988), Roy A. Rappaport, *Ritual and Religion in the Making of Humanity* (Cambridge: Cambridge University Press, 1999), Victor Turner, *The Forest of Symbols: Aspects of Ndembu Ritual* (Ithaca: Cornell University Press, 1967). I have chosen Turner's definition of ritual function as it provides a comprehensive coverage of the issues explored in this study of the efficacy of psalms of distress.

[21] Driver, *Liberating Rites*, 6.

[22] Driver, *Liberating Rites*, 16. It should be noted that while emphasizing the repetitive nature of ritual, Driver also allows for the incorporation of improvisation within the form. Thereby ritual produces another tension for the participant; that of fixed, prescribed activity with the seemingly innate human desire to be creative. According to Driver this should not be ignored but, rather, nurtured.

[23] Theodore W. Jennings, 'On Ritual Knowledge,' *The Journal of Religion* 62.2 (1982): 115.

iting this only to transforming thinking and/or emotions. His conclusion reinforces the perspectives of Driver and Turner in particular.[24] In further clarifying the transformative nature of ritual, Jennings goes on to argue that 'Ritual action does not primarily teach us to *see* differently but to *act* differently. It does not supply a point of view so much as a *pattern of doing.*'[25] Conceptualizing ritual as a 'pattern of doing' highlights ritual as being an important activity which is both planned and ongoing.

Roy Rappaport reinforces Jennings' idea by adding that 'participation is the *sine qua non* of ritual.'[26] That is, ritual cannot simply be observed. If its efficacy is to be fully realized a ritual must involve active participation. Also, Rappaport highlights a further issue stressing the significance of relationship between the person using words and engaging in action. While he does not want to lessen the power of the spoken word in voicing experience he does want to suggest that physical action accompanying words is 'performatively stronger' or 'performatively more complete' than simply speaking.[27] So, for Rappaport, the power of ritual is not found only in words, though these are a helpful vehicle for expression and often the basis for ritual.

While it may be too definitive a stance to argue that word is *always* stronger when attached to action,[28] it is reasonable to view actions with words forming a stronger activity and possibly a more complete 'pattern of doing.' Most importantly, however, if action attached to words in ritual provides a catalyst for deeper understanding then it can be inferred that the combination may potentially be markedly transformative.

Victor Turner, in his formative work on the nature of ritual, argues that ritual is 'prescribed formal behaviour for occasions not given over to technological routine, having reference to beliefs in mystical beings and powers.'[29] In this sense ritual can express an experience of the divine and beliefs about that entity. The action need not be complex or esoteric in nature. In fact, Driver argues that ritual actions are in fact 'elaborations upon simple behaviours already known.'[30] Although the behaviours may be simple, they can express something far deeper and more complex. In fact, Driver suggests that some things can be expressed only in actions. The non-verbal action in ritual can not only reinforce the verbal but may also transcend the verbal. Therefore, while the verbal aspect of ritual is no

---

[24] Jennings, 'On Ritual Knowledge,' 117.

[25] Jennings, 'On Ritual Knowledge,' italics added.

[26] Rappaport, *Ritual and Religion*, 72.

[27] Rappaport, *Ritual and Religion*, 143.

[28] Of course, the expression of words alone can also constitute a ritual act.

[29] Turner, *The Forest of Symbols*, 19.

[30] Driver, *Liberating Rites*, 19.

doubt important, non-verbal aspects cannot be ignored or underplayed.[31]

Jonathan Smith adds to this observation suggesting that ritual is not only about what is performed but about the action of paying attention. He says, 'It is a process for marking interest.'[32] This also is an important observation as it highlights self-involvement within any ritual as being paramount to its efficacy. It requires the participant to be mindful of what the ritual is symbolizing and what the meaning of this may in fact be.

Herbert Levine also offers a perspective on ritual, incorporating the ideas of Rappaport, Turner and Smith, as he comments specifically on potential links between ritual action and use of the Psalms saying,

> ...ritual forms in us 'a complex permanent attitude,' an emotional pattern that governs our individual lives. As metaphor functions within language, so ritual can be a tool for the abstract, symbolic thought. Ritual actions can be regarded as figures of speech, in which a gesture stands symbolically for a complex of ideas and emotions.[33]

Levine's observations suggest, then, that ritual is a form of sign and the sign produced, even if simple, suggests a complex set of thoughts and emotions within the individual. An obvious question arising from these observations is, 'How might the ritualizing of personal distress be efficacious?'

Herbert Anderson and Edward Foley provide one possible response to this question as they build on the work of theorists such as Turner and Driver by adding another emphasis to the rôle of ritual. They argue convincingly that 'Ritual and story are common ways within a particular social context by which we order and interpret our world.'[34] The emphasis here is twofold. First, they clearly define ritual as a vehicle for telling a story, whatever that story might be, and, second, the purpose of telling this story through ritual has a goal of making sense of a person's world.

In expanding on the idea of narrative they make a distinction between two kinds of story being expressed in ritual using the terms 'mythic' and 'parabolic.'[35] A mythic view is characterized as one in which all difficulties are successfully resolved and all ends well. In contrast to this, the parabolic story narrates paradox and contradiction. However, rather than viewing these as being

---

[31] Driver, *Liberating Rites*, 22. As an example of this transcendence Driver cites the example of washing ones hands before a meal saying that he learnt and practiced the ritual of this long before he had a cognitive apprehension of its significance yet he did it because it is 'the way it is done.'

[32] Jonathan Z. Smith, 'To Take Place,' in *Ritual and Religious Belief*, ed. Graham Harvey (London: Equinox, 2005), 33.

[33] Herbert J. Levine, *Sing Unto God a New Song: A Contemporary Reading of the Psalms* (Bloomington: Indiana University Press, 1995), 24.

[34] Anderson and Foley, *Mighty Stories*, xii.

[35] Anderson and Foley, *Mighty Stories*, xi-xii.

irreconcilable opposites Anderson and Foley go on to argue that 'mythic' story provides a sense of hope while 'Parabolic stories invite transformation by opening us to the possibility of something new.'[36] How do they do this? 'Myth may give stability to our story, but parables are agents of change and sometimes disruption.'[37]

Most psalms of distress contain both these elements as they tell the story of distress experienced by an individual.[38] By holding both the 'parabolic' and the 'mythic' together they provide an invitation to 'something new.' They present a world which is not unfolding as desired or perhaps expected by the person in distress. However, in contrast to this these psalms also present a world of possibility where a hopeful future can begin to be imagined.

A ritual can provide a holding space for the tension between the 'parabolic' and the 'mythic,' allowing meaning-making to begin. So, Anderson and Foley conclude this part of their discussion by suggesting that a primary function of combining myth and parable is to 'construct meaning and build community.'[39] They add that,

> We tell stories of a life in order to establish meaning and to integrate our remembered past with what we perceive to be happening in the present and what we anticipate for the future.[40]

What might this mean for an engagement with personal distress? It is important to stress that meaning is not homogeneous in nature. Reflecting this Leonel Mitchell employs the term 'multivalent'[41] to express the idea that a ritual can in fact have multiple meanings all at the same time. The stereotypical nature of psalms of distress, and their inherent 'parabolic' and 'mythic' narratives, allows for, and perhaps even promotes, a multiplicity of meanings to emerge from the person's experience.

One conclusion from these observations is that psalms of distress, as a ritualized narrative, may create a place where both the 'parabolic' and the 'mythic' can be brought together in a safe and secure place. They can be allowed and encouraged to co-exist, opening the possibility of engagement with, reflection on, and perhaps even resolution of personal distress. In each case the opportunity for experiencing something different is afforded to the participant in such a process.

Therefore, it can also be assumed that the ritualizing of a story of personal

---

[36] Anderson and Foley, *Mighty Stories*, xi.

[37] Anderson and Foley, *Mighty Stories*, 14.

[38] The interesting exception here is Psalm 88 which could be characterized as being exclusively parabolic in nature.

[39] Anderson and Foley, *Mighty Stories*, 3.

[40] Anderson and Foley, *Mighty Stories*, 5.

[41] Leonel L. Mitchell, *The Meaning of Ritual* (Harrisburg: Morehouse, 1977), 28.

distress which incorporates both myth and parable may be efficacious for a participant. The 'mythic,' it could be argued, provides a hope for the future and perhaps even the present. However, this alone could be viewed as idealistic if it were not balanced with the 'parabolic' which grounds the experience in real life with all its paradoxes, questions and wonderings. So, ritualizing the 'parabolic' and the 'mythic' fosters the existential coexistence of both these experiences reflecting a reality in the face of distress but not hopelessness. It could also be that 'Rituals not only construct reality and make meaning; they help us fashion the world as a habitable and hospitable place.'[42] Such an observation highlights both the proactive nature, and efficacy, of ritual. However, as stressed above, while ritual can be observed, it cannot be engaged with simply through such observation. Ritual calls on the participant to engage actively with the world which the ritual creates by entering as a participant in that world.

Given the connections observed between actions and words, ritual and story, any ritual can be viewed as an 'acted out' response to particular circumstances. For engaging with personal distress this could be significant. Ritualizing distress by using psalms of distress provides prescriptive content for the person to 'act out' their distress in response to a particular circumstance and an opportunity for reflection on that distress. An invitation such as this may in fact be different to the way in which an individual would normally choose to respond to such a circumstance. Jennings characterizes the individual's experience as 'knowing' through acting out a ritual. However, 'knowing,' for Jennings, is not a cognitive apprehension which is independent of the experience but, rather, a consciousness of what is happening to the self as a significant by-product of the experience.[43] This consciousness or self-awareness through ritualizing appears to be a key for a transformative process to be precipitated in the person.

Ritual opens possibilities of telling both the mythic and parabolic stories and acting out through ritual can bring about a deeper consciousness, or 'knowing.' This raises an important question. What might this transformation process be like when it takes place? By integrating the ideas of narrative and consciousness Stephen Crites is helpful in suggesting that in ritual, 'action and experience interpenetrate.'[44] Edward Canda explains the idea further suggesting that,

> Transformation is a process involving a period of de-structuring of a stable condition a period of extreme fluidity and openness to new possibilities, and a period of

---

[42] Anderson and Foley, *Mighty Stories*, 20.

[43] Jennings, 'On Ritual Knowledge,' 112.

[44] Stephen Crites, 'The Narrative Quality of Experience,' *Journal of the American Academy of Religion* 39.3 (1971): 291. In doing this Crites wants to inextricably link life experience and story to each other. Therefore the articulation of this narrative becomes possible *because* the experience is a story.

restructuring a new stable condition.[45]

It is reasonable to infer from these observations that a regular practice of praying psalms of distress could provide a forum for articulating the 'de-structuring' envisaged by Crites. While at any given point an person's situation may in fact be stable, a ritual focusing on personal distress may offer an opportunity for the formative process of 'de-structuring' and 'restructuring' to take place. In this sense a ritual of lament might even act as a 'shelter,' as described by Driver above, which concurrently offers safety with an opportunity for change.[46] Driver also suggests,

> The elaborations produced by ritualizing activity have the intention of leading somewhere, of going from one condition to another, even though the end may not be clearly in view. Although the process employs randomness, it is not itself random.[47]

So ritual cannot simply be viewed as 'going through the motions' or even merely an expression of emotions. It can in fact be a reflective space which promotes transformation.[48] To capture the idea Driver coins the term 'transformance.'[49] His idea of transformance requires active involvement, not passivity.[50] However, in building on 'transformance' Driver argues for ritual being more than simply participation. He suggests that ritual actions can be 'confessional.' That is, the person taking part in the ritual takes on responsibility and volitional activity in response to the situation. He summarizes saying,

> The confessional mode transcends the ritual mode inasmuch as the performers recognize and speak out (confess) their moral responsibility for the rituals they perform.[51]

An important part of the confessional nature of ritual is honesty in expression of the heart. Driver says that in ritual we '*act* what we feel, not what we ought to do.'[52] Expressing emotion, questioning and the wondering, help to locate both the human and the divine existentially. The ritualizing of this confession can also

---

[45] Canda, 'Therapeutic Transformation,' 206.
[46] Cf. n. 3.
[47] Driver, *Liberating Rites*, 28.
[48] Driver uses a helpful analogy comparing the function of ritual to that of a washing machine which actually takes dirty clothes and washes them, as opposed to a book about washing machines which simply informs.
[49] Driver, *Liberating Rites*, 28.
[50] Virginia H. Hine, 'Self-Generated Ritual: Trend of Fad?,' *Worship* 55.5 (1981): 412. She argues that, 'the greater the psychic change required, the greater the investment in ritual must be.'
[51] Driver, *Liberating Rites*, 113.
[52] Driver, *Liberating Rites*, 5.

be viewed as an acknowledgment of relationship with oneself, God and others and 'is to place oneself in the presence of others, whether human or divine, making of oneself a very word of address inviting response.'[53] In contrast to this Lynne Texter and Janine Mariscotti suggest that ritual can in fact result in a multidimensional alienation from self and others which may, in addition, extend to a sense of distance or alienation from God.[54] So, rather paradoxically, a sense of relationship *with* oneself, God and others, and alienation *from* oneself, God and others can co-exist. However, rather than viewing this as a negative outcome they see it as an integral part of the process of engagement and eventual transformation.

These observations resonate with qualities often found in psalms of distress.[55] Immediately on using the psalms of distress verbally as a ritual one is engaged in a confessional process. Although the psalms were originally authored and performed by others these psalms can become the performer's own confession. They are no longer simply about expressing the *idea* of personal distress. Rather, they become an expression and confession of the person's *own* experience of personal distress.

The distress expressed in the ritual use of psalms of distress may not in fact need to be a present reality for the person. In fact Quentin Quesnell argues that,

> It is not everyday reality, but re-presentation so a past reality may be experienced more profoundly; in fact, that it may no longer be past, but the most present reality of all.[56]

Quesnell's statement offers two significant observations relevant to the experience of using psalms of distress. First, it assumes that a 're-presentation' of a past reality is an important activity that ritual facilitates and, second, there is value in a past reality becoming 'the most present reality of all.' In other words a revisiting of past distress in a ritual manner opens the opportunity for that past distress to become profoundly available for meaning-making in the present. However, all this, as argued above, assumes self-involvement of the person. It also assumes the ritual participant holds a particular posture towards the activity. Robert Sweetman describes such a stance as being one of 'permeability' describing the

---

[53] Driver, *Liberating Rites*, 117.

[54] Lynne A. Texter and Janine M. Mariscotti, 'From Chaos to New Life: Ritual Enactment in the Passage from Illness to Health,' *Journal of Religion and Health* 33.4 (1994): 326.

[55] E.g. Ps. 10:1, 'Why, O LORD, do you stand far off? Why do you hide yourself in times of trouble?' Ps. 13:1-2, 'How long, O LORD? Will you forget me forever? How long will you hide your face from me? ² How long must I bear pain in my soul, and have sorrow in my heart all day long? How long shall my enemy be exalted over me?' Ps. 22:1, 'My God, my God, why have you forsaken me? Why are you so far from helping me, from the words of my groaning?' *et al*.

[56] Quentin Quesnell, 'Interior Prayer and Ritual Drama,' *Dialogue and Alliance* 3.4 (1989-90): 70.

concept as, 'the reader's openness to allow what she (sic) reads to get under her skin, to change her essential posture towards the text at hand, or perhaps even in life.'[57] In succinct language Sweetman identifies an aspect of potential transformation in the ritual process. Ritual is not simply about participation but about change.

The final issue concerning ritual is the idea of divine involvement in the process. As highlighted earlier, Victor Turner, in his formative work on the nature and function of ritual, concluded that ritual, as he viewed it, assumed 'reference to beliefs in mystical beings and powers.'[58] So, this being the case we will now explore the implications of his observations for understanding psalms of distress.

Anderson and Foley also address the notion of divine involvement in the ritual process suggesting that ritual

> is significantly magnified when the divine and human intersect in our storytelling and ritualizing. We are transformed in part because we begin to understand our particular story as part of a larger, transcendent narrative. God has chosen to co-author a redemptive story for us and with us in human history, and in so doing has invited us to reshape radically the horizon of all other storytelling and ritual making.[59]

One might ask at this point, 'Is this intersection with the divine necessary as part of the process of storytelling and ritual?' In one sense answering such a question is dependent on how the term 'divine' is defined.[60] However, this study assumes that people of faith will inevitably, by definition, incorporate thinking about how the Divine is, or is not, involved in various life experiences. It seems that experiences of distress, perhaps even more than other experiences, may heighten levels of thinking and expression about divine involvement.

If the intersection of human and divine involvement for the person of faith of experiencing distress is a given, then this intersection can paradoxically be both comforting *and* problematic. The ritualizing of lament offers a process whereby the intersection can be recognized and a forum within which the resulting tensions can be voiced. Anderson and Foley argue this in narrative terms saying that,

> The integration between the divine and human narratives is necessary so we will have a language to speak about our human struggles that will, at the same time,

---

[57] Robert Sweetman, 'Thomas od Cantimpré: Performative Reading and Pastoral Care,' in *Performance and Transformation*, ed. Mary Suydam and Joanne Ziegler (New York: St Martin's, 1999), 134.

[58] Turner, *The Forest of Symbols*, 19.

[59] Anderson and Foley, *Mighty Stories*, 37.

[60] A discussion of various perspectives on defining 'divinity' or God is beyond the scope of this study.

open us to possibilities beyond the present struggle.[61]

Robert Jenson goes even further than Anderson and Foley in suggesting that ritual opens the possibility of a sacramental word from the Divine to the one in distress.[62] His observation supports the argument that a meaningful ritual engagement with personal distress is the most powerful way of approaching this common human experience. Ritual, then, presents an opportunity for weaving the human and the divine story together while attempting to make sense of the distress being experienced. In addition Gary Brock argues that,

> If in ritual we encounter the Ultimate, if in liturgy we meet God on the brink of chaos, then the sacramental response becomes a way of talking about what one took into the Presence of the Holy, what one anticipated happening and what really and finally happened.[63]

These observations return us to the 'transformative' potential of ritual not *despite* distress, or chaos as Brock describes it, but *because of* distress. The issue of divine involvement in the matters of life, particularly when there is chaos or distress, is clearly obvious in psalms of distress. Driver offers a somewhat dogmatic but nonetheless significant conclusion arguing that, 'Without ritual, the divine-human relationship is broken, and in the break everything that can be truly identified as either divine or human dies.'[64]

Summary

To this point our attention has focused on the use of the Psalter, including psalms of distress, in cultic settings, particularly in ancient Israel, and the possible implications of its use with ritual. We have also explored the potential significance and implications of ritual people of faith. From this survey it can be supposed that the Psalter gained and maintained a prominence in both corporate worship and personal devotion within ancient Israel and beyond through its integral connection with ritual which reinforced the content in various ways. Self-evidently the connection between psalms and ritual included individual psalms of distress. Connecting psalms of distress with ritual allows for enacting words which tell the story of personal distress and allowing for reflection which can lead to making meaning out of the experience. This action and reflection process in turn offers the possibility of personal transformation. In light of these observations we need to go beyond examining the use of psalms of distress in ritual to exploring the nature of the discourse found in the text.

---

[61] Anderson and Foley, *Mighty Stories*, 41.
[62] Robert W. Jenson, 'The Praying Animal,' *Zygon* 18.3 (1983): 314-16.
[63] Gary Brock, 'Ritual and Vulnerability,' *Journal of Religion and Health* 29.4 (1990): 291.
[64] Driver, *Liberating Rites*, 98.

Signpost 3 – Discourse and dialectic

To examine the discourse of psalms of distress I will approach them from two distinct and yet interrelated perspectives; narrative and poetry. However, before discussing these two types of discourse it is necessary to locate the current discussion within the broader context of the discipline of discourse analysis studies. Jan Renkema provides a helpful working definition saying that discourse analysis provides 'an explanatory description of systematic differences in forms and functions and the relation between them.'[65] This definition reflects the location of this study, in terms of discourse, where the focus is more on the *form* and *function* of the discourse rather than on philosophical issues behind creating the text.[66] With these observations in mind we will now examine the narrative and poetic features of psalms of distress in turn.

Narrative

Individual psalms of distress possess a distinctive narrative quality. In other words they do not simply record an isolated complaint or even just a specific request of God. Rather, they are examples of richly textured, and at times complex, stories of personal distress and responses to such experiences. They tell the story of the experience of distress by identifying the characters,[67] sometimes describing any precipitating events as a plot, providing a climax[68] and often a resolution in the imagination of a hopeful future. This narrative, expressed in poetic language, gives shape and substance to the distress and subsequently promotes the freedom of emotional expression.[69] With this freedom of emotional expression a strong sense of movement is obvious through the presenting story.[70] This movement often appears to gain impetus by a reflection on the past,[71] and the

---

[65] Jan Renkema, *Discourse Studies* (Amsterdam: John Benjamins, 1993), 2.

[66] While the philosophical basis for the discourse found in psalms is a significant issue it is outside the parameters of this study. Having said this, Jan Blommaert, *Discourse* (Cambridge: Cambridge University Press 2005), 14, makes an observation which is worth noting as background to the current discussion saying, 'We can, and must, start from the observation that language matters to people, that people make investments in language, and that this is a crucial part of what they believe language does for them and what they do with language.'

[67] Of course, in individual psalms of distress all the characters are anonymous, including the person in distress, but are nonetheless portrayed as characters.

[68] The climax could be articulated in a variety of ways including the 'plea' or a cry of imprecation against the enemies.

[69] More will be said about the nature and function of poetic language later.

[70] E.g. Psalm 22 is one of the most dramatic examples of this kind of movement; however, others also reflect similar movement.

[71] E.g. Psalm 22:4-5, '…in you our ancestors put their trust, they trusted and you set them free. To you they called for help and were delivered; in you they trusted and were not put to shame.' Psalm 44 also provides an example of an extended appeal to history as the basis of lament. Though this is generally categorized as a communal lament psalm its content

capacity to engage in a re-authoring, which leads to imagining a new future. The movement described here could be viewed broadly as movement from desolation to consolation.

Of particular significance is the interplay between the characters represented in psalms of distress; namely, the 'self,' God and others (often characterized as the 'enemy'). Westermann, in his formative work on the Psalms, identifies this interplay as a dialectic style of communication.[72] The dialectic reinforces the significance of the relationships between the individual, God and enemies in an experience of distress, admitting the struggle and tension in relationships between these characters.[73] Evidence in psalms of distress themselves suggests the dialectic also provides a pathway, or even the impetus, for movement from expressing desolation to finding consolation.[74] The term dialectic is helpful in that it also highlights the often confrontational nature of the encounter between the person, God and the enemy. The words of the distressed person to God and the enemy's words are particularly strong at times.[75]

A second aspect to understanding the narrative nature of individual psalms of distress is to view it as a story of disorientation— reorientation— new orientation.[76] This terminology is helpful in highlighting the relational shifts which occur alongside the dialectical expressions of thought and emotion in a process of lament. Taking these two ideas together, dialectic and relationship, alerts us to

---

clearly emphasizes a historical focus on the action of God as a starting point for expressing distress. The individual lament psalms tend not to describe history in such detail as found in Psalm 44 but still seem to be focused on the idea that because God has saved in the past (e.g. as in Psalm 44) it is worthwhile calling on God in the present.

[72] Westermann, *Praise and Lament in the Psalms*, 193-94. The term 'dialectic', as opposed to 'dialogue,' is helpful in this context as it highlights the tension between the voices active within the lament.

[73] Martin Buber, *Between Man and Man*, trans. Ronald Gregor Smith (New York: MacMillan, 1965). In discussing this concept Buber refers to the definition of dialectic provided by Feuerbach as far back as 1843 who said, 'True dialectic is not a monologue of the solitary thinker within himself, (sic) it is a dialogue between *I* and *Thou*.'

[74] In this sense desolation and consolation can be viewed as two sides of the one coin.

[75] For example, in Psalm 10:4 the enemy of the distressed person quotes the enemy who says, 'There is no God,' and '... we shall not be moved.' In Psalm 22:14-17 the distressed person says, 'I am poured out like water, and all my bones are out of joint; my heart is like wax; it is melted within my breast; my mouth is dried up like a potsherd, and my tongue sticks to my jaws; you lay me in the dust of death. For dogs are all around me; a company of evildoers encircles me. My hands and feet have shriveled; I can count all my bones. They stare and gloat over me.'

[76] P. Ricoeur, *The Rule of Metaphor, Multidisciplinary Studies in the Creation of Meaning in Language* (London: Routledge & Kegan Paul, 1978). Note my usage of this concept in a different sense to Brueggemann (Brueggemann, *The Psalms in the Life of Faith*, 8.) He uses Ricoeur's terms as descriptive categories for whole psalms.

the potential dynamic of psalms of distress in recounting distress. It also highlights the potential to move the person towards greater understanding of their story of distress and/or resolution of their distress. Entering into a dialectic and, thereby, exploring relationship, seems to find its impetus through an intentional engagement with distress by recounting the experience. The precise nature of the dialectic identified by Westermann and its connection with exploring relationship will be discussed later. However, before we do this it is also important to examine the significance of these psalms as *narrative in the form of poetry*.

Poetry

Poetry is the chosen language of the discourse in psalms of distress. In commenting on the poetic language of the psalms William Brown has observed that, 'The power of the Psalms lies first and foremost in its evocative use of language. The psalms at once caress and assault the soul.'[77] Ricoeur argues that in this type of process, 'The word forms our feeling in the process of expressing it.'[78] He also contends earlier in the same book that, 'Everyday reality is metamorphosed by... imaginative variations that work on the real.'[79] In other words, Ricoeur astutely points out that a discourse does not represent some fanciful wondering about what life experience might be like but can provide a metamorphic language to describe one's actual view of reality. In this sense poetry is complementary to narrative. It assists telling the story of distress through a metaphorical picture formed by a perception, or set of perceptions, arising from real life experiences *and* the language for imagination of a different reality. However, to more fully appreciate the nature and psychodynamic function of psalms of distress we need to appreciate some of the unique qualities of Hebrew poetry. For this investigation we turn to a selection of biblical scholars who have explored Hebrew poetry in various ways and with some rigour. Robert Alter helpfully describes Hebrew poetry as,

> working through a system of complex linkages of sound, image, word, rhythm, syntax, theme, idea... an instrument for conveying densely patterned meaning, and sometimes contradictory meaning.[80]

James Kugel adds to this by underlining the prominence of 'patterns' and 'regularity' within Hebrew poetry.[81] In individual psalms of distress this type of poetry

---

[77] William P. Brown, *Seeing the Psalms: A Theology of Metaphor* (Louisville: Westminster John Knox, 2002), 2.

[78] P. Ricoeur, *Essays on Biblical Interpretation*, ed. Lewis S. Mudge (Philadelphia: Fortress, 1980), 90.

[79] Ricoeur, *Essays on Biblical Interpretation*, 80.

[80] Robert Alter, *The Art of Biblical Poetry* (New York: Basic Books, 1985), 112.

[81] James Kugel, *The Idea of Biblical Poetry: Parallelism and Its History* (New Haven: Yale University Press, 1981), 69-70. While his comments describe poetry in the Hebrew Bible generally they obviously include the material of Psalter as significant examples.

provides the linguistic parameters for creating a functionally rich literary tapestry. It is important to note that the features identified by Alter and Kugel are not only salient to the composition and literary nature of such psalms but also to the performative nature of the psalms.[82] Throughout history coupling psalms with various musical forms has enhanced the efficacy of poetic language in the Psalter.[83]

The coalescing of 'patterns' and 'regularity' using devices such as parallelism[84] creates a unique genre of poetic or dramatic literature which is not simply to be heard but to be entered by performance.[85] The presence of parallelism serves to enhance, contrast, re-emphasize or rephrase the ideas being expressed by the person. In experiencing psalms of distress the reader or person praying is presented with confronting words and imagery which provoke powerful mental pictures. The emotive qualities of the experiences are also prominent in the foreground. The poetry of the psalms of distress provides an incomparable medium for telling the story of distress by offering a 'languaging' which is defining but not constrictive to the imagination. Therefore, while powerful in its capacity to carry emotion and image it is by no means restrictive to expression. Rather, poetic language provides freedom for expression and safety in using a familiar mode.[86]

As well as this, Brown suggests that psalms have a didactic function and are, therefore, 'poetry with a purpose.'[87] He concludes that in poetry 'metaphors *do* something to enable the reader to perceive something differently.'[88] If this is the case it suggests that continuing ritual use of psalms, as a way of responding to personal distress, may also intentionally provide participants with education in how to perceive differently and respond fittingly to such experiences. Another significant function of poetry, as observed in the Psalms, is what Brown refers to

---

[82] By using the word 'performative' here I am suggesting that the language of Psalms was composed with the intention of being read or sung/chanted aloud as a form of ritual in itself or part of a broader ritual process rather than being simply read silently.

[83] It is beyond the scope of this study to explore implications of these kinds of connections. However, the concept of verbalizing the words of psalms of distress will be explored further in a later section of this chapter focusing on speech act theory.

[84] Much debt is owed to Robert Lowth for his seminal work on Hebrew poetry: *De Sacra Poesie Hebraeorum Praelectiones Academicae*, published in 1783. Lowth coined the term *parallelism* as a way of describing the two line couplets prominent in Hebrew poetry where the second line in some way reflects the content of the first.

[85] Gerstenberger, *Psalms Part 1*, 14. He suggests the presence of a five syllable stress feature which he identifies as a 'dirge rhythm' in the lament psalms.

[86] Assuming here the usage of the psalms in a regular ritual manner.

[87] Brown, *Seeing the Psalms*, 7. It should be noted that Brown does not limit the function of any psalms to didactic function. However, what he helpfully highlights is the potential effect this kind of discourse might have on those who engage with it.

[88] Brown, *Seeing the Psalms*, 7.

as 'iconic metaphor' where he convincingly argues that combining language and image presents 'powerful ways to stimulate reflection and emotion.'[89] The connection here with ritual acts discussed earlier is made plain by Earl MacCormac who makes the observation that, 'Metaphors not only communicate suggestive and expressive meaning but they also become iconic objects through their fusion of sense with sound.'[90] Janet Soskice, on the basis of work by cognitive literary theorists, describes the use of metaphors as 'cognitive meditation' suggesting that poetic metaphor engages both affective and cognitive responses.[91]

I have chosen to identify the text of psalms of distress as poetic narrative in an attempt to capture both characteristics of the discourse. Now we turn to examine further implications of viewing the text as the type of discourse described above. Jurie le Roux points out that 'the written... word is only a partial reflection of the inner word.'[92] His perspective here is an important acknowledgment that any set of words presented in text, as rich as they may be, are a reflection of something far greater. So, whether psalms of distress are viewed as narrative, poetry or both, the ideas hold. While the words act as a sign or symbol of what le Roux calls 'the ineffable inner word' they can in no sense be viewed as a comprehensive exposure of a person's inner thinking and feeling. As he relates his thinking to the psalms, le Roux's emphasis here is more effectively characterized as a dialogue of questions and answers.[93] This is helpful in underlining the flexibility of the discourse in psalms. While it is a fixed text and a fairly fixed form it does not 'fix' affect and cognition. On the contrary, it appears to free these up through a dialectical process which could be characterized as a continual progression of reflective questioning and answering.

When poetic narrative is viewed as this dialogue between question and answer the reader is not left to just contemplate words-signs but a world which opens because of expressing these word-signs. Wade Wheelock perceptively calls this

---

[89] Brown, *Seeing the Psalms*, 5.

[90] Earl R. MacCormac, *A Cognitive Theory of Metaphor* (London: Massachusetts Institute of Technology, 1985), 192-93.

[91] Janet Martin Soskice, *Metaphor and Religious Language* (Oxford: Clarendon, 1985), 38-39.

[92] Jurie H. le Roux, 'Augustine, Gadamer and the Psalms (Or: The Psalms as the Answer to the Questions),' in *Psalms in Liturgy*, ed. Dirk J. Human and Cas J.A. Vos, (London: T&T Clark, 2004), 124.

[93] In doing this le Roux acknowledges the formative work by Gadamer in this regard. In saying this le Roux is not suggesting that the text is therefore a close-ended discourse such as a cathechismic question and answer process. He elucidates this by arguing that, 'The dialogue does not comprise of propositions but of questions and answers, which *always give rise to new questions and different answers*'—le Roux, 'Augustine,' 127, italics added.

'[an] entry into the world of ideas.'[94] But how is this 'world of ideas,' presented as a discourse, inviting engagement? Interestingly, Kenneth Quinn argues that story is dispensed with when poetry is employed. However, it is debatable that such a strong distinction can be made between the function of poetry and the function of narrative. Nonetheless he does go on to suggest the primary function of poetry is expressing emotions which he views in contrast to the function of narrative.[95]

While Quinn's distinction between the function of poetry and the function of narrative may be too definitive it is reasonable to conclude that poetic language makes a more explicit attempt to facilitate expressing emotions. Despite these comments, I would argue for a significant connection being made between the poetic expression of distress and a narrative of distress based on the content of psalms of distress in the Psalter. However, his comments should not be dismissed out of hand because at least they highlight the emotional nature of poetic discourse.[96] Quinn then takes his thinking a step further making the connection between poetry and ritual suggesting that such a connection 'sets up a counterpoint between sound and sense that refuses to be ignored. The pattern of sound provides the structure and a pattern of thought.' This sits well with the idea that perhaps human beings do not invent rituals as much as rituals invent human beings.[97] It is a cyclical process at work which also reflects the question and answer process identified by le Roux.[98]

A specific focus on relationship between characters emerges from the powerful combination of narrative and poetic discourse in psalms of distress. Levine is also helpful at this point in drawing together the ideas of ritual theorists and the perspectives of Martin Buber[99] and Mikhail Bakhtin[100] on discourse. He highlights the significance of relationship *as a foundation for understanding the function of the poetic narrative discourse* we see in the psalms. These approaches

---

[94] Wade T. Wheelock, 'The Problem of Ritual Language: From Information to Situation,' *Journal of the American Academy of Religion* 50.1 (1982): 49.

[95] Kenneth Quinn, *How Literature Works: The Nature of the Literary Experience* (Sydney: Australian Broadcasting Corporation, 1982), 93.

[96] Roman Jakobson, 'Linguistics and Poetics,' in *The Discourse Reader*, ed. Adam Coupland Jaworski, Nikolas (London: Routledge, 1999), 60. As an example of one aspect of emotion evoked by poetry Jakobson highlights the idea that, 'Ambiguity is an intrinsic, inalienable character of any self-focused message, briefly a corollary feature of poetry.' He goes on to say that 'Not only the message itself but also its addresser and addressee become ambiguous.'

[97] Driver, *Liberating Rites*, 31.

[98] Cf. n. 84.

[99] Buber, *Between Man and Man*.

[100] Mikhail Bakhtin, *Problems of Dostoevsky's Poetics*, ed. Wlad Godzich and Jochen Schulte-Sasse, trans. Caryl Emerson, 8 vols., vol. 8, Theory and History of Literature (Minneapolis: University of Minnesota Press, 1984).

underline the idea that in discourse the sum of the parts is greater than the whole in significance for the person. For Buber the 'in between,' or the relationship between entities, is as important as the discrete entities involved in any discourse.[101]

For Bakhtin the dialogical relationship between the entities creates a continuing process of defining the characters in terms of their relationship with one another.[102] As an example of this Levine offers a helpful insight into the manner in which the discourse found in the psalms of distress can promote a deeper understanding of oneself. He states,

> I can experience myself on my own terms— feel pain, feel happiness, and so forth— but I cannot perceive or understand myself except from some point of view outside myself (though any one external point of view will necessarily be limited).[103]

So, in Levine's view, this kind of discourse, the 'self' as a character in dialogue with others, can promote a deeper self-awareness *by* the engagement with others in the process.[104] The dialogical engagement provides the opportunity for the 'in between' to be experienced, recognized and reflected on. To this end Bakhtin argues that,

> Dialogic interaction is indeed the authentic sphere where language *lives*. The entire life of language, in any area of its use... is permeated with dialogic relationships.[105]

Interestingly in psalms of distress the other characters are God and often an enemy. Bakhtin refers to God as a '"super-addressee" who transcends the present, seeing us from the vantage point of eternity.'[106] Levine argues that the reason for the divine character in psalms of distress is a recognition that a deeper sense of self-understanding can ultimately only come from including the divine other in the process. It seems acknowledging someone or something greater than the individual may be one outcome of engaging with personal distress. For the person of faith this acknowledgment is foundational; necessitated by the belief in a god and the relational connection with that god.

While a superficial reading of the individual psalms of distress might suggest

---

[101] Levine, *Sing Unto God a New Song*, 81.

[102] Although it must be acknowledged that Bakhtin developed these ideas primarily from analysing fictional novels, namely those written by Dostoyevsky, a number have seen the relevance to the psalms (Bakhtin, *Problems of Dostoevsky's Poetics* and Patricia K. Tull, 'Bakhtin's Confessional Self-Accounting and Psalms of Lament,' *Biblical Interpretation* 13.1 (2005): 41-55.)

[103] Levine, *Sing Unto God a New Song*, 82.

[104] In some ways this reflects what could be characterized as the difference between a biographical view of self which views others, and relationships with those others, in a different way to an autobiographical view of self and relationships with others.

[105] Bakhtin, *Problems of Dostoevsky's Poetics*, 183.

[106] Levine, *Sing Unto God a New Song*, 82.

that they are formed purely by the words of the distressed person this is not always the case. The discourse found in the psalms of distress also quotes the words of God and the enemy. The technique of 'doublevoicedness,' to use a Bakhtinian term, where the words of God and/or the words of the enemy are quoted by the person in distress appear to perform two significant functions.[107] First, they provide an opportunity for those in distress to stand somewhat 'detached' from their experience of distress and view it from another perspective (that is, God and/or the enemy). Second, doublevoicing provides the opportunity for reflecting on the 'in between' as it articulates the nature of the relationship between the person in distress with God and/or the enemy. Levine also argues that this provides the added force of the text having a 'rhetorical use... intended to persuade [God to respond]'.[108]

The upshot of this dialogical process and the use of doublevoicing is the creation of a polyphonic discourse which ultimately promotes the emergence of more richly textured self-expression and deeper self-understanding.[109] Patterson calls this 'a movement inward through a movement outward, into the open, to a position of vulnerability.'[110] Bakhtin argues that

> What is important to Dostoyevsky is not how his hero appears in the world but first and foremost how the world appears to his hero, and how the hero appears to himself (sic).[111]

While acknowledging again that Bakhtin has a specific genre of literature in mind, which is in many ways different to psalms of distress, the principle seems equally applicable to psalms of distress. As one reads these psalms there is no sense in which the writer (author) is presenting other than the authentic self (hero) as perceived by self, God and the enemy or enemies. The discourse tells it like it is in the language of poetic narrative. However, Levine adds that, 'The Psalms are... concerned with establishing a dialogic relationship and, in that relationship, with being heard and answered by a Thou.'[112] So, the discourse is simply about 'telling;' it is also about hearing and responding.

---

[107] Bakhtin, *Problems of Dostoevsky's Poetics*, 72, 73 and 185-86. For example, God is quoted in Psalm 35:3b saying, 'I am your salvation,' while the enemy is quoted Psalm 10:11 saying, 'God has forgotten, he has hidden his face, he will never see it.' There are many other examples of these kinds of quotes throughout individual lament psalms.

[108] Levine, *Sing Unto God a New Song*, 115.

[109] This deepening of self-understanding seems to derive in part from individuals being able to articulate both their own words about themselves and the words of God and others about them.

[110] David Patterson, 'The Religious Aspect of Bakhtin's Aesthetics,' *Renascence* 46.1 (1993): 63. In this article Patterson is specifically dealing with the relevance of Bakhtin's theories to religious understanding.

[111] Bakhtin, *Problems of Dostoevsky's Poetics*, 47.

[112] Levine, *Sing Unto God a New Song*, 105.

Dialogue or dialectic?

While the emphasis by Levine and Patterson is on the discourse being in the form of a dialogue I have chosen to define the idea of dialogue more narrowly in the context of psalms of distress. The dialogue which takes place between the 'self,' God and the 'enemy' is, in my view, more accurately described as dialectic. The choice of this term is based on the content of the discourse found in psalms of distress. Rather than the three characters conversing with each other— an implication of using the word dialogue— there is a decidedly argumentative tone to the discourse better described as dialectic. We now turn to discuss dialectic in greater detail.

The work of Westermann in highlighting the dialectic and, by definition, the relational features of psalms of distress provides a helpful picture of the dynamics of the discourse present in psalms of distress. Clearly from the text a tripartite relationship is obvious. The person is relating to the 'self,' God and an anonymous 'enemy.' Only the dialectic between the person and God is literally articulated in the psalms of distress. However, as well as this, the words of God[113] or the words of the enemy[114] are not infrequently quoted by the lamenter as part of the dialectic. Therefore, it is not unreasonable to infer that the person is also engaged in dialectic internally with self and externally with the enemy.

In sum then the dialectic is indicative, and perhaps symptomatic, of distress being experienced by the person. It also presents a structure for the discourse through which distress seems to be best expressed; that is, in the context of relationship. The dialectic voices the distress being experienced, the nature of the relationship, or lack of relationship with God and others, and suggests a struggle with personal disempowerment in the face of distress. Each of these three aspects will be examined in detail in chapter five.

However, it is important, at this point, to examine further Westermann's identification of dialectic within psalms of distress and the implications for our understanding of the nature of relationship in the process of engaging with distress. In exploring Westermann's ideas it is helpful to bear in mind the significance of ritual action and poetic narrative discourse.[115]

The first relationship obvious within the tripartite dialectic is that which exists between the person and the 'self.' A simple reading of psalms of distress reveals

---

[113] E.g. Ps. 12:5, 'Because the poor are despoiled, because the needy groan, I will now rise up,' says the LORD; 'I will place them in the safety for which they long' *et passim*.

[114] E.g. Ps. 22:8, 'Commit your cause to the LORD; let him deliver— let him rescue the one in whom he delights!' *et passim*.

[115] Leslie C. Lewis, 'Continuity and Meaning,' *Journal of Religion and Health* 37.2 (1998): 151. He notes interestingly that 'Both narrative and ritual contribute to continuity with others, self, time, and God.'

a distressed person who often describes the 'self' as one who is in need.[116] Alongside this the person also often characterizes the 'self' as faithful, innocent and upright.[117] Another self-description is found in a subcategory of psalms of distress usually referred to as penitential psalms where the psalmist describes self as having sinned, recognizing the need to confess and repent. These are all attempts by the person to come to terms with the 'self' in the face of personal distress. However, these thoughts and emotions are not experienced in isolation. A psalm that is used as a form of prayer is, in a sense, speaking to oneself *and* to God about oneself and about God. Psalms of distress are self-directed in two ways. First, they are a mode of expressing thoughts and feelings about oneself and a situation of personal distress generated from the 'self,' by the 'self' and for the 'self.' Second, they are also self-directed in that they are expressed by the distressed person rather than by someone else on the person's behalf. They are directed towards God in that they are a form of prayer which is expressed to the 'self' and towards a divine other.[118] As the psalms are self-directed and God-directed in these senses they are, by definition, also expressions of relationship, with the 'self' and with God.

Expressing relationship in the psalms of distress is not often one of harmony but, rather, an expression of tension and struggle amid distress. A significant aspect of this struggle appears to be elusive nature of self-empowerment, or control, which can form part of a person's response to distress. The person reflected in psalms of distress desires control over their life and the situation but is confronted with a reality where there is a distinct lack of self-control and a resulting sense of disempowerment. Ambivalence and ambiguity are obvious but there is no attempt to deny the experience. In psalms of distress the struggle over ambivalence and ambiguity is clearly verbalized to oneself in the face of intense distress. A clear example of this is found in Psalm 13:4 where the distressed person expresses a sense of total disempowerment. The psalmist states, 'I will sleep the sleep of death' and then quoting the words of the 'enemy' who says, 'I have overcome him....'[119]

---

[116] James L. Mays, *The Lord Reigns: A Theological Handbook to the Psalms* (Louisville: Westminster John Knox, 1994), 30. He discusses this description at length. See for example Psalm 34:6, 'This poor soul cried, and was heard by the LORD, and was saved from every trouble'; Psalm 40:17, 'As for me, I am poor and needy, but the Lord takes thought for me. You are my help and my deliverer; do not delay, O my God,' and Psalm 69:29, 'But I am lowly and in pain; let your salvation, O God, protect me.'

[117] E.g. Psalm 4:3, 'But know that the LORD has set apart the faithful for himself; the LORD hears when I call to him;' Psalm 7:10, 'God is my shield, who saves the upright in heart,' and Psalm 10:8, 'They sit in ambush in the villages; in hiding places they murder the innocent. Their eyes stealthily watch for the helpless.'

[118] The idea of these psalms as a form of prayer directed towards God will be explored in a later section of this chapter.

[119] Cf. Pss. 38:12-14, 'Those with designs on my life lay snares, those who wish me ill

The second part of the tripartite dialectic is that which occurs between the person and God. God is the significant other in relationship with the person. A profound question such as, 'My God, my God, why have you abandoned me?'[120] is both an expression of relationship *and* alienation where the person is attempting to make sense of the relationship in the face of distress. The feelings of alienation also appear to be a key feature of the existential experience of distress.

A person may feel that control of the situation does not lie within themselves, when confronted with distress. Instead, control may be viewed as something which can be vested in God.[121] This includes an assertion that God is present and that this presence guarantees divine control of the situation. It also implies that the person will be protected. Even this assertion, however, is accompanied by ambivalence at times. Broyles highlights the way in which God's disposition is often described in psalms of distress in terms of wrath, rejection, forgetting and hiding of the face.[122] A confronting example of this is Psalm 17:1-5 where the 'faithfulness' of the person in distress is pitted against the implied 'unfaithfulness' of God.[123] The relationship is uncomfortable where God is viewed concurrently as the solution *and* the problem.

Despite this dilemma, the authenticity of relationship between the person and God facilitates the possibility of reaching a deep level of honesty. There is not simply a tacit recognition of God's presence in the situation. Nor is the person dumbstruck in their predicament. The person is asserting innocence and a substantial plea for God's action in the situation. This assertive position displays great courage and self-assuredness in speaking *to* God which has its foundation in the freedom to express oneself *before* God *about* oneself and *about* God. Kathleen Farmer encapsulates the picture well by observing that,

---

speak of violence and hatch treachery all day long. But I hear nothing, as though I were deaf, as though dumb, saying not a word. I am like the one who, hearing nothing, has no sharp answer to make,' and 130:3, 'If you, O LORD, should mark iniquities, Lord, who could stand?' *et al.*

[120] Ps. 22:1, 'My God, my God, why have your forsaken me?'

[121] E.g. Psalm 4:8, 'I will both lie down and sleep in peace; for you alone, O LORD, make me lie down in safety' *et passim.*

[122] Broyles, *The Conflict of Faith and Experience*, 62-63.

[123] Ps. 17:1-5, 'Hear a just cause, O LORD; attend to my cry; give ear to my prayer from lips free of deceit. ² From you let my vindication come; let your eyes see the right. ³ If you try my heart, if you visit me by night, if you test me, you will find no wickedness in me; my mouth does not transgress. ⁴ As for what others do, by the word of your lips I have avoided the ways of the violent. ⁵ My steps have held fast to your paths; my feet have not slipped.'

> They (the psalmists) do not wait passively for God to notice their pain and come to their aid. Rather, they cry out as an act of faith in the steadfast love of the one they confidently trust will not reject them for what they feel or say.[124]

The expression is one of freedom to be open and authentic in voicing the story of personal distress and what it is like for the one encountering it. However, Farmer also highlights the sense of risk of possible rejection which may well be imagined by the distressed person engaging in such a process.

The third aspect of the tripartite relationship is that which exists between the person and the 'enemy.' However, before exploring this aspect, it is important to note that there is some evidence within psalms of distress suggesting the presence of others who are supportive towards, rather than opposed to, the person in distress. For example, Gerstenberger highlights the presence of the community and a figure he refers to as a 'ritual expert.'[125] Typically, then, a lament process does not appear to be something which occurs for the person in isolation. Rather, it is a process which involves the community acting in a supportive rôle.

Despite this, dialectic between the person and the 'enemy' is clearly obvious.[126] Although there does not appear to be physical confrontation or direct conversation between the two the relationship is implied. Part of the story of distress is recognizing that initially, at least, control is located with the 'enemy.' Often the thought is expressed, in psalms of distress, as what the 'enemy' has done or may do to the person and the powerlessness the person feels in the situation. This sense of disempowerment can also extend to the person's relationship with God, at least initially. Neither is responding in the way desired or perhaps expected.

Much internal evidence from the psalms describes the source of distress in terms of the 'enemy's' activities.[127] The anonymity of the 'enemy' contributes to

---

[124] Kathleen A. Farmer, 'Psalms,' in *The Women's Bible Commentary*, ed. Carol A. Newsom, Sharon H. Ringe (London: SPCK, 1992), 140.

[125] Gerstenberger, *Psalms Part I*, 14.

[126] In Psalm 3:2-3, for example this dialectic can be observed. '...many are saying to me, 'There is no help for you in God.' Selah ³ But you, O LORD, are a shield around me, my glory, and the one who lifts up my head.' It is not in the form of a direct conversation between the two parties but, rather, the enemy's jibes are quoted and then the distressed individual's contrary viewpoint on the situation.

[127] Cf. Pss. 3:1-2, 'O LORD, how many are my foes! Many are rising against me; ² many are saying to me, 'There is no help for you in God.' Selah' and Psalm 10:2-11, 'In arrogance the wicked persecute the poor— let them be caught in the schemes they have devised. For the wicked boast of the desires of their heart, those greedy for gain curse and renounce the LORD. In the pride of their countenance the wicked say, 'God will not seek it out'; all their thoughts are, 'There is no God.' Their ways prosper at all times; your judgments are on high, out of their sight; as for their foes, they scoff at them. They think in their heart, 'We shall not be moved; throughout all generations we shall not meet adversity.' Their mouths are filled with cursing and deceit and oppression; under their tongues are mischief and iniquity. They sit in ambush in the villages; in hiding places they

the stereotypical nature of lament. By the 'enemy' being portrayed in this way I can agree with Patrick Miller that 'the enemies are in fact whoever the enemies are for the singers of the Psalms.'[128] In fact the 'enemy' may even be oneself, or God, in some circumstances.[129] Perhaps penitential psalms are the clearest examples where the psalmist views the 'self' as 'enemy.' It seems that in the process of lament there is an inherent 'need' for an 'enemy' as a direction for emotion to be vented. The specific identity of the 'enemy' is a subordinate issue.

Summary

The notion of psalms of distress being used ritually has been connected with the nature of the discourse constituting these psalms. The particular discourse found in psalms of distress is a fusion of poetic and narrative features creating what I have identified as a poetic narrative. It is text which tells the story while employing metaphor and repetition, among other poetic devices, to express the experience set in motion by personal distress. The power of the poetic narrative style found in psalms of distress is its capacity to express concurrently 'mythic' and 'parabolic' thinking. Psalms of distress present us with a 'mythic' image where distress is successfully resolved. However, they also highlight a 'parabolic' reality, where distress may not have immediate resolution, producing residual ambiguity in the person's experience.[130]

As well as this, the nature of the discourse found within psalms of distress can be characterized as dialogical in form. I have further refined this dialogical form as dialectic. The sharper definition is due to the dialogue in psalms of distress being argumentative in nature. This dialectic is characterized as being an expression of a tripartite relationship between the person in distress, God and the enemy.

When the ideas of ritual and discourse analysis, of the kind just discussed, are viewed alongside one another it could be concluded that fusing poetic language and performance of some form contributes to the forging of a powerful form for expressing thought and emotion. This fusion produces material which cannot be simply examined, analyzed or explained from an 'objective' standpoint. It must, by necessity, be experienced. While the poetic narrative provides the medium, it is the dialectic quality which provides the impetus for an authentic expression of thinking and emotion around experiences of distress. These features are embedded in the form of psalms of distress which provides a structured literary space in which genuine expression can take place. We will now explore the form this

---

murder the innocent. Their eyes stealthily watch for the helpless; they lurk in secret like a lion in its covert; they lurk that they may seize the poor; they seize the poor and drag them off in their net. They stoop, they crouch, and the helpless fall by their might. They think in their heart, 'God has forgotten, he has hidden his face, he will never see it.' *et al.*

[128] Patrick D. Miller Jr., *Interpreting the Psalms* (Philadelphia: Fortress, 1986), 50.

[129] An interesting example of this if found in Psalm 130:10 where the individual, by implication, is an enemy to self, due, in this case to ones 'sins' (TNIV).

[130] See the discussion Anderson and Foley's ideas in the previous section.

poetic narrative takes in psalms of distress and discuss the possible implications of the form for meaning-making.

Signpost 4 – Form and meaning-making

Form

The form of psalms of distress is another signpost on the landscape of lament. Form provides the framework for the discourse within which expressions of various kinds can most effectively take place. The form-critical approach to the Psalms provided the foundation for identifying and describing the major constituents of individual lament in contrast to other *Gattungen*. Gerstenberger embellished the formative work of Gunkel and others arguably producing some of the most comprehensive and helpful research in relation to the form of psalms of distress. He identified the presence of up to ten discrete elements found within the classic individual lament form of the Psalter.[131] The elements are as follows:

1. Invocation
2. Complaint
3. Confession of sin/affirmation of innocence
4. Plea/petition for help
5. Imprecation against enemies
6. Affirmation of confidence
7. Acknowledgment of divine response
8. Vow/pledge
9. Hymnic blessing
10. Anticipated thanks

While identifying these elements is helpful in describing the content of the form it also implies a potential function for the ten discrete elements, as expressions of prayer, within the overall form. Do the ten elements identified by Gerstenberger encapsulate possible responses of individuals to existential distress? If so, does the existence of these elements in the form of a psalm of distress suggest a model for engaging with distress intentionally? To respond to these two questions I have further distilled these elements into four constellations which incorporate all ten elements identified in typical lament form by Gerstenberger. The four constellations are:

- **Expressing**
  - Invocation

---

[131] Gerstenberger, *Psalms Part I*, 12. It should be noted that these ten elements are also present in communal laments. However, not all ten elements identified by Gerstenberger appear in every lament psalm. Westermann, *Praise and Lament in the Psalms*, 52, suggests five elements as constituents of individual lament identifying the presence of— address, lament, confession of trust, petition, vow of praise. While this is also a helpful way of viewing the form of lament Gerstenberger's approach is more comprehensive.

- Complaint
- **Asserting**
  - Confession of sin
  - Assertion of innocence
  - Plea
- **Investing**
  - Imprecation
  - Affirmation of confidence
  - Acknowledgment of divine response
- **Imagining**
  - Vow
  - Pledge
  - Hymnic blessing
  - Anticipation of thanks

This further distillation above of Gerstenberger's ten elements goes beyond simply identifying and describing the elements of lament form as found in individual psalms of distress. Each constellation denotes different functional aspects of the psalm in responding to distress. When viewed together the constellations make up a matrix of lament which is a helpful way of viewing lament form in this study. Although expressed in a diversity of ways within the text of individual psalms of distress, essentially these constellations reflect a dynamic process of engagement with phenomenological distress. The distillation of Gerstenberger's ten elements into the four constellations, creating a matrix of lament, will be explicated more fully with examples in the following chapter.

Classifying individual lament as a discrete form within the Psalter and the subsequent attempts to identify the discrete elements of this form by Gerstenberger, Westermann and others presents us with two important questions. Why would experiences such as distress, which could be characterized as causing feelings of a lack of control, anxiety and hopelessness, be formulated and expressed in a stable literary form? Also, why have they been enshrined in Judeo-Christian ritual? There are two major responses to these questions which again contributes to an understanding of the potential psychodynamic effects these psalms may have for those who engage with them.

Structure

It has been recognized above that not all psalms of distress contain each of the ten elements identified by Gerstenberger. However, when lament is viewed as a collection of constellations (expressing — asserting — investing — imagining) it is evident that each psalm of distress consistently incorporates all four constellations.[132] Therefore, the constellations viewed together highlight the structure of

---

[132] The only notable exception to this is Psalm 88 which will receive special attention in chapter six as one of the psalms selected for use in this study.

individual psalms of distress and a consistency of content, although ordering of these constellations can vary. Brueggemann has called this form 'structure-legitimating.'[133] He goes further to argue specifically that psalms of distress legitimate one who 'struggle[s] to be free [and] is open to *the embrace of pain.*'[134]

In addition to this, the structural nature of psalms of distress, as a form, can be viewed as juxtaposed with the lack of structure resulting from personal distress. Presenting this paradox to the distressed person in the form of a psalm invites them to engage with the lack of structure caused by distress *through* a structure.[135] Not only is the experience then structure-legitimating but Leslie Lewis adds that structure also provides a sense of continuity of experience saying,

> Continuity is a collective set of experiences that in the best of circumstances results in a feeling that one's life has purpose and meaning, and in the worst of circumstances provides a container for despair and loss.[136]

To further define this picture of structure without it seeming too clinical, Martha Robbins employs the image of a divine dance or *perichoresis* to describe the form of psalms of distress. In summarizing her use of this imagery she says that, 'We want to stick to the dance steps we know and the dance partners we choose.'[137] Psalms of distress provide a form in which this can occur. So the form provides an important space for self-expression and the parameters for that expression but it also offers a liminal space for exploring and, perhaps, even making meaning out of the distress being experienced by the person. It is to the issue of meaning-making that we now turn.

Meaning-making

In addressing the issue of meaning-making the underlying assumption is that individual psalms of distress are in fact an attempt to do just that; make meaning. I would argue that the value of a lament process, as an attempt to make meaning, is self-evident in its continuing use throughout much of Judeo-Christian history. John Swinton supports this notion in a general sense arguing that, 'We cannot be

---

[133] Walter Brueggemann, 'Shape for Old Testament Theology, 1,' *The Catholic Biblical Quarterly* 47.1 (1985): 31. Admittedly here he is addressing the theology expressed in psalms rather than directly describing the emotional experience of distress from phenomenological distress.

[134] Brueggemann, 'Shape for Old Testament Theology, 1.'

[135] It is interesting to note Mitchell's (Nathan D. Mitchell, 'The Amen Corner,' *Worship* 76.1 (2002): 67.) observation at this point that 'our participation expresses both our worship of God and solidarity with one another.' Notwithstanding the fact that this study is focussing on individuals as they engage with personal distress through individual psalms of lament the aspect of communal resonance, in whatever form that takes, cannot be ignored.

[136] Lewis, 'Continuity and Meaning,' 143.

[137] Martha A. Robbins, 'The Divine Dance: Partners in Remembering, Revisioning, and Reweaving,' *The Journal of Pastoral Care* 51.3 (1997): 344-46.

anything other than interpretive beings.'[138] Coining the phrase 'hermeneutic phenomenology' he says that participation in various phenomenological experiences *assumes* the process of meaning-making.[139]

Another significant aspect of meaning-making is the concept of understanding. Graham Hughes, for example, characterizes understanding as 'comprehension' referring to the Latin root of the word meaning 'grasping together.' In summarizing his thoughts he suggests that,

> when we strain for the meaning of something, we are attempting to find the ways in which its parts form some kind of significant whole and then the ways in which that whole hangs together with whatever else we know of the world.[140]

A significant part of this process is engaging oneself in a process which can lead to a deepening self-awareness for the person in relation to the events experienced. Dialogue, or dialectic in the form of psalms of distress, can be a most effective structure in which this deepening of self-awareness might occur.[141]

A cautionary comment is warranted here. It could be concluded from these thoughts that the goal of meaning-making is to make complete sense of an experience such as personal distress. However, this is to focus solely on a goal of resolving distress. Potentially a goal such as resolution may overshadow the *form of engagement* and a *focus on the process* of engaging with, reflecting on and, ultimately, growing because of the personal distress without necessarily experiencing any form of resolution.

Anne Sutherland, in her work on trauma and suffering further elucidates the challenge of meaning-making by using the paradigm of 'world-frames' to describe a person's response to distress. She suggests that, 'The problem comes when something happens in life and a person is unable to find a sense of meaning and purpose that incorporates that event.' She goes on to suggest that a change

---

[138] John Swinton and Harriet Mowat, *Practical Theology and Qualitative Research* (London: SCM, 2006), 107.

[139] Swinton and Mowat, *Practical Theology*, 106. In presenting this idea Swinton and Mowat consider that, '*Phenomenology* is a philosophy of experience that attempts to understand the way in which meaning is constructed through human experience.'

[140] Graham Hughes, *Worship as Meaning: A Liturgical Theology for Late Modernity* (Cambridge: Cambridge University Press, 2003), 79. As part of his discussion Hughes relates the ideas of understanding and comprehension to the work of Mink on the function of narrative in the meaning-making process.

[141] In this regard Hughes (Hughes, *Worship as Meaning*, 90) refers to Derrida's comments on dialogue: 'I must first hear myself. In soliloquy as in dialogue, to speak is to hear oneself. As soon as I am heard, as soon as I hear myself, the I who hears *itself*, who hears *me*, becomes the I who speaks and takes speech from the I who thinks that he speaks and is heard in his own name.'

of 'world-frame' may be needed to promote meaning-making.[142] If the change identified is to take place a liminal space may facilitate such a movement. Individual psalms of distress may provide such a space or structure for this to occur.

In such a process it is significant that individual psalms of distress themselves, while potentially being used with non-verbal ritual processes, are, by definition, verbal expressions containing significant responses to distress. By it, they give language and voice to the distress experienced. Patricia Byrne states that,

> when the crisis occurs, the person is pushed to the edges of the previous way of being. To push through to the next space, language is essential. This speech will be more than an articulation of ones circumstances, but will have actual creative function. Heidegger says it beautifully, "the poet is the shepherd of being."[143]

Summary

So, in summary, individual psalms of distress represent a structured form for engaging with personal distress by recounting distress using the metaphorical power of poetic narrative language. The form of the psalms of distress is fairly stable across the Psalter in that they almost all contain the four constellations (expressing — asserting — investing — imagining). When employed, as a form of prayer, the form offers a liminal space as an opportunity for reflection and meaning-making. While the poetic narrative language has certain mimetic qualities attached to it there is also space for a hopeful imagination both *within* and *beyond* the experience of existential distress. The particular form of psalms of distress also contributes to a process of meaning-making for the distressed person.

A further important consideration in any discussion of the use of psalms of distress must be a recognition that these psalms are also shaped as prayers. In light of this observation we will now consider the implications of the words of the text being viewed as a form of prayer formed by the four constellations described above.

Signpost 5 – Speech act and prayer

To this point we have discussed the function of individual psalms of distress with ritual, the nature of these psalms as discourse, and described their form as a means of providing both literary and existential structure for meaning-making. Psalms of distress can also be characterized as a series of speech acts which collectively can be characterized as prayer.

---

[142] Anne V. Sutherland, 'Worldframes and God-Talk in Trauma and Suffering,' *The Journal of Pastoral Care* 49.3 (1995): 285-86.

[143] Patricia Huff Byrne, "'Give Sorrow Words': Lament— Contemporary Need for Job's Old Time Religion," *Journal of Pastoral Care and Counseling* 65.3 (2002): 262.

Speech acts

The formative work by J.L. Austin entitled *How to Do Things With Words* set the course for many subsequent studies in speech act theory.[144] As Wade Wheelock puts it,

> His [Austin's] key insight was to recognize that utterances could be not only statements of fact but also the *doing* of something.... Austin came to the realization that all utterances have a performative aspect. To make any utterance is to perform an act.[145]

This being the case, Austin's observations can be understood as highlighting various effects of speech on both the speaker and the hearer.[146] Implicit in such a view of language is this idea that words, when spoken, can be viewed differently from words that are bound to a page. Second, speech acts involving both speaker and hearer infer some kind of relationship between the two.[147]

Though a consensus has been reached regarding the idea that speaking words does something to speaker and hearer that is where the consensus ends. However, focusing on the idea that speaking words *does* something is helpful when examining the function of psalms as they are prayed aloud. As a beginning point, viewing the psalms of distress as a collection of speech acts, we will take up John Searle's classification of five distinct types:[148]

- **Assertives** – we tell people how things are
- **Directives** – we try to get them to do things
- **Comissives** – we commit ourselves to do things
- **Expressives** – we express our feelings and attitudes[149]

---

[144] J.L. Austin, *How to Do Things with Words*, ed. J.O. Urmson, Marina Sbisà 2nd ed. (Cambridge: Harvard University Press, 1975).

[145] Wheelock, 'The Problem of Ritual Language,' 52.

[146] Judith Marie Kubicki, 'Using J.L. Austin's Performative Language Theory to Interpret Ritual Music Making,' *Worship* 73.4 (1999): 312. She sees that spoken language cannot just be language of assertion but also language of action. This reinforces both the idea of speech acts *doing something* and also the ubiquitous reality of relationship between speaker and hearer.

[147] In fact on the issue of speech and relationship, Day (James M. Day, 'Speaking of Belief: Language, Performance, and Narrative in the Psychology of Religion,' *The International Journal for the Psychology of Religion* 3.4 (1993): 215.) states categorically that, 'language arises and is meaningful in and because of relationship, and there is no place outside the social realm where it could function.'

[148] Richard S. Briggs, *Words in Action* (Edinburgh: T&T Clark, 2001), 51.

[149] The idea of a 'permissive' could be included in this category as well indicating a nuanced concept of expression where the individual's speech act is present by virtue of a form (i.e. in this case lament form) which gives permission for such an utterance to be made.

- **Declarations** – we bring about changes through our utterances

The reason I have chosen this approach is twofold. First, the emphasis of each category is clearly on the *effect* that the particular speech act has as a speech act.[150] Second, all these speech act types are found to be present in the individual psalms of distress. This reinforces two important concepts underpinning this exploration. First, that the individual psalms of distress when prayed become, in fact, a collection of speech acts rather than simply words confined to a page. Second, that the function of the speech acts may do something to the speaker to promote reflection.

Before exploring what speech acts in psalms of distress might do it is important to bear in mind that Austin and subsequent theorists, such as John Searle,[151] only focused on speech acts as normal speech. They focus did not concentrate specifically on what might be described as ritual speech. Wheelock is helpful at this point in describing the contrast between the two speech types which he refers to as ordinary (normal) speech and ritual speech. He states:

> My proposal is that one must make a broad distinction between all those speech acts whose fundamental intention is the communication of information between a speaker and a hearer, and those speech acts whose intention is to create and allow the participation in a known repeatable situation. This thesis implies that the language of any ritual must be primarily understood and described as 'situating' rather than 'informing' speech.[152]

This distinction between speech acts that are 'situating' and speech acts that are 'informing' is important in relation to the individual psalms of distress. In a primary sense psalms of distress could be viewed as a collection of speech acts which inform the person of certain issues (i.e. normal speech). However, when incorporated into a ritual process, which implies repetition, the 'informing' nature of the speech acts becomes secondary, as the information is already known. Then the 'situating' of the speech acts becomes the primary focus each time the psalm is spoken or prayed (ritual speech). In other words the function shifts from what could be viewed as assertives about a situation to include the other types of speech acts identified by Searle. Interestingly, as noted above, each type of speech act identified by Searle can be found throughout psalms of distress. Below I have listed examples of each type taken from psalms of distress to be used in this study.

---

[150] Terms such as locutionary, illocutionary and perlocutionary as developed and used by Austin (1975) and Searle (1970) *et al* need to be carefully defined and there is still some disagreement as to definitions presented by the various theorists.

[151] John R. Searle, *Speech Acts: An Essay in the Philosophy of Language* (Cambridge: Cambridge University Press, 1970).

[152] Wheelock, 'The Problem of Ritual Language,' 59.

- **Assertive** - Psalm 10:2 - 'In arrogance the wicked persecute the poor.'
- **Directive** - Psalm 22:19 - 'But you, O LORD, do not be far away! O my help, come quickly to my aid.'
- **Comissive** - Psalm 35:18 - 'I will thank you in the great congregation; in the mighty throng I will praise you.'
- **Expressive** - Psalm 55:4, 5 - 'My heart is in anguish within me, the terrors of death have fallen upon me. Fear and trembling come upon me, and horror overwhelms me.'
- **Declaration** - Psalm 55:16 - 'I call upon God, and the LORD will save me.'[153]

James Day elucidates the rôle of speech acts further by arguing that,

> to speak means both to be spoken into being and to transform what it is that being and speaking can mean; language always involves both interlocution and appropriation.[154]

By employing the concept of 'appropriation' Day highlights the *active* nature which speech acts can take on. This idea is encapsulated most simply in the title of Austin's formative work on speech act theory, *How to Do Things With Words*. 'Doing things with words' in some respects undergirds the process of meaning-making addressed in the previous section. As experiences are *articulated and reflected on* in a favourable environment meaning-making has the opportunity to emerge. Kubicki suggests that

> performative language theory is a helpful tool in liturgical studies because it provides a method which examines the relationship of *meaning* and *text* in the context of ritual. In addition, the theory is pertinent to the study of liturgy because it views language more as 'doing' than simply communicating *about* a state of affairs.[155]

Again the emphasis here, as with Day, is on the idea that speech can both 'situate' and 'appropriate' change. Kubicki expands on the connection between speech and ritual arguing that it is not physical action alone which acts but also any words that are spoken. This connection also highlights the power of speech acts

---

[153] The implication here is that the request itself brings about the action on another's part (in this case God). It is notable that while the first four categories of speech are almost innumerable within the psalms of distress declaratives are not so prevalent. Rather than declare change through one's own words the change is expressed as a direct request (plea) or a wish for something the individual desires God to do. In biblical Hebrew this is most often expressed by using the jussive form of the verb in either the singular or plural which specifically identifies the idea as a wish or desire. It is a nuanced, softer form of the imperative.

[154] Day, 'Speaking of Belief,' 217.

[155] Kubicki, 'Using J.L. Austin's Performative Language,' 320.

to go beyond simply describing events (that is, as in Searle's 'assertive') to viewing speech as proactively bringing meaning about for the speaker.

The observations of Day and Kubicki prompt a question about the potential effects speech acts may have on a person. At a fundamental level speech act theory is a way of talking about the nature of the voice which is given to the speaker.[156] This voice is, by definition, a voice of self-involvement when the text is expressed as a speech act or prayer. Richard Briggs, as a caution, rightly argues for a distinction in levels of self-involvement in speech acts recognizing that participation in any speech act suggests at least a superficial level.[157] However, given that some self-involvement by the speaker in speech acts is necessary we must ask what the implication of such involvement might be. Wheelock is again helpful at this point suggesting that

> The speaking of the text *presents* the situation. It facilitates recognition of the situation...., it expresses this recognition..., and it actually helps to create the situation...[158]

The emphasis here is on process rather that a particular result. The situation created may well be simply a more realistic picture of reality rather than a picture of resolution. However, whatever the picture, the speech act has performed the rôle of at least doing something by situating the speaker in relation to the circumstances.

While the emphasis in speech act theory is on speaking a word or set of words, it is also important to bear in mind that the spoken word can also be viewed as a type of sign. However, as mentioned earlier, le Roux notes that 'The... spoken word is only a partial reflection of the inner word.'[159] He goes on to argue that this inner word is ineffable.[160] In this sense the individual psalms of distress could also be viewed as an opportunity to *articulate the experience of distress* in speech acts even though such speech acts are only partially representative in themselves. However, when these speech acts are employed with ritual the ineffability is provided with a further forum of expression. As the speech acts in ritual are learned by the participant 'the ritual is less an idea to be taught and more a reality to be

---

[156] Day, 'Speaking of Belief,' 215. He suggests that 'Without a voice, there is no reality, let alone the prospect of representing or making it meaningful.'

[157] Briggs, *Words in Action*, 7. Later (148), he argues that, 'The basic point about self-involvement is that the speaking subject invests him or herself in a state of affairs by adopting a stance towards the state of affairs. Where self-involvement is most interesting and significant is in cases where the stance is logically entailed but the utterance itself. This is most obvious in cases where the language is present-tense first person language.'

[158] Wheelock, 'The Problem of Ritual Language,' 60.

[159] le Roux, 'Augustine,' 124.

[160] le Roux, 'Augustine,' 127.

experienced.'[161] In fact Day goes as far as to say that, 'we are created by the words as well as being creators of them.'[162] His observation is particularly important if the speech acts are employed in a continuing process of ritual.

As highlighted earlier all the discrete types of speech acts identified by Searle can be observed in the psalms of distress. From a speech act theory perspective then, their presence suggests that the function of these words, at least in their original context, may have been to *do something*. This idea of *doing something* is in contrast to words being simply a record, informing a reader of events in the past and reflections on those events. It also indicates that if a person were to make these speech acts on their own by verbalizing them and relating them to their own experiences of distress they may provide a ready-made entry point for engagement with personal distress.

While a description of psalms of distress as collections of speech acts is helpful, it is nonetheless deficient if limited only to this perspective. Historical use, and the text itself, show that these psalms are prayers. As we are considering individual psalms of distress as a form of prayer it is important to explore how speech acts function *in the form* of prayer. In addition we will examine how this kind of prayer might function for a person in distress.

Prayer

John Finney and H. Newton Maloney Jnr provide a comprehensive and helpful literature review of empirical studies of prayer over the last few decades.[163] As the basis of their review they provide a helpful working definition of prayer being 'every kind of inward communion or conversation with the power recognized as divine.'[164] The definition is general enough to encompass verbal and non-verbal forms of prayer, highlights the existence of relationship between human and divine and suggests some intentional self-involvement in the process.

During their review two themes became increasingly evident to Finney and Maloney Jnr. First, that prayer is often viewed as petition. That is, it seems from observing people's attitudes towards prayer, researchers have discovered that people pray either to express a desire to change the situation faced or for a change in their own subjective response.[165] The second theme was that prayer helped people engage with experiences of distress and aided them in expressing their desire for comfort and communion with God amid that experience.[166]

As well as this, there appears to be something even more fundamental to the

---

[161] Wheelock, 'The Problem of Ritual Language,' 66.

[162] Day, 'Speaking of Belief,' 214.

[163] John R. Finney and H. Newton Maloney Jr., 'Empirical Studies of Christian Prayer: A Review of Literature,' *Journal of Psychology and Theology* 13.2 (1985): 104-15.

[164] Finney and Maloney, 'Empirical Studies,' 104. This definition is taken from W. James, *The Varieties of Religious Experience* (New York: University Books, 1963), 464.

[165] Finney and Maloney, 'Empirical Studies,' 104.

[166] Finney and Maloney, 'Empirical Studies,' 107.

reasons people in fact pray at all. While not denying the petitionary aspect of prayer, or the desire for comfort and communion, Cynthia Cohen and others argue that 'They come to meet their most fundamental need... the need for God.'[167] The observation suggests that at the core of any prayer is a perceived need for a sense of relationship with the divine *amid life* rather than *despite life*.

The thread of relationship seems to be the unifying factor in the themes described above. Kevin Ladd and Bernard Spilka describe this desire for relationship as 'inward, outward and upward prayer connections.'[168] They go on to argue that, because of that relationship, prayer emerges from the difficulties faced in life because of a perceived need for cognitive and spiritual structure and as a pathway for coping.[169] Interestingly both Cynthia Cohen, and Ladd and Spilka do not see the appeal to the divine as an appeal simply because the divine is viewed as more powerful, or all-powerful, but, rather, an appeal because the divine is God.[170] Again the emphasis in terms of efficacy for the person praying is in the existence of the relationship, apart from what God may or may not do in response to the prayer offered.

According to Ladd and Spilka prayer is a process by which relational connections are made. Again underlining the relational nature of prayer Bruce Epperly describes it as 'an invitation to partnership, activity, and growth.'[171] In fact research by Marilyn and William Saur suggested that for some who prayed regularly the content was of little importance but that 'it was as if the words and the rhythm combined as a vehicle of contact with God.'[172] This reinforces the relational significance of the act of prayer. Volney Gay adds some clarity to the intrapsychic dynamics at work here observing the paradoxical nature of prayer as an expression of relationship stating,

> On an intrapsychic level, the prayerful attitude itself, the salutation of a greater being, and the acceptance of his (sic) will, both impinge upon the state of primary narcissism and yet reinforce self-esteem by establishing, if only temporarily, a kind of idealizing transference in which the self that seeks abasement can also share in

---

[167] Cynthia B. Cohen et al., 'Prayer as Therapy,' *The Hastings Center Report* 30.3 (2000): 3.

[168] Kevin L. Ladd, Bernard Spilka, 'Inward, Outward, Upward Prayer: Scale Reliability and Validation,' *Journal for the Scientific Study of Religion* 45.2 (2006): 234.

[169] Ladd, Spilka, 'Inward, Outward,' 234, 37.

[170] Ladd, Spilka, 'Inward, Outward,' 234.

[171] Bruce G. Epperly, 'To Pray or Not to Pray: Reflections on the Intersection of Prayer and Medicine,' *Journal of Religion and Health* 34.2 (1995): 147.

[172] Marylin S. Saur and William G. Saur, 'Transitional Phenomena as Evidenced in Prayer,' *Journal of Religion and Health* 32.1 (1993): 63. They also concluded that for some body posture was also a significant mode of expressing relational connection in prayer.

the glory transferred to the entity which is hallowed.[173]

The intrapsychic movement identified by Gay comes about not simply because the prayer is a collection of speech acts and a process of doing things with words but emerges from the relationship which is voiced *through* prayer. These observations viewed together highlight the significance of relationship in any process of psychodynamic change for a person in distress.

Margaret Paloma, in her study on the effects of prayer on mental well-being, found that all types of prayer analyzed in her study (colloquial, petitionary, ritual and meditation) were rated by the participants as aiding them to feel closer to God.[174] Interestingly she also discovered that while all types were found to be of value, meditative prayer was most helpful in building a strong sense of positive relationship with God.[175] In a previous study of a similar kind Paloma, with Bruce Pendleton found that out of the various types of prayer analyzed (colloquial, petitionary, ritual and meditation) 'ritual prayer was the lone type of prayer effecting negative affect.'[176] If ritual prayer is the mode which most effectively connects with 'negative affect,' and psalms of distress are largely occupied with 'negative affect,' then this indicates that praying psalms of distress ritually may in fact be the most propitious use of such material.[177]

The primary reason for prayer seems to be an expression of relationship and, in terms of distress, to be a coping mechanism with the potential for resolution. It appears that prayer, understood as speech act and used with ritual, suggests at least a theoretical basis for arguing that one significant goal of prayer might be personal change of some kind. As well as this, a significant result of prayer appears to be deepening intimacy with the divine even if it is not a primary goal.

Patrick Miller also adds that the goal of prayer can be viewed as a direct response from God saying that 'God responded to the prayers, and the suppliant's need, in some fashion, was met. A movement has taken place, from plea to praise, from weeping to laughter.'[178] Despite all the significant observations above,

---

[173] Volney P. Gay, 'Public Rituals Versus Private Treatment: Psychodynamics of Prayer,' *Journal of Religion and Health* 17.4 (1978): 250.

[174] Margaret M. Paloma, 'The Effects of Prayer on Mental Well-Being,' *Second Opinion* January (1993): 41.

[175] Paloma, 'The Effects of Prayer,' 41.

[176] Margaret M. Paloma and Brian F. Pendleton, 'The Effects of Prayer Experiences on Measures of General Well-Being,' *Journal of Psychology and Theology* 19.1 (1991): 80-81.

[177] I would not choose to use Paloma and Pendleton's description of affect here as 'negative.'

[178] Patrick D. Miller, *They Cried Unto the Lord: The Form and Theology of Biblical Prayer* (Minneapolis: Fortress, 1994), 134.

Harry Meserve convincingly argues that the primary rôle of prayer is for promoting reflection and resultant meaning-making.[179]

There seems to be no real consensus on the goal of prayer, apart from the fact that there is probably more than one. However, clearly, prayer is an expression of self-involvement and relationship. It is, to reiterate the words of Ladd and Spilka, an expression of connection inward, outward and upward.[180] The empirical research undertaken on the effects of prayer for individuals supports this relational view of prayer and deepening relationship because of such practices.

Because of a relational view of prayer, and since prayer can be an avenue for expressing personal distress, Felicity Kelcourse suggests that,

> Suffering deliberately faced, through the dialogues of the soul in prayer, makes us co-creators with God. Like Wisdom herself, we hover over the primordial face of the deep, trusting that creation, and the light it brings, will be good.[181]

This view holds together the mystery of experiencing personal distress, in the context of relationship with God, and that distress being voiced through the language of prayer.

Summary

Signpost five suggests that it may be helpful to view the psalms of distress as a collection of speech acts unique in that they can form the basis for prayer to God. If each speech act *does something* by being spoken and the psalms of distress can be viewed as a collection of such utterances then what these speech acts do must be contemplated.

When thinking about how psalms of distress connect with the practice of prayer another collection of concepts becomes apparent. The discussion above has highlighted the efficacy of prayer in several areas including expression of relationship and as a pathway to reflection and meaning-making. Given these perspectives, any process involving praying psalms of distress can be examined in their light. From this examination the experience of those praying psalms of distress and how it reflects the perspectives presented above can be evaluated.

Reflections

In this chapter we have identified five signposts for understanding the nature and potential function of psalms in a person's life. These signposts are based on biblical scholarship around psalms with input from broader disciplines which enhance our perspective. So far we have described psalms of distress in the following ways:

---

[179] Harry C. Meserve, 'The Human Side of Prayer,' *Journal of Religion and Health* 30.4 (1991): 276.
[180] Ladd and Spilka, 'Inward, Outward,' 234.
[181] Felicity Brock Kelcourse, 'Prayer and the Soul: Dialogues That Heal,' *Journal of Religion and Health* 40.1 (2001): 240.

- As text which has been historically connected with ritual and can continue to be;
- As a particular type of discourse, which could be more accurately described as poetic narrative consisting of dialectic;
- As being present in the biblical text in a particular form which can provide legitimacy to the experience and a catalyst for meaning-making;
- As being a collection of diverse speech acts which do something as they are articulated as a prayer.

We have noted that research on the rôle of the Psalter in Israel's cult firmly establishes its legitimacy as an intentional expression of distress for individuals and communities. It also alerts us to the connection between the use of these psalms and acting ritual.

The psalms of distress, being communicated through a medium of poetic narrative, have been described as an opportunity to tell the story of distress and as opening the possibility of re-authoring the narrative with a view to the future. Therefore, this narrative encapsulates the distress and a sense of hope side-by-side. Poetic language has been characterized as an ideal medium for expressing emotions and vivid imaginings. In doing this it incorporates an expression of past, present and future. Therefore, psalms of distress are not simply raw complaint about a particular set of circumstances or platitudes with no significant substance. Any imagining of a hopeful future seems to be based firmly on a recounting of the past and an authentic expression of the present as a forerunner.

The form of psalms of distress suggests that the literary mode for articulating distress through cult and ritual was far from haphazard. Rather, it consists of particular elements which are obvious in the form of most of these distress. The stable form of psalms of distress, as illustrated in the constellations (expressing— asserting— investing— imagining), also contribute to the process of meaning-making promoting the individual's ability to make some sense out of the distress experienced.

This brings us back to our original intention; examining the psychodynamic effect on individuals of using psalms of distress (lament psalms) as a form of ritual prayer for engaging with personal distress. Many, or perhaps all, the features of psalms of distress which appear real for those who authored and used these psalms can relate to our present-day experience of distress. While each person's experience of distress is decidedly unique there are aspects of general commonality to all experiences simply because the forum is real life and the participants are human. Hans-Joachim Kraus expresses it this way saying,

> What is typical and paradigmatic in the statements of suffering and praise in their

recourse to conventional means of speech and conception, catches hold of something that is archetypal and supraindividual.[182]

If present-day experiences of distress do hold this commonality with the authors of the biblical psalms then the model of lament found in the psalms of distress may in fact offer us a healthy way of engaging with personal distress. If it does provide a pathway for healthy engagement with distress, how can this be done most effectively and what effect is it likely to have? The five signposts I have identified in this chapter provide markers for traversing the landscape of distress and an important foundation on which praxis involving psalms of distress can be established.

In the following chapter we will encounter the matrix of lament, which is made up of the constellations introduced briefly earlier. The matrix of lament will offer a framework for praxis involving psalms of distress. It incorporates all the features of psalms of distress highlighted so far. The exact nature of each constellation and the elements that form them will be described in detail with examples of each one. The matrix of lament will then be used as a model to examine the efficacy of using psalms of distress. In this way it will respond to questions such as, 'Does the shape and content of psalms of distress in fact provide a helpful and healthy way of engaging with distress?' If it does, then what might this engagement look like and how can it be most effectively promoted? As well as this, what effect is this kind of expression likely to have on a person engaged in such a process?

---

[182] Hans-Joachim Kraus, *Psalms 1-59*, trans. Hilton C. Oswald (Minneapolis: Augsburg, 1988), 301.

CHAPTER 3

The Matrix of Lament: A Model

The multifaceted nature of psalms of distress must now be examined in further detail to develop the model introduced as the matrix of lament in the previous chapter. This in turn will contribute to a greater understanding of the potential function of psalms of distress for the individual. The rationale for using this model is simple. The significant features are comprehensively identified, named and described in a way which presupposes a functional purpose. The model will also provide a specific way of looking at and using the psalms of distress which can then be examined through intentional action research.

Matrix of lament

I have chosen the term 'matrix' to identify a model of engaging with distress found in the psalms of distress. The rationale behind using this term is twofold. First, among the definitions of the term is that of 'container.' This is a helpful image as the psalms of distress, used as a form of prayer, can be viewed as a container which 'holds' the person's experience of distress. This image of 'container' can be further defined as a 'mold'. The implication here is that elements are not simply placed into and held in the container but can undergo a process of shaping into something different as effected by a mold on various substances. Again this is reflective of what can be observed in psalms of distress and alerts us to the potential changes that praying these psalms can cause. Finally, another definition of the term matrix is that it is a kind of 'womb.' Again this imagery is helpful as a 'womb' suggests that these psalms are not just a container which holds or even molds elements but a living space which can give birth to something new.[1] I have chosen to refer to this matrix as a matrix of 'lament' because of the way in which the matrix highlights a *framework* and, additionally, a *process* of expressing experiences of personal distress.

The matrix is constituted by four unique and yet complementary elements introduced earlier as 'constellations' (expressing— asserting— investing— imag-

---

[1] These images and ideas are taken from definitions of the terms as found in the Oxford Dictionary—John Simpson and Edmund Weiner (eds), *Oxford English Dictionary*, 20 vols (London: Oxford University Press, 1989).

ining). The rationale for employing the term 'constellation' is based on its definition as 'a set of ideas, conditions, symptoms, or traits that fall into or appear to fall into a pattern: as a group of stimulus conditions or factors affecting personality and behaviour development.'[2] This working definition highlights some important issues for understanding constellations as found in individual psalms of distress. First, each constellation contains two or more related and yet distinct ideas. Second, there may be a pattern suggested, although this is not necessarily so, and third, the constellations suggest the possibility of psychodynamic change at some level. These constellations can be viewed as the foundational elements which make up the matrix of lament defined and described above.

The matrix of lament and its constellations provide a model, or a broad framework, within which thoughts and feelings associated with distress are expressed safely. God is the chosen significant other for the distressed person and so the 'I-Thou' concept is employed and developed as a helpful way of viewing the divine-human relationship. Various prepositions are supplied between the 'I' and the 'Thou' as a way of describing the changing nature of the relationship in each constellation.[3] It is also important to note that the constellations, as discrete elements, can be encountered more than once as a person engages with distress. It is not so much a linear or sequential experience of the matrix of lament that provides the impetus for moving through distress but, rather, the engagement with and interaction between all four constellations.

Below, each of the constellations will be described in detail. Following the description of each constellation examples from Psalm 22 are used to illustrate. Psalm 22 is a useful example because first, it clearly shows the four constellations of the matrix. Second, the flow of the constellations is not orderly or systematic prompting awareness that the constellations need not be in a specific order as already mentioned.[4] The diversity of expression and the sharp movements of that expression in Psalm 22 may in fact be a helpful reflection of genuine human response in the face of distress. The juxtaposing of distress and praise in the psalm highlights the intensity of the distress fusing with the possibility of hope. Ellen Davis, commenting on Psalm 22, states that it is 'exploding the limits' of how people can express their feelings to God.[5] Although the sense of alienation is clear from the start of this psalm the exact source, or nature, of the distress is

---

[2] Simpson and Weiner, *Oxford English Dictionary*.

[3] I.e. Expressing— I *to* self/Thou, Asserting— I *about* self/Thou, Investing— I *in* self/Thou and Imagining— I *with* self/Thou. The significance of these will be explicated in the discussion to follow.

[4] In fact, the jarring shifts in expression found in this psalm have not passed unnoticed by scholars. As a result some have proposed that the psalm was originally two separate entities which have been fused together. For example see P.C. Craigie, *Psalms* vol. 1, World Biblical Commentary (Waco: Word, 1983), 197.

[5] Ellen F. Davis, 'Exploding the Limits,' *Journal for the Study of the Old Testament* 53 (1992): 93.

not described. The lack of detail in this regard contributes to the psalm's stereotypical nature. Because of these features Psalm 22 brings into sharp focus the paradigmatic function of the matrix of lament.

The third reason for using Psalm 22 as an example is that it is one of the psalms used by the group involved in the action research phase of this study. I have included the full text of Psalm 22 below so the psalm can be viewed in its entirety and the examples of each constellation in the following sections can also be considered in their broader context.

Psalm 22

My God, my God, why have you forsaken me? Why are you so far from helping me, from the words of my groaning?

[2] O my God, I cry by day, but you do not answer; and by night, but find no rest.

[3] Yet you are holy, enthroned on the praises of Israel.

[4] In you our ancestors trusted; they trusted, and you delivered them.

[5] To you they cried, and were saved; in you they trusted, and were not put to shame.

[6] But I am a worm, and not human; scorned by others, and despised by the people.

[7] All who see me mock at me; they make mouths at me, they shake their heads;
[8] 'Commit your cause to the LORD; let him deliver— let him rescue the one in whom he delights!'

[9] Yet it was you who took me from the womb; you kept me safe on my mother's breast. [10]
On you I was cast from my birth, and since my mother bore me you have been my God.

[11] Do not be far from me, for trouble is near and there is no one to help.

[12] Many bulls encircle me, strong bulls of Bashan surround me; [13] they open wide their mouths at me, like a ravening and roaring lion.

[14] I am poured out like water, and all my bones are out of joint; my heart is like wax; it is melted within my breast; [15] my mouth is dried up like a potsherd, and my tongue sticks to my jaws; you lay me in the dust of death.

[16] For dogs are all around me; a company of evildoers encircles me. My hands and feet have shriveled; [17] I can count all my bones. They stare and gloat over me; [18] they divide my clothes among themselves, and for my clothing they cast lots.

[19] But you, O LORD, do not be far away! O my help, come quickly to my aid!

[20] Deliver my soul from the sword, my life from the power of the dog!

[21] Save me from the mouth of the lion! From the horns of the wild oxen you have rescued me.

[22] I will tell of your name to my brothers and sisters; in the midst of the congregation I will praise you: [23] You who fear the LORD, praise him! All you offspring of Jacob, glorify him; stand in awe of him, all you offspring of Israel!

[24] For he did not despise or abhor the affliction of the afflicted; he did not hide his face from me, but heard when I cried to him.

[25] From you comes my praise in the great congregation; my vows I will pay before those who fear him. [26] The poor shall eat and be satisfied; those who seek him shall praise the LORD. May your hearts live forever!

[27] All the ends of the earth shall remember and turn to the LORD; and all the families of the nations shall worship before him.

[28] For dominion belongs to the LORD, and he rules over the nations.

[29] To him, indeed, shall all who sleep in the earth bow down; before him shall bow all who go down to the dust, and I shall live for him.

[30] Posterity will serve him; future generations will be told about the Lord, [31] and proclaim his deliverance to a people yet unborn, saying that he has done it.

This psalm will be overlaid with the four constellations of the matrix of lament:

- **Expressing**
    - Invocation
    - Complaint
- **Asserting**
    - Confession of sin
    - Assertion of innocence
    - Plea
- **Investing**
    - Imprecation
    - Affirmation of confidence
    - Acknowledgment of divine response
- **Imagining**
    - Vow
    - Pledge
    - Hymnic blessing
    - Anticipation of thanks

Expressing constellation

The expressing constellation is formed by the invocation and complaint within the text of a psalm of distress. Normally both these elements are present and often the invocation leads naturally into the complaint as articulations of the person's level of distress. Figure one below shows the constituents of the expressing constellation.

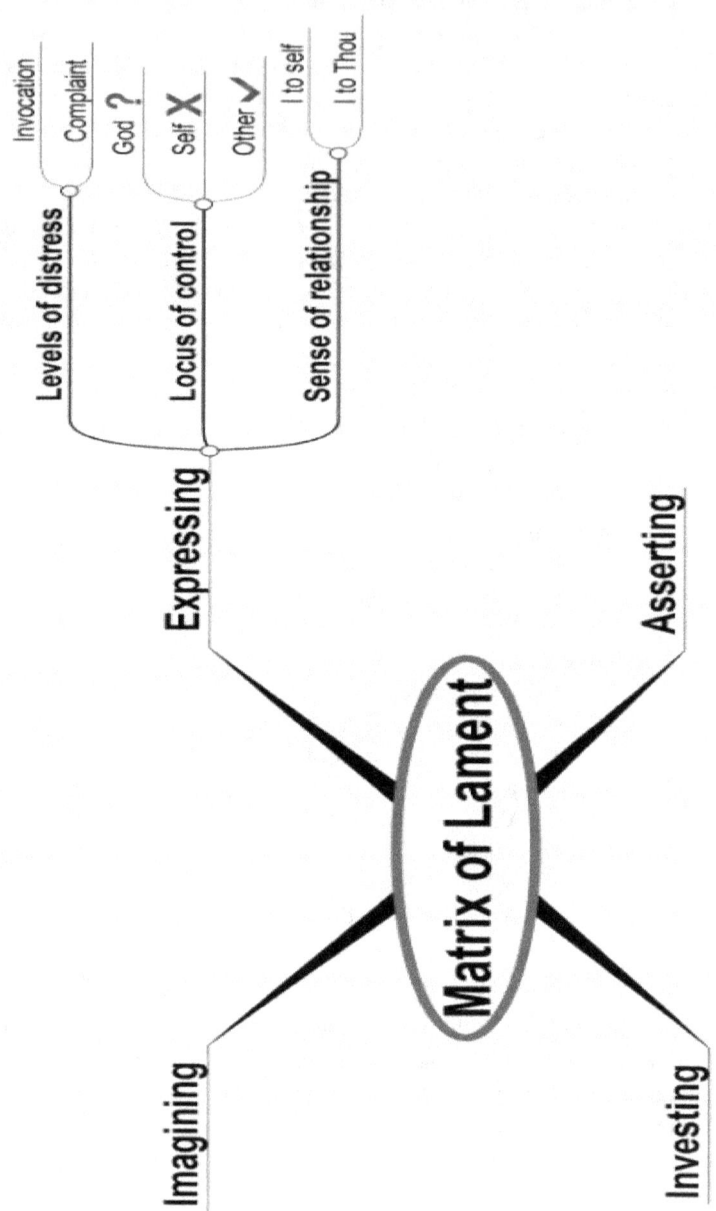

Fig. 1

The invocation sets the tone for the psalm of distress and is integral to the dialectic that the person is initiating. It is often expressed in the form of a question[6] or a request.[7] Immediately, three features of invocation become apparent. First, we are confronted by the emotions evoked by distress. Second, we can observe the struggle for some sense of control in the face of distress and, third, the inherent nature of invocation as an expression of relationship between the person and God.

Despite any seeming incongruity between the person's experience of God's nature and God's perceived inaction there is a strong sense of the 'I' and the 'Thou' of relationship. That this is the starting point of so many psalms of distress affirms that the distressed person has a strong sense of relationship with God in the face of difficult circumstances. Westermann makes an interesting observation at this point noting that the psalmist often uses the more formal address to God. He concludes that such a manner of address recognizes God as the focal point rather than the person.[8] As a result, he proposes the more formal English form of 'Thou' to represent the Hebrew form which accords honour to the addressee. Despite the linguistic form of honour affirming the relationship there is no question that the invocation also clearly voices the fractured nature of that same relationship with brutal honesty. The invocation, taken as a whole, sets out the parameters of the relationship as it stands amid distress from a human perspective.

The invocation can also take either a positive or negative form[9] and can produce a transition into the plea that demands God take, or, not take, a particular path of action for the distressed person.[10] These acts of invocation, whatever the content of the request, firmly thrust the issue into God's realm of activity. The

---

[6] E.g. Pss. 10:1, 22:1 (Why...?) and 13:1 (How long..?) are typical interrogative forms used in lament.

[7] E.g. Pss. 43:1, 'The LORD sustains them on their sickbed; in their illness you heal all their infirmities' (vindication), Psalm 51:1, 'Have mercy on me, O God, according to your steadfast love; according to your abundant mercy blot out my transgressions' (have mercy), Psalm 88:1-2, 'O LORD, God of my salvation, when, at night, I cry out in your presence, let my prayer come before you; incline your ear to my cry' (listening), Psalm 140:1 'deliver me, O LORD, from evildoers; protect me from those who are violent' (deliverance).

[8] Clause Westermann, *Praise and Lament in the Psalms*, 35-36. He cites Psalm 86 as an example of the writer using the Hebrew form *attah*.

[9] E.g. Ps. 102:1, 'Hear my prayer, O LORD; let my cry come to you.' (positive); Ps. 10:1, 'Why, O LORD, do you stand far off? Why do you hide yourself in times of trouble?' (negative).

[10] E.g. Psalm 17:1, 'Hear a just cause, O LORD; attend to my cry; give ear to my prayer from lips free of deceit,' Psalm 55:1, 'Give ear to my prayer, O God; do not hide yourself from my supplication' (positive action), Psalm. 38:1, 'LORD, do not rebuke me in your anger, or discipline me in your wrath' and Psalm 83:1, 'O God, do not keep silence; do not hold your peace or be still, O God!' (negative action) *et al*. It should be noted that this positive or negative is not exclusively found in the invocation of lament psalms.

invocation and pursuant complaint clearly recognize both the state of the person's distress and the perception that only God's intervention can affect resolution.

The complaint contains two obvious features. There is both a raw boldness in the proclamation and graphic descriptions of the situation. This seems to be an attempt to express the gravity of the person's situation to God. The harsh language stands as a sharp juxtaposition to the honorific address in the invocation. Interestingly the graphic nature of address seems to be present *because* of the person's relationship rather than *despite* it. The desired effect of this expression could be an attempt to move God to compassion, elicit action or, alternatively, to simply form a relational conduit through which emotions can be safely expressed.

The invocation and complaint together, being shaped in the form of question, is also significant implicitly requiring a response.[11] This questioning cannot be read simply as the rhetorical musings of one who is distressed. The common interrogative, 'Why?' seems to transcend time, culture and theological perspective when prompted by distress. In psalms of distress it presupposes the presence of distress and the absence of peace.[12] In this lies one provocative aspect of such a process. It suggests empowerment for the person to ask the hard questions produced when people are distressed. Psalms of distress show that these questions can be asked *within* the context of relationship with God, even though there may not be a satisfactory answer. The question recognizes that if there is to be an answer the only source of such a response can be God. Both the invocation and the complaint offer control of the situation to God, hoping that God has power which the distressed person does not have.

The expressing constellation, formed by the invocation and the complaint, voices the person's predicament, as perceived from a human perspective. It is the raw expression of deep emotional torment and questioning. The questions need to be asked even if there appears to be no response. The expressing constellation also focuses on the visceral struggle for control in the situation. Although the expressed desire, within the invocation and complaint, is that God would take control the locus of control is clearly felt to be with the enemy. While the distressed person expresses to God this desire for divine control, God appears to be at best inactive or at worst powerless. Yet, amid distress, the person clearly articulates themselves *to* God and *to* the 'self,' as a beginning point for engaging with distress.

The articulation is in the form of a natural dialectic as an expression of relationship between the person and God. Using Buber's idea of the 'I-Thou' we can see that God is a significant other in relationship to the person amid distress.[13]

---

[11] The desired response is formulated later in more detail with a plea.

[12] Broyles, *The Conflict of Faith*, 80. He explores the 'Why?' question of lament as an expression of an absence of the Hebrew concept of *shalom*.

[13] Martin Buber, *I and Thou* (Edinburgh: T&T Clark, 1970).

However, at this point it could be more precisely expressed as 'I *to* Thou.' Here the person is free to express feelings *to* God even though there is a felt alienation in the relationship. Together with expression to God is an expression of thoughts and feelings to oneself ('I *to* self'). There can be as much implicit questioning of oneself as there is questioning of God. The person is desperately striving to make sense of relationship with God within the maelstrom of distress. A resultant feature of the psalmists' response to distress is an apparent growth in self-awareness.

An example – Psalm 22:1-2

¹My God, my God, why have you forsaken me? Why are you so far from helping me, from the words of my groaning?
² O my God, I cry by day, but you do not answer; and by night, but find no rest.

We find a clear example of both an invocation and a complaint illustrated in verses 1 and 2 of Psalm 22. Together these form the expressing constellation of this psalm. Here the invocation quickly breaks out into a complaint against God. Clearly relationship is expressed through dialectic with God. Amid distress the person, perhaps rather surprisingly, speaks directly *to* God about God's perceived absence from the situation. It is an expression of both doubt and faith. There appears to be a sense of cognitive dissonance where the experience and theology of the person fail to match. At the same time, as the distressed person experiences a sense of abandonment *by* God, their words are directed *to* God. The existential question becomes a theological question for the person of faith. Is God present amid distress and does God hear the individual's cry? Ambivalence overshadows any sense of hope in the expressing constellation.

Implied in the imagery of day and night found in Psalm 22 is the protracted nature of the distress. God's absence is also described here in two distinct ways. First, God is sensed as not acting to help the distressed person and, second, God is viewed as having actively abandoned the person in distress. Despite this, the expressing constellation is still articulated within the context of some form of faith relationship. The person continues to believe that communication with God, as a significant other, is possible. Paradoxically the relationship is obvious despite feelings of alienation and isolation being disclosed. All the questions and statements are expressed *to* God and *to* the 'self' in response to this experience.

⁶ But I am a worm, and not human; scorned by others, and despised by the people.
⁷ All who see me mock at me; they make mouths at me, they shake their heads; ⁸ 'Commit your cause to the LORD; let him deliver—let him rescue the one in whom he delights!'

The expressing constellation is again evident from verses 6 to 8 articulating feelings of worthlessness, being an object of scorn and being despised. Interestingly the words of the enemy are also directly quoted reinforcing the feelings the person has. Terse language used here highlights the often chaotic experience of confronting distress. It also juxtaposes the potential potency of God (vv. 3-5) with the impotency of human beings (vv.6-8). The dialectic at this point is also directed towards the 'enemy' who provides the third aspect to the tripartite relationship in the psalm. Although the 'enemies' are not directly addressed they are characterized as a group actively working against the distressed person. So, the sense of isolation from God and community is exacerbated.

Expressing complaint, as found here, is simply an outpouring of the emotions associated with persecution, alienation, isolation and self-doubt. The 'worm' image is a metaphor describing feelings of lowliness and/or humiliation experienced by the person in distress. These feelings of isolation and powerlessness combine to produce a further struggle to understand the nature of the 'self' and the relationship of oneself to God. The person views the 'self' as unable to cope alone and no more than fair game for the 'enemy's' ridicule.

Asserting constellation

The asserting constellation is a combination of confession of sin, assertion of innocence[14] and a petition or plea for divine help in the situation. The first two elements are not always present but the third is. In fact the petition or plea for divine help is situated at the core of psalms of distress. The makeup of the asserting constellation is illustrated below.

The confession of sin or the assertion of innocence is often disproportionately small compared with the other elements but, nonetheless, noteworthy. They function within psalms of distress in three significant ways. First, they articulate an attempt to take some control back through these assertions. While the expressing elements highlight the dis-ease and lack of control the asserting elements display an attempt to find some equilibrium in the situation. Second, they highlight particular assertions *about* the 'self' and *about* God's rôle in the distress with a broadening awareness of the possible causes of distress. The final function these elements can have is in establishing a 'case' as to why God should respond positively to the person's distress. The act of confession is most commonly found in penitential psalms[15] where the cause of distress is viewed as resulting from offence against God. Conversely the assertion of innocence is expressed often as a

---

[14] Note that in lament psalms one of these is often present but not both.

[15] E.g. Ps. 51:3-4, 'For I know my transgressions, and my sin is ever before me. Against you, you alone, have I sinned, and done what is evil in your sight, so that you are justified in your sentence and blameless when you pass judgment.'

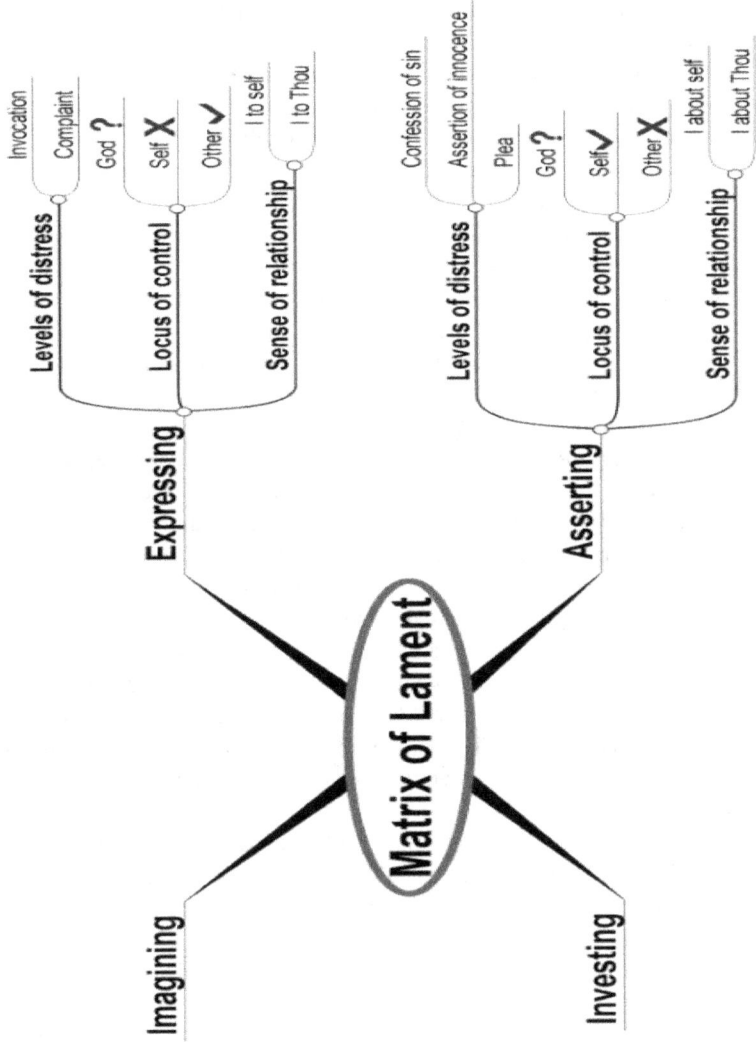

Fig. 2

reaction to action by 'enemies'[16] or God.[17] Regardless of the perceived origins of injustice and resulting distress the elements of the asserting constellation act as a

---

[16] E.g. Ps. 59:3-4, 'Even now they lie in wait for my life; the mighty stir up strife against me. For no transgression or sin of mine, O LORD, for no fault of mine, they run and make ready. Rouse yourself, come to my help and see!' *et al.*

[17] E.g. Ps. 6:5, 'For in death there is no remembrance of you; in Sheol who can give you praise?' *et al.*

persuasive device. This is a direct appeal to the just and compassionate nature of God based on God's past action.

The petition is in effect a plea for help. The nature of this plea is deeply evocative. It carries the intensely painful emotions of disorientation or dislocation in relationship to God and the patent desire for the distress to be relieved and the situation resolved. It also raises the question of what effect an expression of this kind may have for the person. At the very least the picture to this point is one of the distressed person recognizing the significance of the relationship between themselves and God in facing distress together.

The petition/plea acknowledges the sensed latent power of God in the situation to act on the person's behalf and against 'enemies.' The power imbalance between the person and the 'enemy' is not one the person alone has the power to address. Power, at this point, is viewed as hopefully being in God's realm of influence. The pivotal nature of the plea is its recognition that the situation can be changed by God. Again this is clearly asserting a particular belief *about* God.[18]

I characterize the relational aspect of the asserting constellation as 'I *about* Thou' and 'I *about* myself.' The nature of this constellation suggests that a significant aspect of dealing with distress is to assert particular concepts *about* oneself and *about* God as prayer before a significant other (in this case God). This may be an attempt, by the distressed person, to feel justified in seeking action on God's part.[19] It also appears to be an attempt to wrest control from the 'enemy' by asserting that the person can gain some semblance of control over the situation. An assertion is also made that God is not powerless and can respond in an effective way to the person. These assertions stress both the value of human life and the nature of such a life depending on God through a divine-human relationship.

The element of plea, as a part of the asserting constellation, marks a significant transition in the matrix of lament. The transition occurs as the person attempts to take control of the situation by asserting the need of, and substance of, God's response. In the form of a petition/plea the person shows a willingness to begin to recognize the potential for control to be regained through a collaborative effort between self and God. As an explicit attempt by the person to motivate God to action it provides the impetus for moving the distressed person from asserting concepts *about* self and God to investing *in* self and *in* God. The investment, expressed as a petition/plea, voices a belief that God is the one who *will* act on behalf of the distressed person.

---

[18] Due to the historical details surrounding most psalms of distress being sketchy at best it is impossible to conclude whether or not God in fact acted in accordance with the person's petition/plea. However, based on the historical accounts found elsewhere in the Hebrew bible is seems logical to conclude that God would have responded in line with God's compassion, justice and mercy.

[19] When these kinds of psalms were prayed in a communal setting it is also significant that these assertions about self and God were made to the community of faith as well.

The Matrix of Lament: A Model

An example - Psalm 22:11 and 19-21

While there is no example of an assertion of innocence or confession of sin in Psalm 22 a petition/plea for help is clearly evident in the psalm.

> [11] *Do not be far from me, for trouble is near and there is no one to help.*
>
> [19] *But you, O LORD, do not be far away! O my help, come quickly to my aid!*
> [20] *Deliver my soul from the sword, my life from the power of the dog!*
> [21] *Save me from the mouth of the lion!*

Verse eleven marks the first evidence of a petition/plea and this is re-emphasized and expanded in verses 19 to the first part of verse 21 providing a clear example of the asserting constellation (I *to* Thou). This is obviously a concerted plea for action on God's part. The divine name is used here for the first time in the psalm and suggests a greater sense of intimacy, either real or desired. There seems to be a renewed confidence in God's ability to act. In fact the person is asserting that Yahweh is the only hope for resolution in the situation.[20] This asserting reaches a zenith of confidence at the close of verse 21 where the psalmist unambiguously states, 'you have rescued me.' The deliverance is 'completed' despite the circumstances.

Investing constellation

The investing constellation combines imprecation and the acknowledgment of a divine response as a way of voicing the belief that investment *in* God, as the one who can act on a person's behalf, is efficacious. It also affirms an investment *in* oneself as being empowered to ask for help and believe that it would be forthcoming in one form or another. The makeup of the investing constellation is illustrated below.

Often closely accompanying the petition/plea is the language of imprecation[21] used freely and not infrequently within psalms of distress. The language of the imprecations suggests impassioned hyperbole by the psalmist demanding that God take revenge for the one in distress. It should be noted that at no time is there an implication that the person will fulfil the demands of the imprecation by their

---

[20] Note here the use of 'Yahweh' the *name* of the Israelite God.

[21] E.g. Pss. 69:22-28, 'Let their table be a trap for them, a snare for their allies. Let their eyes be darkened so that they cannot see, and make their loins tremble continually. Pour out your indignation upon them, and let your burning anger overtake them. May their camp be a desolation; let no one live in their tents. For they persecute those whom you have struck down, and those whom you have wounded, they attack still more. Add guilt to their guilt; may they have no acquittal from you. Let them be blotted out of the book of the living; let them not be enrolled among the righteous.' See also Pss. 10:9; 137:7-9; 139:17-22 *et al.*

own hand despite caustic attitudes expressed towards 'enemies.' Imprecation is then best defined as an emotional outpouring rather a statement of intended action.

Although the nature of imprecation implies the possibility that God *can* act for the person, an affirmation of confidence often supports this belief within lament. Westermann describes such an affirmation as a 'turning to God' or a 'confession of trust.'[22] The affirmation is often introduced by the Hebrew conjunction *waw*[23] which, in this case, contrasts the sensed inaction of God with the person's desire for God's action. This language form suggests that despite the current distress there is still a willingness to place trust in God. The affirmation of confidence is also, at times, accompanied by an acknowledgment of an *actual* divine response.[24] This acknowledgment is not always a statement describing an existential reality but often takes the form of a vision of future hope where the person's suffering is resolved. This can also be accompanied by thanksgiving to God for divine action.[25] The petition/plea marks a pivotal point in the person's state of mind about the experience of distress. The acknowledgment of divine response is forceful in its emergence from the depths of despair and its graphic description of a hope-filled vision. In a sudden change of direction the distressed person invests *in* God with the possibility of imminent resolution and the firm belief in eschatological resolution.[26]

The investing constellation, below, marks a significant shift in control *and* relationship. I characterize this shift as 'I *in* self' and 'I *in* Thou.' The distressed person invests *in* God by entrusting God with both the ability and willingness to

---

[22] Westermann, *Praise and Lament in the Psalms*, 265.

[23] Paige H. Kelley, 'Prayers of Troubled Spirits,' *Review and Expositor* 81.3 (1984): 377. E.g. Pss. 13:5; 22:3-5, 9-10; 31:14; 39:7 *et al*.

[24] E.g. Psalm 58:10-11, 'The upright will rejoice to see vengeance done, and will bathe his feet in the blood of the wicked. "So", people will say, "the upright does have a reward; there is a God to dispense justice on earth."' See also Pss. 61:5; 130:7-8.

[25] E.g. Psalm 40:1-3, 'I waited patiently for the LORD; he inclined to me and heard my cry. He drew me up from the desolate pit, out of the miry bog, and set my feet upon a rock, making my steps secure. He put a new song in my mouth, a song of praise to our God. Many will see and fear, and put their trust in the LORD.'

[26] It represents an attitude which appears to express the ability of the individual to prevail through the experience of distress *because of* this hope even though the hope may in fact remain unrealized.

The Matrix of Lament: A Model

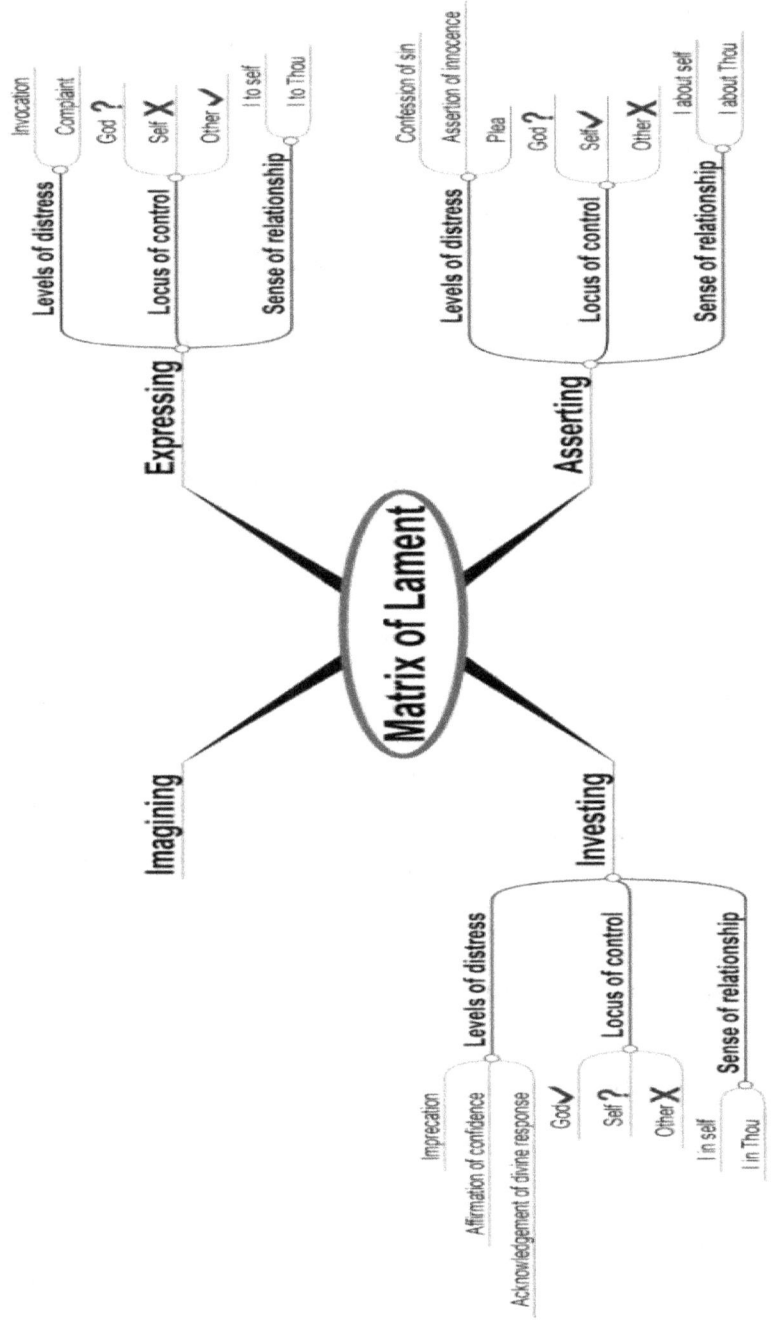

Fig. 3

respond to the situation of distress. Renewed trust enables the person to rest in the confidence that God will act *for* and not *against* the person in the situation. At this point the 'enemy' does not appear to hold the same position of power in the tripartite relationship. In fact a power reversal is suggested by the language of imprecation. The person often attempts to seize control of the situation by pleading for God to act violently towards the enemy commensurate to the violence inflicted by the enemy.

An example - Psalm 22:3-5; 9-10 and 21b

³ Yet you are holy, enthroned on the praises of Israel.
⁴ In you our ancestors trusted; they trusted, and you delivered them.
⁵ To you they cried, and were saved; in you they trusted, and were not put to shame.

⁹ Yet it was you who took me from the womb; you kept me safe on my mother's breast. ¹⁰
On you I was cast from my birth, and since my mother bore me you have been my God.

²¹ᵇFrom the horns of the wild oxen you have rescued me.

Imprecation is not a feature evident in Psalm 22. However, verses 3-5 and 9-10 provide two affirmations of confidence which reveal a key element of the investing constellation. In both instances the affirmations of confidence mark a dramatic shift from the asserting constellation to the investing constellation. Both affirmations stand in stark contrast to the preceding sections which assert both the impotency of the 'self' and an implied divine impotence. This affirmation of confidence is now voiced as a need to invest in God by relying on God for a sense of hope. Investing, at this point, keeps the emphasis on I *in* Thou shifting the onus back to God and God's action. These verses are shaped as a narrative within the broader narrative of the whole psalm. The story of the past is framed in terms of total dependence on God and connectedness with God from birth onwards. Thus personal safety and solidarity with God are equally stressed. Addressing God in the second person reinforces this sense of relational connection as the person reframes the story in the light of their current experience. As well as this, the phrase 'my God' provides an echo which contrasts with verse one. The emphasis here is one of intimacy rather than alienation. This remembrance adds weight to the dialectic directed towards God. The person is voicing a confidence in a god who cannot fail to deliver in the present based on experience.

The acknowledgment of divine response is short here in Psalm 22 is short but nonetheless significant. Use of the perfect conjugation in the Hebrew for the verb 'rescue' marks an event which has already occurred, even though it may not yet have come about. In other words the acknowledgment here could be the distressed person believing in the reality of God's rescuing action as an accomplished *fact* despite the presenting situation.

Imagining constellation

The imagining constellation consists of a vow, or what is sometimes referred to as a pledge, together with a hymnic blessing and/or an anticipation of thanks. This constellation imagines a future which is hoped for and a confidence in God's ability to intervene in the person's situation of distress and make it so. The makeup of this constellation is illustrated in figure four below.

The shift to a hope-filled vision and sense of partnership with God, in the face of distress, displays itself in the form of a vow or pledge. The person, in an empowered manner, voices loyalty to God and often expresses this with a personal testimony of what God has 'already' done. While accepting that in reality there may not have been an *actual* response from God, the vow displays two important characteristics that now form a critical part of the person's perspective on distress. First, it shows their inherent desire to believe that God can change the situation and second, a volitional decision to act on the basis that this belief is already, or will shortly, become fact.[27]

Westermann argues that the presence of praise, such as that found in the vow or pledge, can *only* be understood within a context of lament.[28] In elaborating on this astute observation he also argues that the goal of lament is praise. Perhaps it could be viewed as the ultimate goal. However, the immediate goal appears to be a desire to elicit a response from God so the person can endure their distressing experience. Accompanying the vow or pledge is a significant petitionary expression about the future. Often the petition is expressed in negative terms. In such a case the person is asking God *not* to allow certain things to occur.[29] A hymnic blessing, when present, could be described as an outpouring of praise and thanks that again foreshadows, or possibly suggests, a shift in the person's state of mind.

The imagining constellation, more than any other part of the matrix of lament, marks a return to viewing the relationship between the person and God as being connected and intimate. At this point the relationship is imagined as 'I *with*

---

[27] Westermann, *Praise and Lament in the Psalms*, 58-59. He points out that the confession of trust at times *leads to* a point where the person can actually praise God (e.g. Ps. 74:12, 'Yet God my King is from of old, working salvation in the earth' leading to verses 13-17, 'You divided the sea by your might; you broke the heads of the dragons in the waters. You crushed the heads of Leviathan; you gave him as food for the creatures of the wilderness. You cut openings for springs and torrents; you dried up ever-flowing streams. Yours is the day, yours also the night; you established the luminaries and the sun. You have fixed all the bounds of the earth; you made summer and winter').

[28] Westermann, *Praise and Lament in the Psalms*, 27.

[29] E.g. Pss. 6, 27, 28, 35 *et al.*

Praying Lament Psalms: The Psychodynamics of Distress

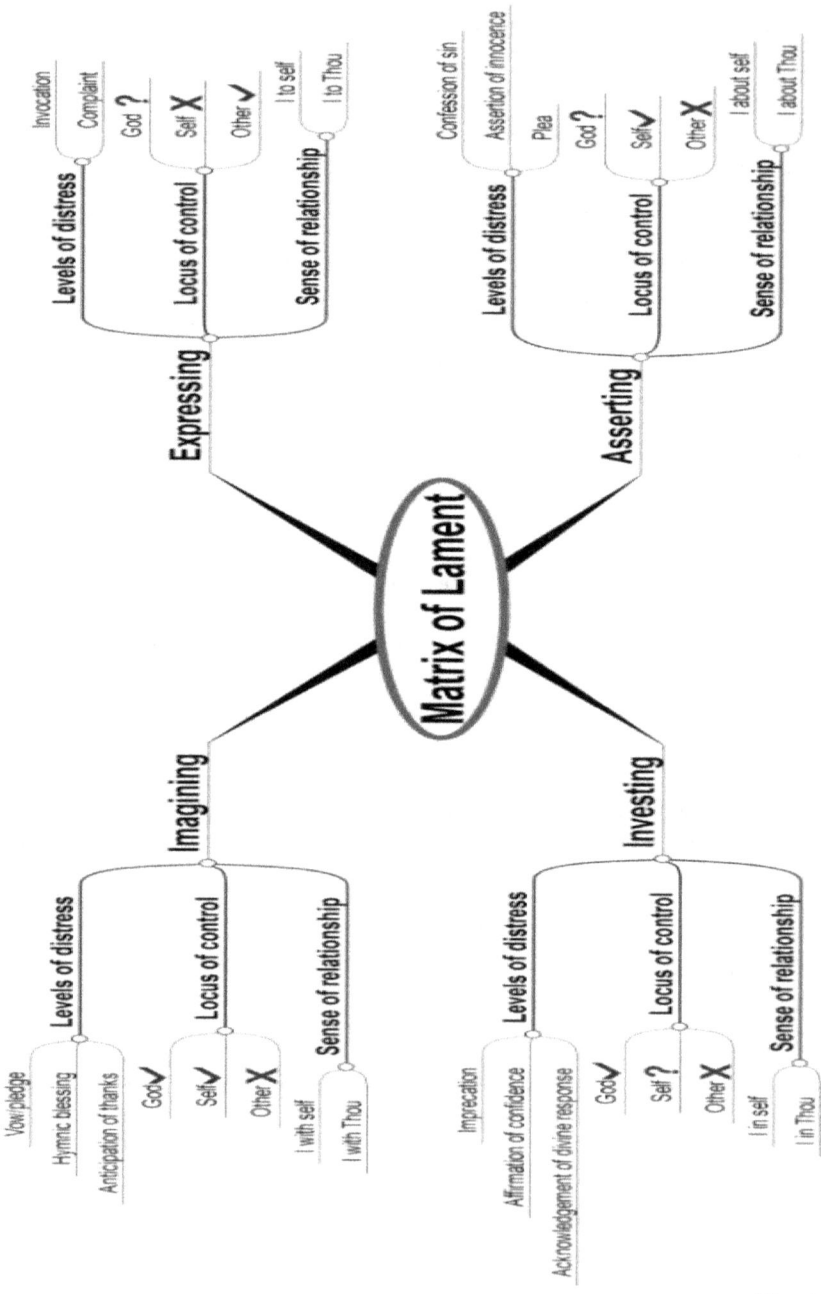

Fig. 4

Thou.' Accompanying this is a sense of oneness with self ('I *with* self'). The elements of this constellation collectively present a picture of hopeful possibility. The distress has been faced, engaged with and endured *with* God and the sense of alienation is dissipating. It is possible that the divine-human relationship is now stronger and deeper because of the process represented by the matrix of lament. It is also interesting to note that the imagining constellation emerges from the relational context of the person confronting personal distress *with* God. The person appears to be empowered by an increasing sense of togetherness with God. There is no suggestion in the matrix of lament that God takes the matter completely out of the person's hands by rescuing them, nor that the distress is resolved. Rather, engaging with distress is depicted as an experience to be faced through divine-human cooperation and collaboration.

An example - Psalm 22:22-31

22 I will tell of your name to my brothers and sisters; in the midst of the congregation I will praise you: 23 You who fear the LORD, praise him! All you offspring of Jacob, glorify him; stand in awe of him, all you offspring of Israel!

24 For he did not despise or abhor the affliction of the afflicted; he did not hide his face from me, but heard when I cried to him.

25 From you comes my praise in the great congregation; my vows I will pay before those who fear him. 26 The poor shall eat and be satisfied; those who seek him shall praise the LORD. May your hearts live forever!

27 All the ends of the earth shall remember and turn to the LORD; and all the families of the nations shall worship before him.

28 For dominion belongs to the LORD, and he rules over the nations.

29 To him, indeed, shall all who sleep in the earth bow down; before him shall bow all who go down to the dust, and I shall live for him.

30 Posterity will serve him; future generations will be told about the Lord,

31 and proclaim his deliverance to a people yet unborn, saying that he has done it.

From verse 22 through to the end of the psalm, perhaps rather unexpectedly, a hopeful imagining emerges from this melting pot of thoughts and feelings produced by distress. The concept of I *with* Thou is voiced through a hymn of thanks. The vision here expresses a sense of solidarity, not alienation, between the person and God. The influence of the 'enemy' has now receded into the background becoming of little or no effect. Control appears to be located jointly with the person and God. Now the psalmist is praising God and surrounded by a community with whom solidarity is possible. So, the imagining is ostensibly an existential reality rather than being relegated to an eschatological ideal.

It is also important to note that the hymn contains two vows in verses 22 and 26. The first is one of personal commitment to share with others what Yahweh has done, and the second describes in more detail the expected response from people who have been satisfied with God's actions. This personal commitment supports the proposal that control is found jointly between the person and God. The hymn of thanks then broadens into a hymn of praise encompassing all creation in verses 27 to 31. Again this forms a part of the imagining for the distressed person. It provides the opportunity for an altered and expanded perspective on both the present and the future. Culminating the imagining elements is an unambiguous, hope-filled pronouncement about the future.

Summary

In summary then, we see an emerging picture of how distress can be engaged with through the matrix of lament and its constellations. As a general observation the matrix of lament appears to depict a decrease in the person's level of distress and a movement towards having a greater sense of empowerment and, therefore, control in the situation. Accompanying these is a deeper intimacy and strength in the divine-human relationship which could now be characterized as a 'partnership.' It is important to note that the experience of distress may not have passed at this point. However, a movement towards integration and resolution of the experience has almost certainly begun.

The characters within psalms of distress

To this point the emphasis has been on the elements which make up the each constellation. We now turn to a close examination of the relationships which are portrayed within the constellations. It is in the context of these relationships that the opportunity is presented for the dialectic to be voiced. This in turn provides the impetus for psychodynamic movement in aspects of distress, control and relationship highlighted in the previous section.[30]

It was noted earlier that the three major figures within the matrix of lament are the individual, God and those who are often characterized as 'enemies.' God is the significant other to whom distress is openly expressed by the psalmist. So, how can we define these three relationships which constitute the dialectic? Westermann provides a helpful beginning point by describing the relationships as psychological (individual's relationship with self),[31] social (individual's relationship with enemies) and theological (individual's relationship with God).[32] It is interesting to note that the only direct communication found within psalms of distress is that of the person in distress with God.[33] With this the communication from God and the 'enemy' is often a quotation of their words. Therefore, the

---

[30] In figures 1-4 the three characters are identified under the feature of control.

[31] Although the term intrapsychic is perhaps more appropriate here 'psychological' is Westermann's preferred way of describing this notion.

[32] Westermann, *Praise and Lament in the Psalms*, 27.

[33] Throughout the psalms of distress, God is referred to in the second person while the 'enemies' are referred to in the third person.

dialectic is constituted by direct speech and quoted speech together with the intrapsychic reflections of the person in distress.

The 'psychological' relationship

The first relational aspect in the matrix of lament is the 'psychological' which highlights how the person views themselves in relation to others and the circumstances which led to distress. Content within psalms of distress reveals particular views of the 'self.' For example, Mays notes the frequent use of the Hebrew term translated as 'poor, needy, afflicted or weak' as a description of the disempowered predicament of the individual.[34] At other points the description is one of the 'self' being faithful.[35] This suggests a shifting, or possibly changing, self-concept for the psalmist through engaging with distress. It also suggests that voicing of emotion and perception, as illustrated in the matrix of lament, may in fact have stimulated this change.

The 'theological' relationship

The second relationship evident within psalms of distress is in the form of a dialectic between the person and God or the 'theological' relationship.[36] Despite the continual cries of suffering by the person in distress there does not appear to be a prevailing belief that God is *not* somehow present in the situation.[37] However, even given a belief in divine presence, psalms of distress express a broad variety of perspectives on God's disposition towards the person. It is variously described as wrathful, rejecting, forgetting and hiding, among others.[38] There is a striking dissonance between these fragmented, negative perceptions and the clear plea for response from a god who the psalmist, at least, believes *can* do something helpful.

In an attempt to understand this incongruity Farmer explains the person's calling out to God as proactive in nature saying,

> They (the psalmists) do not wait passively for God to notice their pain and come to their aid. Rather, they cry out as an act of faith in the steadfast love of the one they confidently trust will not reject them for what they feel or say.[39]

---

[34] Mays, *The Lord Reigns*, 30.

[35] E.g. Psalm 4:3, 'But know that the LORD has set apart the faithful for himself; the LORD hears when I call to him.'

[36] Of course, lament psalms do not record a verbal response from God yet there is an implicit understanding that God has spoken and continues to speak in the situation.

[37] Even in Ps. 22:1 where a feeling of abandonment is expressed it is still, incongruently, expressed to God.

[38] For example, Psalm 88:7, 'Your wrath lies heavy upon me, and you overwhelm me with all your waves;' Psalm 13:1, 'How long, O LORD? Will you forget me forever? How long will you hide your face from me?'

[39] Farmer, 'Psalms,' 140.

Farmer makes a critical observation about psalms of distress with her final comment above. From the individual's perspective the relationship with God is such that nothing seems to be outside the bounds of expression towards God. The dialectic with God is free to contain whatever thoughts and emotions emerge from the distressed person's reflection on their experience. It is also important to note that the dialectic voices real emotions that need to be expressed somewhere. It is in the context of the divine-human relationship that the psalmist chooses to express their thoughts and emotions. As well as these observations Mays suggests an overarching theological theme is present in psalms of distress. He argues that the idea of God's kingship and, therefore, the belief in God's ability to change the situation is significant.[40] In other words the dialectic, as an expression of relationship with God, encompasses thought and emotion which, at some point, assigns power to God as the primary change agent. However, highlighting the paradoxical nature of faith, the dialectic also often juxtaposes the actions of God with the actions of the person. For example, the faithful life of the person is contrasted by an implicit cry that God is not being faithful.[41] Despite these observations, even a cursory reading of the psalms of distress suggests the distressed person ultimately remains steadfast in looking towards God as the only hope for resolution of the situation.

The 'social' relationship

The third facet of relationship in the dialectic is with others around the person who is in distress. Gerstenberger argues convincingly for the significance of the community to the person who is engaging with distress.[42] Although the presence of a 'ritual expert' with a salvation type oracle and 'kinsfolk' is speculative it does highlight two significant functions possibly suggested by the matrix of lament. First, it highlights the traditional place of ritual with psalms of distress as normal practice. Second, the presence of 'other/s' highlights the importance of the faith community to a person in distress.

However, the 'others' within psalms of distress are more often than not characterized as 'enemies.' Though the confrontation which results in distress is not clearly defined the 'enemy' is often viewed as the causal agent and the resultant effects are clearly described. The psalms themselves focus more on the isolation of the distressed person from God and the power of the 'enemy' rather than any

---

[230] Mays, *The Lord Reigns*, 27-30.

[41] This may be indicative of a typical oscillation between faith and doubt in response to distress. For example Psalm 17:1-5, 'Hear a just cause, O LORD; attend to my cry; give ear to my prayer from lips free of deceit. From you let my vindication come; let your eyes see the right. If you try my heart, if you visit me by night, if you test me, you will find no wickedness in me; my mouth does not transgress. As for what others do, by the word of your lips I have avoided the ways of the violent. My steps have held fast to your paths; my feet have not slipped.'

[42] Gerstenberger, *Psalms Part I*, 14.

confrontation. However, given this sense of isolation there is no drawing back from the fact that distress has been caused by a human 'enemy' or, at times, perhaps even God as an enemy.[43] Despite the regular reference to 'enemies' their identity is never disclosed. Day suggests that, 'This is just what we should expect of psalms that were constantly being used in the liturgy of a variety of people.'[44] It may also be that the person who is experiencing distress cannot identify exactly who the 'enemy' is for themselves. This observation underlines the *function* of the 'enemy' in the tripartite dialectic. As discussed earlier the anonymity of the 'enemy' contributes to the stereotypical nature of the matrix of lament.

These observations raise a significant question. 'What is the function of the "enemy" within psalms of distress?' We have already observed how the person wrestles dialectically with the 'self' and God. The distress of the person is obviously heightened by the presence of this 'enemy.' It seems that within the matrix of lament another direction for the venting of emotion apart from the 'self' and God is needed. The precise identity of the 'enemy' or 'other' is subordinate to the function this entity performs in the dialectic produced by distress.

A significant aspect of the dialectic with the 'enemy' is the use of imprecation. Although this element is sometimes placed in the theological 'too hard basket' it nevertheless performs a critical function within the matrix of lament. As already noted, the essence of imprecation is a calling on God to act for the person rather than the person taking responsibility for revenge themselves. Imprecation empowers the distressed person by allowing them to enter a dialectic with those who may well be the cause of personal distress. It also allows confidence to be expressed in a god who is perceived to be able to help. Most importantly imprecation provides an avenue for the venting of vengeful feelings in a non-physical and yet emotionally cathartic manner.

Summary

In summary then, the function of dialectic within the tripartite relationship cannot be underestimated. In all the constellations of the matrix of lament all three relationships are in play in different ways as the dialectic unfolds. The dialectic voiced in the constellations drives the matrix of lament which is indicative of a profound psychological effect on the person praying the psalms of distress. This leads Brueggemann to suggest that,

---

[43] Cf. Psalm 35:11-12, 'Malicious witnesses rise up; they ask me about things I do not know. They repay me evil for good; my soul is forlorn' *et al* and God: Psalm 60:1-3, 'O God, you have rejected us, broken our defenses; you have been angry; now restore us! You have caused the land to quake; you have torn it open; repair the cracks in it, for it is tottering. You have made your people suffer hard things; you have given us wine to drink that made us reel.'
[44] John Day, *Psalms* (Sheffield: Sheffield Academic Press, 1990), 29.

While the experience shaped the pattern of expression, it is also true that the pattern of expression helped shape the experience, so it could be received, understood and coped with.[45]

As people engage with the dialectic through prayer they may discover an effective pathway towards engaging with their experiences of personal distress. This pathway can be best described as a matrix that by nature inevitably births something new. One of the aims of this study is to discover what that 'birthing' process might look like and what might ultimately be 'birthed' as a result.

So, thus far, I have proposed the matrix of lament as a lens through which to view both the content and function of psalms of distress. The matrix highlights distress, control and relationship as three facets of potential psychodynamic change. Before discussing a research methodology to evaluate these potential psychodynamic changes we will consider how lament, as a practice, has been understood. In doing this it should be noted that I am continuing to use both the terms 'distress' and 'lament.' However, their use is *not* interchangeable. 'Distress' is a more apt description of the *content* of the psalm type in focus.[46] The term 'lament' is helpful in identifying the *process* of engaging with the experience of personal distress.

---

[45] Brueggemann, *The Psalms in the Life of Faith*, 69.
[46] This issue of nomenclature was explored in detail in chapter 2.

Chapter 4

Lament Process in Practice

Having established a theoretical basis for praxis involving psalms of distress we now turn to an examination of how these psalms have been understood in pastoral theology and how they have been used in more recent times with people engaging with distress. Earlier in chapter two, I defined more precisely how we might understand the term 'lament psalms,' when used to describe a particular type of psalm, concluding that perhaps a more accurate descriptor might be 'psalms of distress.' Here we will consider lament as a process of engaging with distress and explore the rôle of psalms of distress in such a process. To do this we will focus on the following questions:

- For whom might a process of lament be significant?
- What does a process of lament provide?
- How can one engage appropriately with a lament process?

In addition we will explore some of the theological themes which a process of lament can raise for those who participate in it. An examination of this kind is called for by the fact that this study worked with people who were engaging with their personal experience of distress within the parameters of their theological understanding of themselves, God and the world in which they live. The themes to be explored as we attempt to answer the questions above are:

- The nature of God
- The nature of humankind
- The nature of the relationship between God and humankind

As a result of this examination we will gain a clearer picture of what might occur in a process of lament involving psalms of distress and what kinds of issues such a process might raise for those who participate.

The function of a lament process

As shown in chapter two, it can be convincingly argued that the Psalter, as a whole, has historically been a common constituent of the Judeo-Christian cult. This use of the Psalter, by definition, included engaging with the genre of individual psalms of distress regularly. Self-evidently it can be assumed that, in the past, individual psalms of distress were accepted as a normative and, in fact, necessary part of expressing human experience. While it could be argued that a lament process is only appropriate for people who are facing a particular distress *at a particular time*, the traditional use would suggest otherwise.

Who is a lament process for?

It has already been acknowledged that psalms of distress originated with particular people and emerged from particular experiences of distress. However, including these same psalms within the canon of Scripture and within the liturgy of Temple, Synagogue and Church assumes a validation of continuing use.[1] That is, not only were they used when facing specific distress but also when *not* facing specific distress. Billman and Migliore state that 'for the community of faith it is the living God attested to by the biblical witness who grants the decisive permission to lament.'[2] While I agree with this perhaps it is not strong enough. The prominent place of psalms of distress within the Psalter and the historical use of the same suggests not only *permission* but also perhaps *requirement*, even if a person is not experiencing distress at a particular time. Billman and Migliore perceive the benefit of such a process saying that

> the capacity to grieve deeply is a mark of psychological maturity, rooted in processes that are essential for human life and development. The inability to mourn diminishes human life.[3]

Their observation is important as part of the basis for this study in proposing that a process of lament may be efficacious even if a person cannot readily identify a current experience of specific distress. Billman and Migliore's observation stresses a lament process as a necessity rather than an option for the continuing formation of individuals. It also alludes to the idea that a lack of such a process is not only harmful to a distressed person's experience but also implicitly suggests a deficient view of the value of human expression. This is especially evident in the case of personal distress.

It is also important to note the value that Billman and Migliore place on a process of lament. Their observations can be relevant specifically for people of faith and also for human beings generally. Though psalms of distress assume a context of faith, where God is assumed to exist, this should not preclude the possibility that these psalms may also be useful for people of no particular faith.[4] In other words it may be that the *process* is as important as the *content*.

Despite any distinction between content and process, psalms of distress are clearly relational in nature. That is, they assume some connection with God and others. Therefore, any lament process which utilizes these psalms must also be relational. Craghan says,

---

[1] This is notwithstanding the fact that some settings in the Christian tradition have discontinued their usage in more recent time.

[2] Billman and Migliore, *Rachel's Cry*, 111.

[3] Billman and Migliore, *Rachel's Cry*, 82. Billman and Migliore see here that lamenting can be understood in terms of grief and mourning.

[4] As an example of this one could consider the widespread usage of Psalm 23, though not a lament, has brought comfort to many people regardless of their articulated sense of faith.

> What the laments really presuppose is that my/our problem necessarily becomes God's problem... That there is a God of my/our problem means the death of solitude and isolation. We are linked to Another.[5]

So in the paradigm of a biblical lament process, the relationship with God and the potential efficacy of such a relationship is of supreme importance. An expression of distress being directed towards God could be viewed as initiatory although it could be argued that any human expression is in fact a response to the 'divine word' which has already been spoken. Levine says that 'The world addresses us, and we must answer from our unique place of existence.'[6] Psalms of distress are one way in which this is done. In supporting his argument Levine highlights the theories of both Martin Buber and Mikhail Bakhtin who in different ways emphasize the significance of the relationship *between* the entities as a focus for understanding the relational dynamics in play.[7] He concludes that this focus results in 'producing something further.'[8]

In highlighting the significance of relationship in a lament process Levine goes on to indicate that, for deeper self-understanding, the capacity of the individual to develop 'some point of view outside of myself' is critical.[9] The idea of engaging with 'a view outside of myself' is captured in the presence of dialectic within the tripartite relationship between the 'self,' God and others found within the text of psalms of distress.[10] So, based on the ideas of Buber and Bakhtin, and recognizing a tripartite relationship, an opportunity is provided for the person to see themselves and their world in a different way through God's and their 'enemy's' perspectives.

The resultant broadening of self-understanding emerges from the process of self-reflection by means of those with whom the distressed person has relationship. Reflection on the 'self,' *in* relationship, creates the possibility of a liminal space for meaning-making. Miller makes an astute observation psalms of distress can be viewed as, 'cries for help, and thus as prayers, the laments belong to us in our aloneness and become the voice of that *isolation*. This is not the voice of solitude.'[11] Hence, a process of lament, which employs psalms of distress, is for those who may well be in distress but who are not, by definition, out of relationship. In fact it is only *through* relationship that the self is more fully understood.

---

[5] John F. Craghan, *Psalms for All Seasons* (Collegeville: The Liturgical Press, 1993), 100.

[6] Levine, *Sing Unto God a New Song*, 81.

[7] In doing this Levine takes the 'in between' ideas of Buber, discussed in chapter 2, from being a dynamic of the text to being a function of a process of lament.

[8] Levine, *Sing Unto God a New Song*, 81-82.

[9] Levine, *Sing Unto God a New Song*, 82.

[10] Westermann, *Praise and Lament in the Psalms*, 27.

[11] Patrick D. Miller, 'Heaven's Prisoners: The Lament and Christian Prayer,' in *Lament: Reclaiming Practices in Pulpit, Pew, and Public Square*, ed. Sally A. Brown and Patrick D. Miller (Louisville: Westminster John Knox, 2005), 18.

Therefore, a lament process is for those who want to see themselves more completely, through their own eyes and through the eyes of others.[12]

So, that is the case for people who are experiencing particular distress. However, is a lament process relevant for those who are experiencing more generalized distress in everyday life? As already suggested the liturgy of Judeo-Christian history would suggest that there is also relevance for those experiencing generalized distress. Jacobsen suggests that a process of lament is not only relevant for those experiencing generalized distress but can have value for a person by being intentionally introduced into their experience saying,

> cognitive dissonance can be intentionally introduced into a subject in order to effect a change in behaviour, a change in attitude, or force the addition of a new thought.[13]

Here he is speaking of those not experiencing specific distress. In doing this Jacobsen assumes the potential efficacy of taking such a position irrespective of the circumstances individuals may find themselves in at a particular time.

Of course this could be viewed merely as a contrivance of something which is not real in the person's experience. However, Jacobsen's suggestion can also be understood as an acknowledgment, and validation of the fact, that specific personal distress is nonetheless real for all human beings at one time or another. In addition his comments also allude to the idea that generalized distress is a pervasive aspect of everyday human experience. So, an intentional introduction of a process of lament could be a valuable way for people to learn how to engage with personal distress regardless of whether they are experiencing specific distress or not at the time.

What does a lament process provide?

Given the fact that Judeo-Christian communities have valued the continuing use of psalms of distress by both individual and communities of faith, some inherent value can be assumed. Continuous use, as a ritualized activity, may have served as preparatory to the unavoidable experiences of distress to come. Tanner argues that it is actually easier to pray the psalms of distress *apart from* experiences of specific distress because this then makes it easier to pray them *in* the experience of distress. She says, 'It provides a place to go, a biblical place to stand in the dark valleys of life.'[14] Billman and Migliore also see the function of lament for

---

[12] This draws on the significance of the relationship or the 'in between' highlighted in the writings of Buber and Bakhtin and discussed in chapter 2. It also reflects the functional importance of the tripartite relationship between the self, God and the enemy discussed in chapter 3.

[13] Rolf Jacobsen, 'Burning Our Lamps with Borrowed Oil,' in *Psalms and Practice*, ed. Stephen B. Reid (Collegeville: The Liturgical Press, 2001), 93.

[14] Beth LaNeel Tanner, 'How Long O Lord! Will Your People Suffer in Silence Forever?' in *Psalms and Practice*, ed. Stephen B. Reid (Collegeville: The Liturgical Press, 2001), 150.

engaging with distress in the 'now' alongside hope for the future. In doing this they identify a fundamental existential crisis between present struggle and future hope. Their conclusion is to affirm the helpful function of lament in this situation saying that:

> Two common convictions... are that people are helped when they are encouraged, indeed given biblical authorization, to give voice to the full expression of their experience, and that there is profound connection between healing and participation in the life and worship of a community of faith.[15]

While it is beyond the scope of this study to examine the communal experience of lament the last part of Billman and Migliore's observations is important to note. Any discussion of individuals cannot be completely excised from concepts of community. Even if individuals express and engage with their experiences of personal distress as individuals, the relationships they have with others will inevitably influence their reflections and responses and *vice versa*. In this way any process of lament can be viewed as dynamic relational interaction.

The 'full expression... of experience' described by Billman and Migliore includes expressing distress. But what exactly do the psalms of distress provide in expressing personal distress? The content of these psalms is rather broad. In the discussion on nomenclature for these psalms in chapter 2 we noted that a term which provides a comprehensive description of the content of psalms of distress is not easy to come by. Despite this difficulty, I concluded that these psalms cannot be confined only to expressions of complaint or a sense of hopelessness even though these features are normally a significant part of the content. However, by way of marking out the far-reaching boundaries of biblical lament Billman and Migliore suggest that, 'they evidence at once both the depth of radical suffering and the resiliency of human hope.'[16]

The matrix of lament, with its constellations of expressing, asserting, investing and imaging, provides both the parameters and the boundaries for the concepts described above to be understood, experienced and voiced. Such a view also highlights that form and content ought not to be viewed as mutually exclusive. As Brueggemann points out, an appreciation of the interplay between form and function within these psalms is important for understanding what they actually provide. He argues that the form '*enhances* the experience and brings to it articulation and also limits the experience.'[17]

---

[15] Billman and Migliore, *Rachel's Cry*, 67.

[16] Billman and Migliore, *Rachel's Cry*, 91.

[17] Walter Brueggemann, 'The Formfulness of Grief,' *Interpretation* 31.3 (1977): 265. Notwithstanding this idea of lament form limiting the experience, suggested by Brueggemann, Davis in contrast describes lament as 'exploding the limits.' Her concept is focused on the idea that lament psalms go beyond what some might see as a reasonable

The significance of identifying interdependency between content, form and function is important. These aspects of a text can be viewed as distinct issues for theoretical study but in practice they cannot be divorced from one another. To examine content is to examine how a particular form functions and vice versa. The matrix of lament with its constellations captures both the interplay and the 'in between' of content, form and function.[18]

In expanding further on the relationship between content, form and function Capps makes an interesting observation in comparing the work of Kübler-Ross and Brueggemann saying,

> The differences are due primarily to the fact that the lament expresses confidence in God's ability to intervene in the lives of the sufferers. Thus the major dissimilarity in the two structures is that *confession of trust* leads to *petition*... at precisely the point where, in Kübler-Ross' structure, *bargaining* is followed by *depression*.[19]

While Capps obviously observes some commonalities in structure, or form, between the two programmes the content of the two opens quite different paths. As discussed earlier, the psalms of distress uniquely and intentionally recognize the relevance of divine connection and activity as related to experiences of distress. According to Capps this recognition and acknowledgment leads distressed people to very different conclusions about their situation. While the person in distress may not find immediate resolution to the distress there is, nonetheless, a sense of connection with God and empowerment to continue through the distress. This is in contrast to a passive resignation, resulting in the 'depression' highlighted by Kübler-Ross.

From the observations above about content, form and function it could be inferred that a process of lament is ordered, controlled or even contrived.[20] On the one hand this is true. Any use of individual psalms of distress promotes some level of ordering, control and even contrivance, particularly when specific distress is not being currently experienced. On the other hand, however, Hughes points out that lament can be spontaneous, originating in the depths of our existential experience recognizing that

---

limit in expressing personal experience to God in prayer. So there is a tension here in lament form between limitation and freedom.

[18] I have referred to this idea of the 'in between' previously in regard to the relationship between the entities represented in the dialectic of lament psalms. However, here the idea is related to the movement between the experiences of despair and hope.

[19] Donald Capps, 'Nervous Laughter: Lament, Death Anxiety, and Humour,' in *Lament: Reclaiming Practices in Pulpit, Pew, and Public Square*, ed. Sally A. Brown, Miller, Patrick D. (Louisville: Westminster John Knox, 2005), 71. It should be noted, of course, that, though a comparison is helpful, Kübler-Ross' work was particularly in bereavement and loss whereas Brueggemann is addressing the more generalized issue of distress.

[20] It is interesting to note the use of the term 'structures' by Brueggemann in discussing Kübler-Ross and lament psalms which could give this impression.

Lament is a double-meaning term, presenting at the overt level complaint or accusation, but at a deeper level intending to protest the unfairness of the crisis and to seek relief from God.[21]

He later suggests that lament is in fact a very natural response to distress.[22] If expressing distress can be spontaneous then a process of lament provides a form for that response. A form for expression is important because the experience of distress is normative for human beings and the response is often, at least initially, involuntary, uncontrolled even though completely normal. However, at the same time it 'destroys language.'[23] That is, the experience of distress can be, at least initially, difficult or even impossible to verbalize. So is the experience of distress necessarily ineffable, confining the person to silence, or is any expression limited to a groan or a cry?[24] Billman and Migliore are again helpful at this point identifying the difficulty and suggesting that 'since the capacity to name and to speak is a distinctive mark of human life, being without voice only compounds the anguish of the sufferer.'[25]

A lament process utilizing psalms of distress can provide 'the capacity to name and to speak' identified by Billman and Migliore. The psalms of distress, formed by identifiable elements found in the constellations of the matrix of lament, are not necessarily initial expressions of the experience of distress. Rather, they are examples of reflection on distress experienced by the psalmist and voiced through specific language.[26] So paradoxically, individual psalms of distress provide language for voicing that which can be described, at least in its early display, as 'language shattering.'

Employing such psalms in a ritual manner presents an environment where those in distress use the language of others to voice their experiences of distress which for them may be, ironically, 'language shattering.' Therefore, they are not necessarily engaging with real distress each time but simply seeking to voice a

---

[21] Richard A Hughes, *Lament, Death, and Destiny*, ed. Hemchand Gosai, vol. 68, Studies in Biblical Literature (New York: Lang, 2004), 7.

[22] Hughes, *Lament*, 155.

[23] Elaine Scarry, *The Body in Pain* (Oxford: Oxford University Press, 1985), 4.

[24] Hughes, *Lament*, 155. He says that, 'as a cry, lament originates in sound, whether incoherent groaning or intelligible speech. The varieties of sound make lament polyphonic and susceptible to differing interpretations.'

[25] Billman and Migliore, *Rachel's Cry*, 105.

[26] While the focus of this study is to examine the psychodynamic effect on individuals of utilizing the lament psalms as found in the biblical text, Hoffman makes an important observation saying that one, 'may begin with the text but must eventually go beyond it — to people, to their meanings, to their assumed constructs, and to their ritualised patterns that make their words uniquely their own' — quoted in Don E. Saliers, *Worship as Theology: Foretaste of Glory Divine* (Nashville: Abingdon, 1994), 141. The comment highlights the stereotypical nature of the individual lament psalms and their function as a beginning point but not necessarily an end in themselves.

response to personal distress in a normative way. This leads Tanner to conclude that 'It is easier for people who have heard these prayers before they pray them in times of pain.'[27] Tanner's observation underlines that familiarity can lead to a natural and healthy expression of distress which the person might otherwise find difficult or impossible to voice. It also highlights the notion that the content and form of these psalms may provide a sense of safety and security *within* the distress but not necessarily *from* the distress.

After reviewing the work by pastoral theologians on lament, and by way of summary, Billman and Migliore conclude with a consensus view on what a lament process involving psalms of distress provides for the person in distress:

- 'the conviction that bringing the particularity of one's suffering to voice is vital to healing and hope;'[28]
- 'the biblical laments offer a form or structure for expressing acute suffering that facilitates the turn to hope;'[29]
- 'that community is indispensable to healing.'[30]

These observations also reinforce Reid's idea of the Psalter being pedagogical in function. He says,

> Practice is the intention of the psalms, and that practice includes prayer, praise and piety. The liturgical pedagogy of the psalms comes forth only as you use them. They motivate you to learn more about yourself. The psalms also contain ideas of theology.[31]

Psalms of distress promote expression of distress and can prepare a person for voicing experiences of distress when they occur. If this is so, however, it raises a further issue of how these psalms might be best engaged with to facilitate such a process.

How can a lament process be engaged?

The traditional use of psalms of distress over many centuries suggests that engaging with the content of these psalms was not an *improvised* practice but a *ritual* practice. Therefore, by definition, it was regular and prescriptive. Robbins' use of 'dance' as an image to describe such a practice is helpful. He says ritual is 'the Divine dance through which we are invited and empowered to be partners

---

[27] Tanner, 'How Long O Lord!', 150.
[28] Billman and Migliore, *Rachel's Cry*, 80.
[29] Billman and Migliore, *Rachel's Cry*, 83.
[30] Billman and Migliore, *Rachel's Cry*, 86.
[31] Stephen B. Reid, 'Power and Practice: Performative Speech,' in *Psalms and Practice*, ed. Stephen B. Reid (Collegeville: The Liturgical Press, 2001), 53.

in remembering, revisioning, and reweaving.'[32] As with many forms of dance, the process of lament can be prescriptive and taken up again and again in partnership with God. Such an ongoing use accords with the conclusions of Billman and Migliore who state that,

> while there is common agreement on the normalcy and necessity of intense emotions related to substantial loss, there is no unanimity about the depth and duration of lament, either among clinicians of pastoral theologians. We note, however, a trend toward more openness to the intensity, complexity and longevity of the process of recovering from traumatic experiences.[33]

Of particular note here are Billman and Migliore's observation of 'a trend toward openness to intensity, complexity and longevity.' It seems logical that ritual use of individual psalms of distress may in fact encourage and promote this kind of trend if the engagement is over an indefinite period of time; significant for this study. Rather than attempting to examine a person's response to using psalms of distress in a one-off situation, though this may be valuable, it is perhaps more significant to evaluate their repeated use over an extended period of time.[34] Repeated use also places greater emphasis on the *process* of lament rather than any particular *result* or *set of results* which may emerge from the experience. A continuing ritual of engagement with distress also suggests, in a sense, that experiences of distress are never totally cast off or 'dealt with.' They are experiences with which the person continues to live while ritual provides permission to revisit them regularly. As highlighted earlier, Jacobsen affirms the practice of intentionally introducing people to cognitive dissonance. Specifically, in relation to psalms of distress, he goes on to embellish the idea, suggesting that placing

> words of disorientation in the mouth of the congregation by using a lament psalm liturgically. The pastoral goal here would be to introduce a dissonant cognition of disorientation into the oriented person's mind in the hopes that this new thought would eventually be a catalyst that would cause the person to add new cognitions and new attitudes.[35]

We can observe then that lament may be engaged within separate and yet related real life scenarios:

- Where a person is seeking to engage with specific, identified, current distress.
- Where a person is encouraged to engage with generalized distress even if a specific instance is not identifiable.

---

[32] Robbins, 'The Divine Dance,' 339. It is interesting to note that Robbins calls this Divine dance *the* Divine dance emphasizing the significance of its ubiquitous place in human experience.

[33] Billman and Migliore, *Rachel's Cry*, 81.

[34] The exact detail of this will be discussed in chapter six on research design.

[35] Jacobson, 'Burning Our Lamps,' 95.

- Where a person is encouraged to revisit and engage with a specific, identifiable but past experience of distress.

The experience of the person in each scenario will of course be different. However, the commonality between them is twofold. First, it allows for the 'normalcy and necessity' of response to distress but does not limit the 'depth and duration of lament'. In fact, if the psalms of distress are used regularly, as part of a personal or communal ritual process, it *assumes* that the duration of lament is not only inexact but perhaps also never having an end. Second, it also validates the importance of intentional revisiting of, and reflection on, existential distress.

It might be argued that this kind of revisiting could simply be an excuse for the person never leaving the place of distress or, to use common language, simply provides an opportunity for 'getting stuck.' However, this is to misunderstand the underlying function of a lament process. If these psalms are viewed only as a process of how to resolve distress then 'getting stuck' is a real possibility and the most significant function of the psalms has been bypassed. However, the process can transcend feelings of 'getting stuck', by providing a pathway for beginning to make sense of the distress being experienced. Revisiting can then promote movement and eventually growth. Resolution may, or may not, be a by-product of this.

The revisiting process could be described as an opportunity for 'restorative retelling.'[36] But, how then does this 'restorative retelling' play out through ritual? As the psalms of distress transition from text on a page to spoken, sung or chanted prayers, and connected with other symbols such as body movement and/or icons, they become a dramatic 'retelling' of the psalmist's distress. As a result the person praying can become engaged in intentional rôle-taking. It may be that this rôle-taking enables the person to then retell and act out their own distress. Through this expression the person cannot remain detached from revisiting and retelling the experience of distress through the ritual. Rôle-taking can also act out hope amid distress which past generations experienced.[37] In describing the efficacy of rôle-taking Jumonville and Woods explain the possible outcomes of such an action saying,

> A Role-taking or co-orientation paradigm of prayer thus draws upon a past situation or promise, enabling a person to anticipate the divine response in the present. Since it takes seriously the traditions of the community and the promises of God's word, it avoids any uncontrollable subjectivism. On the other hand, co-orientation still

---

[36] Hughes, *Lament*, 165. Admittedly Hughes is referring specifically here to a response to violence in lament and the distress caused by it. However, the term is useful in describing the restorative nature of re-visiting the distress whatever it might have been. The terminology used also reflects the narrative nature of psalms of distress explored in chapter 2.

[37] E.g., Psalm 22:22, 'I will tell of your name to my brothers and sisters; in the midst of the congregation I will praise' *et al*.

leaves room for individual religious experience.[38]

A ritual rôle-taking can then, 'give deliberate structure to our lives. Structure gives us as sense of security. And that sense of security is *the ground of meaning*.'[39] The last observation made here is especially significant in recognizing an important result of a lament process. A *one-off* revisiting of an experience of distress requires reflection which is a forerunner to significant meaning-making. However, a continual revisiting and retelling through a ritual facilitates the powerful possibility of a layering of meaning over the one event through repeated reflection. In other words, each time the event is revisited and retold a new insight can arise or a fresh reflection can be experienced.[40] Even if this does not occur on every occasion it at least allows for the possibility. Hughes summarizes by stating that 'the retelling becomes a life-long task with ongoing reformulations of the narrative.'[41] The ritual itself becomes a 'crucible of meanings.'[42]

Stopping at this point could leave us in a position of viewing the psalms of distress and a lament process as simply a pathway to find meaning but not offering any opportunity for resolution of the distress. However, I have stated above that the emphasis of individual psalms of distress used as ritual is focused on *process* rather than *result*. Notwithstanding this, it must be recognized that there is a self-evident expectation of some kind of result within most psalms of distress and, at times, an indignant response when results are not forthcoming.[43] This

---

[38] Robert Moore Jumonville and Robert Woods, 'The Role-Taking Theory of Praying the Psalms: Using the Psalms as Model for Structuring the Life of Prayer,' *Journal of Biblical Studies* 3.2 (2003): 43.

[39] Robert Fulghum, *From Beginning to End: The Rituals of Our Lives* (Sydney: Bantam, 1995), 21, italics added.

[40] Peter L. VanKatwyk, 'Healing through Differentiation: A Pastoral Care and Counseling Perspective,' *The Journal of Pastoral Care* 51.3 (1997): 286. He goes even further than this suggesting that 'This baseline in the wounded person is represented by a line of interaction between *suffering* and *knowing* the wound. Knowing is found in the ongoing process of naming, interpreting, and representing the wound through such narrative and symbolic expressions as story, lamentation, prayer and symptom. The knowing and suffering interaction keeps the wound, though dated in precipitating events in the past, hurting in the present and projected through anticipation into the future.'

[41] Hughes, *Lament*, 166. It should also be noted that the words as ritual are a useful tool for reflection and meaning-making. However, it is also important to consider the combining of words with ritual symbols. This then adds a 'multivocality' as identified by Turner, *The Forest of Symbols*, 1-47. This indicates that there is the possibility of multiple levels of reflection and, therefore, meaning-making for different individuals from the same ritual process.

[42] Saliers, *Worship as Theology*, 145.

[43] E.g., in Psalm 10:17 the psalmist clearly states an expectation of a result saying, 'O LORD, you will hear the desire of the meek; you will strengthen their heart, you will incline your ear.' In Psalm 42:9, indignation is clearly evident through usage of the interrogative as the psalmist struggles with distress: 'I say to God, my rock, "Why have you

brings us to the final section concerning lament in practice; the meaning-making in which people of faith may engage as they respond to personal distress.

Lament process and meaning-making

Identifying individual psalms of distress, as a part of what Judeo-Christian tradition recognizes as sacred Scripture cannot be ignored in examining any process which uses them. Definitions for the terms 'sacred' and 'Scripture' will, no doubt, vary from person to person. However, the terms allude to a recognition that, at the very least, individual psalms of distress are uniquely and inherently theological in contrast to a range of other literature.[44] Psalms of distress represent, in part, attempts to make meaning of such sacred Scripture in the light of experiences of personal distress. Therefore, a final consideration in relation to the process of lament is an examination of meaning-making in the light of psalms of distress. This meaning-making can be categorized into distinct and yet related areas foreshadowed at the start of this chapter and expanded here:

- What the lament process and psalms of distress suggest about the nature of God;
- What the lament process and psalms of distress suggest about the nature of humankind;
- What the lament process and psalms of distress suggest about the relationship between God and humankind.

The nature of God and psalms of distress

As one reads through the psalms of distress acknowledgment of God's existence is obvious and pervasive, even when the divine presence is not immediately obvious to the psalmist. As well as this, psalms of distress are shaped as prayers *directed towards* a specific divine entity.[45] It must be recognized that these psalms do not attempt to present propositional statements about God, humankind and the relationship between the two. Rather, they present a prayerful reflection on the issues highlighted above as an attempt to make sense of what is happening to the person in distress. Not only this, but they also assume that there is an openness, or even a willingness, on God's part to be involved with a person in the situation of distress.

These two underlying assumptions give rise to a freedom to question the presence of God at the time of distress and to seek a response to these situations with an air of confidence. This theological need according to Billman and Migliore,

---

forgotten me? Why must I walk about mournfully because the enemy oppresses me?'"

[44] While other literature may also be pertinent and helpful to the process of lament it would not be considered Scripture.

[45] As discussed in detail in chapter two.

present[s] an image of a God who prefers opening oneself unashamedly in relationship to God rather than keeping polite distance, and they convey the sense that others have travelled the road of terror and rage thereby mitigating some of the isolation of grief.[46]

So the view of God is one which *allows* rather than *discourages* expression when a person feels disaffected from God through distress. That this kind of expression is embedded in the sacred text of Judeo-Christian heritage validates such an expression from both the human *and* the divine perspective.[47] The process, then, provides a catalyst for the distressed person to attempt to make sense of God's response in the situation.

Of course, the individual psalms of distress go beyond validation and attempt to make sense of the situation. That individual psalms of distress do not end at the point of voicing distress, but go on to make specific requests for a divine response, raises questions about the effect that these prayers may have on the god who hears them.[48] Does God *in fact* respond in appropriate ways to the person in distress or is the process of lament more about the person's experience of trying to make sense out of their distress irrespective of the ultimate outcome? Theologically speaking, the text of the psalms shows that, for those who prayed to God in their distress, there was a strong sense that God could, and God would, respond favourably.[49]

Billman and Migliore are again perceptive at this point arguing for the passibility and mutability of God because 'they trust that God has the power to save them even as they ask why God has not yet acted.' They go on to conclude that 'God's power is different to unilateral/absolute power but is seen as something engaged by the lament prayer.'[50] Two observations are important here. First, there is an assumption that the distressed person's prayer can affect God's re-

---

[46] Billman and Migliore, *Rachel's Cry*, 83.

[47] My point here is based on my evangelical perspective that the Scriptures were in some sense inspired by God. It is outside the scope of this study to examine the range of views addressing what the concept of 'inspiration' might actually mean. Suffice to say that here I take inspiration in a general sense to mean that the Scriptures, which of course include psalms of distress, originated with God and were communicated through the agency of human beings. Therefore, I would suggest that we have a text which has divine origins being produced in partnership with humankind, self-evidently assuming the imprimatur, so to speak, of both God and humankind.

[48] This, of course, points up an important aspect of theology which is beyond the scope of this study.

[49] Cf. Howard Neil Wallace, *Words to God, Word from God* (Aldershot: Ashgate, 2005), 79. He says of Psalm 13, 'In this prayer there is the assumption that God is powerful enough to effect some change in the psalmist's plight. It is the way of God to effect transformation in life.'

[50] Billman and Migliore, *Rachel's Cry*, 114.

sponse in some way. Second, it assumes that the transformative power of a lament process is not God's sole responsibility, but rather, within the parameters of a divine/human relationship. While the first of these may potentially resolve distress it is the second which leads to transformative meaning-making. However, before we can examine the dynamic of the divine-human relationship we will briefly explore the nature of humankind as found in psalms of distress.

The nature of humankind and psalms of distress

As highlighted in chapter two, psalms of distress, though anonymous and lacking historical information, emerge from the crucible of real human experiences of distress. I also proposed that the presence of individual psalms of distress and their frequency within the Psalter suggests that it is normal and natural for human beings to express these experiences in the form of prayer.[51] The fact that psalms of distress exist suggests that 'What we believe, acknowledge, and become by praying are deep features of what we profess about God.'[52] In this sense then individual psalms of distress, and a person's ability to use them as their own prayer, say much about how we make sense of ourselves as human beings and our experiences.

In a fundamental way the psalms of distress voice the possibility of faith and doubt coexisting for a person. It is the coexistence of faith and doubt in tension, produced by the distress itself, which results in the individual cry from the person of faith. The cry emerges as a reflection on this tension which then, in turn, gives impetus to the meaning-making process as the person attempts to make sense of the experience.

In an existential sense this tension is also produced by a clash between what the person thinks life *ought to be like* and what it *is actually like*. Hughes puts it this way saying,

> moral emotions are the practical vehicles of lament. As an example, anger is not simply an outburst of hostility for its own sake but a sign of an ethical gap between what is (e.g. unfairness) and what ought to be (e.g. fairness). Anger bears a moral intentionality of protest and search, and this fits the function of biblical lament.[53]

Tension of this kind, between faith and doubt, and the clash between what is and what ought to be, could be viewed as a response to specific situations of personal distress. Alternatively it could be viewed as a continuing response to life as a whole, recognizing that by being human we are never in a situation where distress of some kind is absent and the tension non-existent. Saliers calls this a 'crucible of testing' arguing that it 'brings us to face the truth about ourselves.'[54] In this

---

[51] Over a third of the Psalter is constituted by lament psalms of the individual or communal kind.
[52] Saliers, *Worship as Theology*, 69.
[53] Hughes, *Lament*, xvi.
[54] Saliers, *Worship as Theology*, 119.

sense, psalms of distress could be characterized as subversive as a form of prayer which may reveal facets of our human nature which we might seek to ignore or conceal intentionally. However, as the full gamut of our humanity is voiced in the context of relationship with God it becomes personally confronting and yet, at the same time, facilitates the possibility of personal transformation through reflection and making greater sense of the 'self.'

So how do these perspectives on the nature of God and the nature of humankind play out in terms of the divine-human relationship? We now turn to this aspect in psalms of distress.

The relationship between God and humankind and psalms of distress
What we observe in the biblical psalms of distress is not unprecedented as an articulation of distress. In fact articulations of distress occur in all religious traditions and are widespread in secular settings.[55] However, the biblical laments are unique in that they are expressed in prayer, to a particular god, based on the belief that this god has been intimately involved with the community of faith throughout their history. In other words, the divine-human relationship is assumed.

In this lies the challenge. In the face of distress, how does a person reconcile the idea of divine-human relationship with God's perceived lack of response? Clearly the psalmist in distress found in these psalms was not calling out to an anonymous or detached God. Viewed within the broader context of the Psalter and the Hebrew Bible the God is Yahweh, God of the Hebrew people. In commenting on the nature of this relationship Reid uses the biblical image of covenant suggesting that the practice of questioning and challenging God is inherent in this kind of relationship.[56] His stance accords with what we observe in the story of Israel throughout the Hebrew Bible. Rather than a relationship of either passive subservience or of total rebellion we see the ebb and flow of a relationship based often on question and challenge.[57]

This observation contributes to Reid's argument that the Psalter provides appropriate articulation of what the relationship between God and humankind is like. It also offers a pedagogical tool which aids in discovering how the relationship might work, particularly amid distress.[58] However, a conclusion that meaning becomes obvious from such a process is perhaps premature. Billman and

---

[55] See Terry Muck, 'Psalm, *Bhajan* and *Kirtan*,' in Reid, *Psalms and Practice*, 7. He says that, 'from the history of religions point of view, psalm, bhajan, and kirtan are religious devotional songs used in liturgical and individual's worship by adherents of Christianity, Hindu, and Sikh, respectively, as aides to think, feel and act in ways appropriate to their traditions' understanding of transcendent reality.'

[56] Reid, 'Power and Practice,' 54.

[57] It is interesting to note that this concept is possibly embedded in the name Israel itself. One of its possible translations is 'one who struggles with God.'

[58] Reid, 'Power and Practice,' 53.

Migliore offer the caution that,

> Prayers of lament honestly acknowledge that we may now experience God as hidden, absent or silent. In such prayer God is not experienced as familiar, predictable, or comforting but as shattering different and 'other'.[59]

So the relationship between God and humankind that is engaged with through individual psalms of distress presents another theological tension not uncommon to the rest of Scripture. God is freely related to in prayer but is concurrently viewed as in some sense possibly unaffected by human experience. Yet at the same time God appears open to respond to the human experience of distress. In the light of this paradox, God can be viewed as both the potential solution to the problem of human distress and the problem itself.[60] Jumonville and Woods offer a practical response to the tension arguing that prayer is about 'how we perceive God working in the world.'[61] They go further in suggesting that the prayers we pray, in this instance, individual psalms of distress, 'restructure' the situation and then 'one experiences "interaction" in relation to God.'[62] An 'interaction' process, such as that suggested, opens an avenue for reflection and potential meaning-making rather than silent resignation which could, in contrast, lead to 'stuckness' described earlier

Summary

We began this chapter by exploring the importance of lament as a process in response to experiences of personal distress. A process of this kind is not only relevant to people of faith, but to all. I have suggested that if such a process is engaged with, particularly as part of a ritual, the value of revisiting distress in reflection can lead to productive meaning-making for a person. What's more, this meaning-making can take place even if the distress is never fully resolved.

From this discussion I then highlighted the significance of psalms of distress as material relevant to and useful for a person engaging in a process of lament. While individual psalms of distress originated from deeply personal encounters with distress they have been shaped into profound expressions of the experience of distress within the context of relationship with God. Despite the nature of the divine-human relationship being mysterious and at times enigmatic, from a human perspective, the psalms of distress do manifest particular perspectives on

---

[59] Billman and Migliore, *Rachel's Cry*, 112. They are referring here in part to the observations of David Tracy, 'The Hidden God: The Divine Other of Liberation,' *Cross Currents*, Spring (1996): 5-16.

[60] In this sense the lament psalms approach the age-old dilemma of theodicy. Again it is beyond the scope of this study to explore this in depth. However, Richard Hughes presents some helpful historical perspectives on this issue together with the emergence of a doctrine of providence evident in the Christian Scriptures and developing significantly in the writings of biblical scholars and theologians ever since (Hughes, *Lament*.)

[61] Jumonville and Woods, 'The Role-Taking Theory,' 36.

[62] Jumonville and Woods, 'The Role-Taking Theory,' 36.

God, humankind and the relationship between the two. These perspectives are formed as a result of a person being faced with and courageously engaging with existential distress. Psalms of distress may also suggest that making sense out of one's experience, and gaining a deeper theological understanding and appreciation of God, can actually and only come through *an engagement* with distress *because* of the experience's tensions and mysteries. A process of lament using biblical psalms of distress can facilitate this kind of reflection and meaning-making.

Our examination now moves to a more detailed discussion of the psychodynamics embedded within the matrix of lament together with any potential implications for a process of lament using the psalms in focus.

Chapter 5

The Psychodynamics of Lament

Before proceeding it will be useful to summarize where we have come to so far. To this point we have explored the significance of several signposts in psalm's research for more effectively understanding the nature of psalms of distress. I then proceeded to describe the formulation of the matrix of lament as a working model for praxis involving these particular psalms. Following this, we considered the potential function of lament as a process for engaging with personal distress. The final step in this first section is to examine the potential psychodynamic movements embedded in the matrix of lament. These considerations taken together will form a helpful backdrop to the action research part of this study. Three specific potential psychodynamic movements are proposed and explored in this chapter. They are:

- Levels of distress
- Locus of control
- Sense of relationship with God

Support for these particular potential movements are drawn from the text of individual psalms of distress and represented in the matrix of lament. However, this study is not limited to the function of the text *as text*. It also considers the potential effects of this kind of text when it is being used ritually, as a form of prayer.[1]

Before addressing the psychodynamic effects one by one, however, we need to briefly explore the nature of humanity. This, of course, is a complex and much broader discussion. Here I want to make a few observations regarding the nature of humanity, particularly in aspects of cognition, affect and experience in relation to the use of these psalms as ritual prayer.[2] An appreciation of how they relate to an individual's levels of distress, locus of control and sense of relationship, together with material in the preceding chapters will then form a more complete basis for understanding the research design proposed below.

---

[1] The idea of psalms of distress functioning within a ritual context has been explored as one of the significant signposts in chapter two.

[2] Todd W. Hall and Margaret Gorman, 'Relational Spirituality: Implications of the Convergence of Attachment Theory, Interpersonal Neurobiology, and Emotional Information Processing,' in *Annual Convention of the American Psychological Association* (Chicago: American Psychological Association, 2003), 6. They view human spirituality as an aspect of human nature which 'arise[s] from a search for the sacred' and also something which is 'fundamentally relational.'

Implications for processing distress

Despite various ways of describing human beings in discrete terms as being cognitive, emotional, physical *et al*, a foundational perspective of this study is an appreciation of the wholistic nature of individuals. This is in keeping with a Hebraic world view which does not appear to 'compartmentalize' human beings as one thing or another but treats each individual as a whole in and of itself. As a helpful way of incorporating these ideas, Boivin employs the term 'psychophysical organism' to describe human beings, arguing that 'when it came to the living person, the Hebrews took a wholistic approach.'[3] In addition, this study involved people of faith.[4] By direct implication a significant aspect of being human for the participants is recognition of the existence of a divine other and some kind of relationship with that divine other, or God.

On this basis the study asks the participants to engage in the activity physically and verbally, rather than simply to *theorize* about the text as text or how they imagine they might experience praying psalms of distress. As a further response to the observations above, this study also asks participants to use verbal expression *together with* physical activities as part of their use of psalms of distress. In this way the participation becomes more of a whole person experience.[5]

From the 'wholistic' involvement of the person the study will be able to explore the individual's different perspectives on the 'self.' Through using psalms of distress, perspectives on the 'self' can be formed by viewing the 'self' through one's own eyes, God's eyes and even through the eyes of others most often characterized in the psalms as 'enemies.'[6] Rollo May emphasizes the importance of a developing concept of the 'self' which can ultimately lead to 'the capacity of the human organism to have conscious awareness of its activities and, through this awareness, to exercise a measure of freedom in directing these activities.'[7] It could also be argued that the sense of self-awareness and self-understanding in fact emerges from people who are able to see themselves more clearly when viewed through relationship with another. As noted in previous chapters the views of writers such as Buber, Bakhtin and Levine conjecture that this is the

---

[3] Michael J. Boivin, 'The Hebraic Model of the Person: Toward a Unified Psychological Science among Christian Helping Professionals,' *Journal of Psychology and Theology* 19.2 (1991): 161.

[4] In this case people who would identify themselves as people of Christian faith.

[5] The exact nature of whole person involvement in this study will be explained in chapter six on research design.

[6] The concept of the 'enemy' and the significance of the relationship to the individual in distress was introduced in chapter three as one aspect of the matrix of lament.

[7] Rollo May, *The Meaning of Anxiety* (New York: W.W. Norton, 1977), 390. It is also interesting in the light of this study to note that May's comments are made in relation to individuals who are experiencing some kind of anxiety.

case. In addition, a formulation of self-concept can also be enhanced by a dialogical or, in the case of psalms of distress, a dialectical process between the entities in relationship with one another.[8]

The idea of the 'self' in a faith context is important in this study. McDarrgh stresses the importance of interpersonal relationships in forming who the self is, *à la* Buber, Bakhtin and Levine, while at the same time not seeing the individual as an entity totally subsumed by the 'other;' divine or human. This is significant in any engagement with distress in the context of a divine-human relationship. He makes an interesting observation that,

> many Christian spiritual writers have been insistent that while God is the ultimate reality, that in which we 'live and move and have our being,' the graced awareness of our *participation in God* is one that does not dissolve the *otherness of God or ourselves*.[9]

These observation suggest that the healthy 'self' engaging with the divine other preserves the integrity of the 'self' without abrogating a sense of responsibility for the 'self.' However it may, at the same time, recognize a certain inadequacy to cope with distress alone. A balance between *individuation* and *relationship with God*, recognizing the significance of a human-divine relationship, is an important foundation for understanding the psychodynamic movements embedded in the matrix of lament.

Within the context of faith, a fine balance is apparent between the discovery of the 'self' within oneself and discovering the 'self' within God. If May is correct in stressing the significance of 'participation in God,' yet at the same time not losing our sense of 'otherness' from God as a pathway towards self-discovery, then an experience of wholeness appears to be equally dependent on the 'self' and God mutually engaging in relationship. Merton goes even further than this suggesting that any such discovery of the 'self' must begin with God, prioritizing the person's relationship with God over that with self or other people saying,

> In the 'prayer of the heart' we seek first of all the deepest ground of our identity in God... We seek... to gain a direct existential grasp, a personal experience of the deepest truths of the life and faith, finding ourselves in God's truth.[10]

Clearly, whatever position is taken, the importance of recognizing oneself and God as distinct and yet coexisting entities in relationship with each other presents the context within which distress can be expressed using psalms of distress. Then, not only can the distress be expressed but it can also contribute to a healthy self-

---

[8] For a fuller discussion on this refer to the previous section on narrative in chapter two.

[9] John McDarrgh, 'The Life of the Self in Christian Spirituality and Contemporary Psychoanalysis,' *Horizons* 11.2 (1984): 355-56, italics added.

[10] Thomas Merton, *Contemplative Prayer* (London: Dartman, Longman and Todd, 1981), 82.

understanding and experience of intimate relationship between oneself and God.

Of course, what one experiences by engaging with distress in a faith context will necessarily vary from person to person. However, Gerald May offers an important caution suggesting that,

> For a long time people thought of spiritual experience as the achievement of a new or different perspective on reality. Something to be achieved. Something which takes us *beyond* the usual world. But in fact it seems that spiritual experience is more a vision *of* the usual world; a clearing away of the distortions and confusions which normally cloud our vision of the world.[11]

The goal, so to speak, of a spiritual experience such as praying psalms of distress could be viewed as a kind of 'reality check' or even an engagement with the disavowed self. In this view the world of the distressed person is accepted as 'usual' and something to be embraced rather than avoided. Therefore, the experience of distress and an engagement with it can be experienced as an opportunity, rather than an obstacle, and a process of learning, rather than a problem to be resolved.

Cognition

The language of psalms of distress expresses a specific world view and thinking about God, the 'self,' others, and the experience of distress itself. On the one hand psalms of distress can be viewed simply as the expression of distress by an anonymous individual bearing no existential relationship to the reader. As a result, the way one thinks about the text can take a more objective form. On the other hand, when a person *engages* with the text by employing it as an expression of personal thinking about their own distress through prayer and ritual, the content will be viewed in a significantly different manner. So, it could be argued that the thinking of a person praying the psalm can be affected by the particular perspective being taken. With the addition of ritual D'Aquili, in examining the cognitive effects of ritual on its participants, describes the potential 'cognitive transformation' being:

- 'possible alteration or substitution of one element for another'
- 'addition of new elements of content which were not previously present'
- 'specific rules of reorganization of all the elements of content'[12]

In other words, for D'Aquili, adding ritual action to a text necessarily adds a further dimension to a person's cognition. This appears to be, at least in part, because ritual action engages the whole person in the process. In terms of cognitive dissonance D'Aquili goes on to suggest that ritual can influence cognition at

---

[11] Gerald G. May, 'The Psychodynamics of Spirituality,' *The Journal of Pastoral Care* 31.2 (1977): 185.

[12] Eugene G. D'Aquili, 'The Myth-Ritual Complex: A Biogenetic Structural Analysis,' *Zygon* 18.3 (1983): 256.

this point saying,

> it is solved by some resolution or unification of the seemingly irreconcilable opposites which constitute the problem... the most meaningful resolution of the problem presented in the surface structure of a myth is usually achieved by *expressing* the myth in the form of ceremonial ritual. (Italics mine)[13]

So, thinking about a distressing event is most fully marked and resolved by the expressing through ritual action. Whatever the person's thinking about the cause/s of distress, the acting out of the myth shows at least an acknowledgment of the cognitive processes within the individual whether these be consonant or dissonant.[14] It also allows for theological thinking and reflection together with an opportunity for meaning-making to take place. As an example of cognitive dissonance Ritzema notes that,

> Christians, most of whom perceive God as having considerable control over their lives, are probably uncomfortable with the notion that he can produce negative outcomes. They might thus avoid attributing causality for negative events to God.'[15]

It cannot be denied that people do sometimes attribute the cause of their distress to God. Praying of psalms of distress, by virtue of their content, encourages thinking around the idea to be voiced within the relatively safe confines of sacred Scripture. An absence of such a pathway could leave the person in distress with no voice to express his or her thoughts. In explaining the connection between ritual and cognition further, Hall and Gorman suggest that ritual is able to facilitate a connection between the 'subsymbolic' and the 'symbolic'. They argue that the absence of ritual may produce 'The disconnection between subsymbolic and symbolic experience prevent[ing] integrating and processing negative aspects of spirituality.'[16] Therefore, it could be that a lack of ritual and a person's continued disconnection between the subsymbolic and symbolic could lead to an ignorance of the disavowed self.

---

[13] D'Aquili, 'The Myth-Ritual Complex,' 259. Note here that D'Aquili's use of the term myth is in a more general sense that that of Anderson and Foley discussed in chapter two.

[14] It should also be added that this combining of text and ritual also acknowledges affective processes.

[15] Robert J. Ritzema, 'Attribution to Supernatural Causation: An Important Component of Religious Commitment?,' *Journal of Psychology and Theology* 7.4 (1979): 288.

[16] Hall and Gorman, 'Relational Spirituality,' 7. It should be noted here that while agreeing with the sentiment expressed at this point the usage of the term 'negative' is not altogether helpful. Use of this term can suggest a pejorative standpoint whereas I see distress, for example, as a given, not needing a value judgment to be added. It should also be noted that Hall and Gorman's usage of the terms 'symbolic' and subsymbolic' appear to be based on Fowler and Newell's earlier work in distinguishing between thoughts that simply exist in the mind (non-symbolic or subsymbolic) and thoughts that are then expressed through speech or act (symbolic).

Despite the importance of cognitively processing the experience of distress, this alone is not sufficient. D'Aquili is again helpful at this point seeing the connection ritual can make between a person's cognitive and the affective experience. He says that

> a powerfully affective resolution arises primarily from ritual and rarely from a cognitive fusion of antinomies alone, although such cognitive fusion may be a necessary precursor to human religious ritual.[17]

To this point I have emphasized the significance of viewing a person wholistically and the importance, in a faith context, of viewing individuals as being in relationship with God yet at the same time individuated from the divine other. An awareness of this means that while the cognition of distress is significant it cannot be viewed in isolation from the person's affective response. We now turn to a brief examination of human affect in response to personal distress.

Affect

It may be that some 'affect resolution' can emerge from ritual action as cognitive dissonances are engaged. The textual evidence within psalms of distress supports the view that the distressed person most certainly engages with God at both a cognitive and affective level. There is an openness and honesty by the psalmist and no sense of this merely being an intellectual exercise or a 'going through the motions' activity.[18]

The affect brought to the ritual, together with cognition, may find its expression and articulation in the words of psalms of distress and any associated ritual activity. As mentioned earlier Hall and Gorman highlight the significance of language for articulation pointing out that cognitive *and* affective control over sub-symbolic experience is difficult without language. They conclude that 'language, or explicit, conceptual knowledge... gives us more control over the emotional information that is processed.'[19]

On the basis of their observations then, the function of psalms of distress, used as prayer in a ritual manner, presents an opportunity for connecting the symbolic and subsymbolic. As a result, a pathway can be opened for the potential transformation of both the cognition and the affect. It may be that participants can find 'symbolic' articulation for affect through the language and action of ritual and, as a result, can become 'assertive participants in [their] future.'[20]

---

[17] D'Aquili, 'The Myth-Ritual Complex,' 260.

[18] This openness and honesty is perhaps even more graphically illustrated in the Jeremianic laments found in Jeremiah, chapters eleven to twenty or in the book of Lamentations.

[19] Hall and Gorman, 'Relational Spirituality,' 8.

[20] James D. Whitehead and Evelyn Eaton Whitehead, *Shadows of the Heart: A Spirituality of Negative Emotions* (New York: Crossroad, 1994), 139. They use the specific emotion of anger as an example here concluding that the articulation of this particular emotion

This could well be effective in the presenting situation if it were a once-off experience. However, embedding this subsymbolic/symbolic connection within a repeated ritual presents another possibility. Hall and Gorman go on to suggest that 'repeated new experiences create new implicit memories; at the neurobiological level this is the increased likelihood for a particular neural network to fire in the future.'[21] It appears that the ritualizing of a person's engagement with distress can become a practiced response to such events which produces a normative response pattern for the articulation and possible transformation of both cognition and affect.

Experience

Ritual, as described and discussed earlier, implies the acting out of something. Cognition and affect can be represented by actions. D'Aquili argues that 'there is a powerful inbuilt mechanism encouraging us to act out our thoughts.'[22] This being the case, engaging with distress through ritual becomes of critical importance to the individual. It suggests that whether a constructive and meaningful ritual is employed to engage with distress or not some active response will necessarily follow any experience of distress. Ritual could be viewed as a proactive response to distress while a spontaneous response could be viewed more as a reaction which may impact the person and those around them either positively *or* negatively.

Embedding the distress within ritual action also presents an opportunity for theological reflection and meaning-making around the experience of distress for the person, allowing for a possible integration of the experience with the divine-human relationship. Hall and Gorman call this integration 'implicit knowledge' although Polanyi helpfully adds that 'knowledge is an activity which would be better described as a *process of knowing*.'[23] For this integration to occur a process of action and reflection is necessary. Ritual experience may therefore help to shape the experience; providing a space for reflection and an opportunity to make sense of what is being ritualized. Hall and Gorman conclude that

> we have very little *direct* control over implicit spiritual processes; however, we do have *indirect* control over them through spiritual practices. The purpose of a spiritual discipline is to do something we can do... in order to develop the capacity to

---

'separates a person from the protective cocoon of depression' and, instead, present a different pathway with hope for the future.

[21] Hall and Gorman, 'Relational Spirituality,' 10. Another perspective on this is provided by Michael Polanyi, *Personal Knowledge: Towards a Post-Critical Philosophy* (Chicago: University of Chicago Press, 1958), 303. Here he describes this as the 'coherence of commitment' which comes about through a process of intentional reflection.

[22] D'Aquili, 'The Myth-Ritual Complex,' 261.

[23] Hall and Gorman, 'Relational Spirituality,' 9. See also Michael Polanyi, *Knowledge and Being* (Chicago: University of Chicago Press, 1969), 132, italics added.

do something that we are currently unable to do.[24]

In this sense, using psalms of distress as a form or ritual prayer in response to distress, could assist a person in developing an intentional, engaging, meaningful and perhaps even transformative response to their experiences. With the implications of ritual for cognition, affect and experience we now turn to specific areas of psychodynamic change suggested by the text of these psalms.[25]

Aspects of psychodynamic change

Levels of distress

As has become clear thus far, I have favoured to use the term distress when referring to the experience expressed in the psalms under examination. Distress refers to an experience which has been caused by something or someone external to the person. The resulting thinking, feelings and experience associated with a particular distress could be characterized as stress and anxiety.[26]

Psalms of distress display a movement of what biblical scholars often refer to as lament to praise.[27] Although I have already cautioned against seeing the matrix of lament as a sequential process the constellations of the matrix do generally reflect the lament to praise movement of the text.[28] As a result, and taken on face value, the text suggests a potential decrease in the level of distress being experienced by those praying psalms of distress. The praying of these psalms could be characterized as a mode of 'religious coping' which Meisenhelder and Marcum found to be 'associated with reduced stress and other forms of improved mental health.'[29] They go on to add that,

Turning to religious faith brings an omnipotent and ever-present Partner to one's

---

[24] Hall and Gorman, 'Relational Spirituality,' 8.

[25] I have purposely chosen the term psychodynamic rather than intrapsychic as the former term incorporates more comprehensively the significance of relationship beyond the individual as reflected in the individual psalms of distress.

[26] In the following chapter the *Depression, Anxiety and Stress Scale* will be discussed as a psychometric test which will be used to assess level of stress and anxiety; thereby, providing some insight into the effects of the distress and the praying of the designated psalms.

[27] Cf. comments on Westermann in chapter three. In this study it is interesting to note the one exception to this being Psalm 88. I will explain the rationale for the use of this psalm in the next chapter on research design.

[28] See my comments on this in chapter three in describing the four constellations.

[29] Janice Bell Meisenhelder and John P. Marcum, 'Responses of Clergy to 9/11: Posttraumatic Stress, Coping, and Religious Outcomes,' *Journal for the Scientific Study of Religion* 43.4 (2004): 548. This is based on studies by Koenig, McCullough and Larson in 2001. The basis for this idea of 'religious coping' and psalm usage is found in chapter two which highlights in part the ongoing liturgical usage of all the psalms, including psalms of distress as a ritual expression of diverse experiences of life.

life, lending a greater sense of control, which is a critical element to decreasing posttraumatic stress.[30]

While posttraumatic distress is outside the parameters of this study their observation would also possibly hold for those expressing less acute levels of distress.

In terms of the matrix of lament, defined earlier, it is suggested that within the constellations of expressing and asserting the level of distress is acute. The invocation and complaint, which characteristically constitute this constellation, are evidence of deeply felt distress. The confession of sin, assertion of innocence and, ultimately, the plea (which is always present in psalms of distress) are also an articulation of deep distress. However, the plea that God would do something in response to the situation of personal distress may signal the beginning of a diminishing level of personal distress with a commensurate increase in hope for divine action.

The presence of the investing constellation with its characteristic acknowledgment of divine response, imprecation and affirmation of confidence seem to mark a decrease in distress. The imagining constellation may also provide an articulation of decreased sense of distress through a vow or pledge, a hymnic blessing and an anticipation of thanks. Again it is important to emphasize that it is not assumed that the constellations follow a prescriptive order. However, there is a general movement from expressing to imagining, or, a psychodynamic shift from high levels of distress to lower levels of distress.

Locus of control

The observations by Meisenhelder and Marcum point up the further issue of control, or more particularly, locus of control. This is the second key potential psychodynamic shift evident in psalms of distress. It could be concluded from acknowledgment that God is involved in the experience of personal distress may mark a surrendering of a personal duty to do something about the distress being experienced. In fact Jackson and Coursey in their study on control in relation to coping and life purpose found the opposite, noting that, 'A common secular perspective on religion assumes that believing God is an active agent in one's life requires relinquishing a sense of personal or internal control.'[31]

However, they go on to conclude in their study that, 'the findings... indicate the exact opposite of the traditional psychological position that God control is

---

[30] Meisenhelder and Marcum, 'Responses of Clergy,' 553.

[31] Laurence E. Jackson and Robert D. Coursey, 'The Relationship of God Control and Internal Locus of Control and Internal Locus of Control to Intrinsic Religious Motivation, Coping and Purpose in Life,' *Journal for the Scientific Study of Religion* 27.3 (1988): 399.

equivalent to an external locus of control.'[32] In contrast to the view that religious people might 'relinquish' personal control in response to distress Jackson and Coursey acknowledge the importance of a sense of collaboration with God, for people of faith, concluding that, 'effective coping is achieved via personal control *through* God, as opposed to believing in an externally controlling God, is suggested by the data in this study.'[33]

In a later study, Douglas Richards agrees with Jackson and Coursey but also provides an additional insight saying that, 'individuals reporting a deeper sense of change of state in prayer are particularly low in this [external locus of control] trait.'[34] He concludes that,

> The group that might need special counseling on prayer are not the Internals, but the Externals who perceive powerful others and chance as controlling their lives and, in the data, who are subjectively less successful in prayer.[35]

Richards' observations suggest that those who fail to acknowledge a collaborative approach to experiences of distress between themselves and God actually disadvantage themselves. As a result, they risk forgoing the potential efficacy of acknowledging their experience to God while, at the same time, recognizing their rôle in engaging with and reflecting on their experience.

The general movement from personal disempowerment towards joint empowerment with God, is highlighted by the 'locus of control' aspect of matrix of lament. This aspect suggests that praying psalms of distress may aid in recognizing the trait identified by Richards and possibly moving the distressed person towards a greater level of internal locus of control. In the expressing constellation, control seems to be resident with the enemy of the person in distress. God and the person are present but seem powerless in dealing with the distress. The asserting constellation displays a shift in this. Voicing a plea, in particular, suggests that the person *does have* control enough to voice what he or she wants from God and that God may in fact be able to respond in some helpful manner.

The investing constellation suggests that the person in distress now senses some self-empowerment to rely on God, who is viewed as empowered to wrest control from the enemy and, by it, relieve the distress. Finally, the imagining constellation sees a level of self-control and God-control articulated in balance as the person and God are described as jointly engaging the presenting distress.

---

[32] Jackson and Coursey, 'The Relationship of God Control,' 407. These conclusions are also supported by Adrian F. Furnham ('Locus of Control and Theological Beliefs' in *Journal of Psychology and Theology*, 10.2, 1982, 130-36) in his literature review of research on this issue concluding that numerous studies demonstrate the same result.

[33] Jackson and Coursey, 'The Relationship of God Control,' 407.

[34] Douglas G. Richards, 'The Phenomenology and Psychological Correlates of Verbal Prayer,' *Journal of Psychology and Theology* 19.4 (1991): 361.

[35] Richards, 'The Phenomenology and Psychological Correlates,' 361.

The text echoes Jackson and Coursey's observation that 'effective coping is achieved via personal control *through* God.'[36]

A final helpful observation about locus of control is of interest at this point. Mitchell notes that 'locus of control is a learned approach to assigning cause to outcomes.'[37] If this holds true then it can be concluded that the process of lament as ritual prayer, with its accompanying potential psychodynamic shift in locus of control, could aid in reinforcing a healthy balance in the person's outlook between God-control (that is, a more external locus of control) and self-control (that is, a more internal locus of control).

Sense of relationship

The third aspect of potential psychodynamic change is in the person's sense of relationship with the 'self' and between the 'self' and God. While the divine-human relationship could be viewed as different from any human to human relationship, because it is self-evidently between a divine other and a human being, Hall *and others* argue for some similarities. Based on the work of Benner they agree

> that psychological and spiritual functioning are inextricably related because people relate to God through the same psychological mechanisms that mediate relationships with other people. If spiritual and psychological functioning, understood from an object relations perspective, are intricately related as suggested above, the positive relationship between the level of object relations development and spiritual maturity would be theoretically expected.[38]

In essence they highlight the idea that both psychological and spiritual maturity is embedded in the experience of relationships; be they human-human or divine-human. In addition they point out the interconnectedness between human relationships and relationship which might be found with God. As a result of this line of argument they conclude their own findings about links between relationship and spiritual maturity by saying that

> in general, the quality of one's relationship with God is more highly related to the quality of relationship with others than it is to one's awareness of God's promptings, presence, and responses.[39]

These observations and conclusions underline two significant concepts. First, that while divine-human and human-human relationships can be distinguished

---

[36] Jackson and Coursey, 'The Relationship of God Control,' 399.

[37] Christina E. Mitchell, 'Internal Locus of Control for Expectation, Perception and Management of Answered Prayer,' *Journal of Psychology and Theology* 17.1 (1989): 21.

[38] Todd W. Hall et al., 'An Empirical Exploration of Psychoanalysis and Religion: Spiritual Maturity and Object Relations Development,' *Journal for the Scientific Study of Religion* 37.2 (1998): 304.

[39] Hall et al., 'An Empirical Exploration,' 310.

substantively, they cannot be separated in terms of their implications for the person in distress. Second, if Hall and others are correct in their conclusion about the person's sense of relationship with God being contingent on their relationship with others, then it also implies that any process which addresses *both* the divine-human and the human-human aspects of relationship will ultimately strengthen the divine-human relationship.[40] Therefore, any personal reflection on human-human relationships will potentially lead to a greater quality in the relationship with God. It would be logical to conclude that any positive outcomes in the divine-human relationship would also be reflected in the person's relation to others.

Other considerations

The greater quality of relationship highlighted above may also lead to increased meaning-making and a deepening of spirituality. This deepening of spirituality could be the result of an increased engagement with the conflicted self through distress. Gerald May identifies this as a key aspect of human spirituality saying 'a conflictual drive which threatened self-identity and was therefore defended against in a variety of ways.'[41] Engaging with distress may in fact open a pathway for a substantial exploration of issues of self-identity including the conflictual drive. This shifts the possible focus of engagement with personal distress towards a greater understanding of self. One consequence of this might be that an 'integrated spiritual experience tends to move an individual away from the importance of need-satisfaction.'[42]

The matrix of lament captures the way in which many of these shifts can be observed in psalms of distress. Psalms of distress are clearly engaged in the divine-human and the human-human relationships. Self-evidently the author, and the one praying psalms of distress, sees some kind of significant existential connection between the 'self,' God and the enemy, even if it is displayed simply as a cry for divine intervention. The initial production of such a psalm and its subsequent use may in fact have been just that, a cry for divine intervention. However, when these kinds of psalms are ensconced within ritual they may take on another, more profound, trajectory providing a pathway for greater reflection and meaning-making which moves beyond a more primal cry of distress. In line with May's observations the 'conflictual self' may be a significant aspect to such a process and can be observed in psalms of distress.

In addition to how a person relates to themselves, relationship with an 'enemy' is also critical to the process of lament. Although the identity of this entity may be unclear, the existence of the relationship is something which provides a catalyst for the conflictual self. Part of this conflict is the triggering of the deeper

---

[40] On the other hand Hall *et al* also suggest that individuals with 'disturbed relationships with other people' are more likely to display a more 'pathological relationship with God' ('An Empirical Exploration,' 311.)

[41] May, 'The Psychodynamics of Spirituality,' 84.

[42] May, 'The Psychodynamics of Spirituality,' 85.

questions of life are prompted such as 'Who am I?' Or, perhaps, 'Who am I in relation to God and others?' In this sense the conflict for the person, evident in psalms of distress, is a necessary contributor towards spiritual growth. Being used repetitively as ritual reinforces continual reflection leading to a deeper level of meaning-making mentioned earlier.

Summary

So in summary this study proposes that an engagement with distress, by praying psalms of distress in a ritual manner, makes it a wholistic approach. The significance of the need for a wholistic approach is based on the perspective that these psalms emerged from a historical-cultural setting which inherently valued the whole person. On this basis I propose that use of psalms of distress, prayed by individuals, may well influence cognition, affect and, ultimately, the overall experience of distress.

While this chapter has examined each of the identified psychodynamic movements— level of distress, locus of control and sense of relationship— it has not been suggested that they be viewed independently from one another. This study seeks to examine whether there is any change in these psychodynamics, or not, for those who engage with personal distress by praying the psalms of distress.

Chapter 6

Research Design

The initial aim of this study, identified in chapter one, was to examine the psychodynamic effect on those using individual psalms of distress intentionally in the form of ritual prayer as a way of engaging with experiences of personal distress. This chapter will present a methodology for the examination, reiterate the specific foci of the study and describe the research instruments employed to facilitate the evaluation. In addition, a rationale for selecting particular psalms of distress and the choice of participants will also be established.

Before doing this I will briefly map out where we have come from so far. Chapter two presented several signposts in research which, viewed together, underline the importance of the Psalter as a whole, and psalms of distress specifically, within the Judeo-Christian context as a significant avenue for expressing both personal devotion and corporate worship.[1] The signposts also highlighted several significant textual features which could have implications for the function of such a text as a form of prayer. The narrative and poetic features of individual psalms of distress and the tripartite dialectic identified between the 'self,' God and the 'enemy' were of particular significance. Chapter two also identified a raft of literary features found in individual psalms of distress, as described by Gerstenberger which I then further distilled into four constellations forming the matrix of lament which highlights the functional nature of psalms of distress.

In chapter three the matrix of lament was more fully developed. It was defined as being a kind of container, mold or womb, which emphasizes the potential it may have for providing a holding space for distress and, potentially, a place for transformation of some kind. With the constellations of expressing, asserting, investing and imagining, the matrix of lament was proposed as a working model through which a person might view and understand psalms of distress. With this perspective and understanding the person may then enter a process of engagement with personal distress *through* psalms of distress.

Chapter four reviewed the ways in which the process of lament has been understood more broadly within pastoral theology. This drew attention to a diversity of approaches to understanding the nature of the lament process, what the process could look like and the effects such a process might have. It also highlighted the efficacy and need for such a process to promote healthy engagement

---

[1] This is notwithstanding the fact that in the introduction I stressed that in settings such as the evangelical church this avenue has become decreasingly well explored.

with personal distress.[2] Considering this background, the research design provides a method for examining any psychodynamic change evident as participants pray selected individual psalms of distress as a regular ritual. The approach highlights both the efficacy of a process involving praying these psalms and the value of the matrix of lament as a lens through which psalms of distress can be both understood and examined.

Research methodology

The general approach to research for this study is qualitative. The rationale for selecting a qualitative approach is based on the perceived importance of *process*, identified in previous chapters, and the subjective meanings which the participants may bring to the process. This approach also allows a closer examination of why participants respond in the ways they do and how they reflect on the responses they have. The qualitative approach being focused primarily on a journaling and one-on-one interview process provides two distinct ways in which the language of response and reflection can be examined.

Based on this qualitative approach I work within an *interpretive* paradigm. A paradigm such as this is helpful in this study for three specific reasons:

1. It focuses on the nature of the person's internal experiences and their external responses to those experiences.
2. It opens the possibility of being able to examine the person's meaning-making process and themes which might emerge for the individual and/or within the group of participants.
3. It provides an opportunity to interact with the person's responses and reflections.

As a pathway for working within the paradigm described above the major focus will be on the narrative aspects of the person's responses. The focus on narrative, in this study, expressed through journaling and one-on-one interview, aided in empowering the participants to *tell their own story*. In chapter 2 the 'narrative' nature of psalms of distress was described and discussed at length. The approach being proposed here provides a process whereby the interweaving of the person's narrative and the narrative of the psalms of distress can be observed and examined ultimately facilitating an interpretive approach to the data.

Specific psychometric testing is also be employed alongside the approach described above. The purpose of this is to provide a more 'objective' perspective on the participant's responses to the process and highlight any congruence or incongruence between their test results and their reflections.

---

[2] Although outside the scope of this study, it should also be noted that the findings are not limited to efficacy and necessity for individuals engaging with experiences of personal distress but also communities facing distress.

Method

Having established a rationale for the method used in this study we will now examine the foci of the method, the instruments used and the process of selection of participants for the study.

Specific foci

The method for this study was designed to focus specifically on an examination of any changes in the psychodynamics highlighted in chapter five:

1. Levels of distress
2. Locus of control
3. Sense of relationship.

However, as well as this, several more general aspects are also examined. These will include:

- How individuals find the matrix of lament as a model for understanding and engaging with psalms of distress;
- How individuals respond to using content such as that present in psalms of distress as a way of praying;
- How individuals respond to this approach to prayer being prescriptive in content and intentional in planning and execution;
- How individuals respond to the idea of experiencing these psalms as a wholistic expression of prayer through ritual.[3]

General requirements

The participants, once selected, were expected to attend an initial group meeting. At this meeting each person was invited to read and sign the consent form.[4] Once this has taken place the group completed the three psychometric tests[5] and were then briefed on the process. To help the participants to become oriented to the requirements they were provided with a short summary of the aims of the project and colour-coded copies of the psalms of distress to be used.[6]

---

[3] The details of the ritual's content will be explicated below in the section 'Participation in the process.'

[4] Ethics permission for this study was granted by the *Human Research Ethics Committee* of *Murdoch University*, Perth, Western Australia in 2007.

[5] The *Depression, Anxiety and Stress Scale* and the *Locus of Control* tests will be administered and evaluated Dr. Alex Main (Clinical Psychologist). The *Spiritual Assessment Inventory* will be administered and evaluated by me as this instrument does not require a qualified administrator. Each of these tests will be discussed in detail below.

[6] The short summary can be found in appendix two and the full text of the psalms of distress, used in this study, are located in appendix four. The colour-coding was provided to indicate which parts of each psalm belonged to which constellation of the matrix of lament. However, you will note that the colour coding in appendix four has been replaced.

Explaining the matrix of lament

Following the testing I took approximately 30 minutes to explain the concept of the matrix of lament and provide examples of the constellations from the psalms to be used in the study. Participants were encouraged to ask any relevant questions about the process and clarify what was expected of them.

Explaining the ritual

As well as this, details of the ritual to be followed were provided and explained with any necessary clarifications being made at that time.[7] A request was made that the participants stay as close to the prescribed ritual of prayer as possible. The rationale for this was threefold. First, as part of the aim of the study, these psalms were not to be prayed in an extemporary manner but, rather, as a systematic, regular ritual. Second, the study was seeking to examine any psychodynamic change that may occur when the action of praying the psalms is *connected with* ritual action. Third, the closer all the participants came to replicating the ritual process the easier it would be to form a basis of comparison between their discrete experiences.

The ritual prescribed was be provided in written form as follows:

- **Step 1:**
    - Find a comfortable and safe place for prayer.
    - Sit with your back straight and your feet on the floor.
    - Focus on your lower abdomen breathing in through your nose.
    - Hold for 4 seconds and then breathe out through your nose for 6 to 9 seconds.
    - Pause before repeating.

- **Step 2:**
    - Say the words of the prayer: 'I am ready to begin...'[8]

- **Step 3:**
    - Think about your point of distress or imagine one from the past before you begin praying.
    - Pray aloud slowly through the designated psalm pausing or changing pace when and where necessary.
    - Use appropriate body movements for each constellation.

- **Step 4:**
    - Journal your reflections based on the questions provided.[9]

---

[7] Details of the ritual can be found in appendix three and also listed below.

[8] The full prayer can be found in appendix three.

[9] These questions have been listed prior to this as part of the discussion of this research instrument.

Research Design

Step 1:
The first step above was designed to provide both space and a framework for centring before undertaking the task of praying the designated psalm. By keeping the same position and the same procedure as a preparation, it was intended that this aspect of the ritual will assist the participant to focus on the task and be able to do this without other distractions.

Step 2:
Each time this process begins the participant was asked to pray the prayer 'I am ready to begin....' The purpose of this was to provide a regular and defined starting point for the process of prayer to begin, which is common to all the participants. The content of the prayer is also general in nature placing the immanent experience of praying the designated psalms of distress in the context of a divine-human relationship. The construction of the prayer and its wording emphasizes the divine-human relationship as one of safety where the authentic self could be expressed freely and without concern.

Step 3:
Step 3 leads into the engagement with the designated psalm. It was important for the participant to focus on the psalm itself and on either their generalized experiences of distress at that moment or a specific experience of distress from either the present or the past. This encouraged each person to seek a connection between the words of the psalm and their own experience and avoid any detachment from the content. It was prescribed that each psalm should be prayed aloud. Praying the psalms aloud is based primarily on the historical practice of using psalms performatively and the notion that psalms are a series of related speech acts.[10] As well as this an oral praying of the psalms, by definition, slows the person down allowing participants to hear the words of the psalms *as if* they are their own.

The body movements, named in the third step are a further development of the centring activities of step one. So that the experience of praying these psalms was a more wholistic experience a specific movement was designated for each constellation of the matrix. The movements suggested are as follows:

- **Expressing:** hands by sides with palms facing outwards
- **Asserting:** hands with palms facing upwards
- **Investing:** hands lifted with palms pressing upwards
- **Imagining:** hands lifted above head with palms facing upwards

These movements were demonstrated as part of the initial group meeting and explanation.

Finally, it should be noted that each psalm was to be prayed for five days in a row. Following each five-day period a two-day break was observed before beginning praying the following psalm for the next five days and so on through all six psalms. The repetition allowed time and space for the experience of each

---

[10] These perspectives were discussed in detail in chapter two.

particular psalm to be revisited and an opportunity to reflect on various issues. The two-day break following each psalm also allowed space away from the constant focus on personal distress.

Step 4:
The final step summarized above is the intentional journaling process based on a set of designated questions. While the questions are specific and detailed, the participants were encouraged to reflect and respond intuitively, keeping the ideas raised by the questions in the background of their thinking. The exact format of the journaling was not specified but each participant was encouraged to use a format which they found suitable for themselves.

One-on-one interview

During the six week process of praying the psalms I kept regular contact with each participant and also conducted the one-on-one interview with each person before convening the group for the last time. The one-on-one interview consisted of a series of questions exploring participant's responses to various aspects of the whole experience. The questions did not address particular issues in particular psalms. However, some of these issues arose during the interview. The questions focused on the following issues:

- How the participant responded to the prescribed manner of praying
- How the participant found the content of psalms of distress
- How they participant found the ritual aspect of the experience
- How the participant found the reflection activity in the form of journaling
- Issues relating to their understanding of the matrix of lament as a concept and the usefulness of using the psalms of distress

The participants were free not to respond to any of the questions posed and to add any further observations that they may find relevant in their experience.

Group debriefing

Following the one-on-one interviews the group was reconvened to complete the post-psychometric testing and then to debrief the process.[11] The focus of the discussion was on the three aspects of psychodynamic change being explored: levels of distress, locus of control and sense of relationship. This was a guided discussion with specific questions in the hope that sharing experiences within a group setting might evoke further observations from the participants.[12]

---

[11] Note again that the *Depression, Anxiety and Stress Scale* and the *Locus of Control* test was administered and collated by Dr. Alex Main (Clinical Psychologist). I administered and collated the *Spiritual Assessment Inventory*.

[12] The interview questions can be found in appendix 6.

Follow-up

Each participant was offered the opportunity for further one-on-one discussion about their experience if they so desired. In addition professional one-on-one counseling from someone other than myself was offered had they wished to pursue any of the issues raised for them by the experience.[13] As well as this I provided each participant with a summary of the general findings of the study once the results have been collated and analyzed.

Having outlined the method employed to pursue the aims of this study we will now examine the research instruments to be used for the method in greater detail.

Research instruments

As already alluded to, several research instruments were employed to provide data for an evaluation of the various aspects of the process highlighted above. This section will discuss the nature and structure of the journaling process and the one-on-one interview with each participant. It will also identify the specific psychometric tests used, offering a rationale for their choice.

Personal Journal

The personal journal was focused around several questions to be reflected on, based on the participant's experience of praying each individual psalm of distress. These questions were designed to help the participant reflect on what happened for them and how the process helped or hindered them in their engagement with distress. The questions are as follows:

Reflection questions:
1. What did the psalm enable me to express to myself and to God about my distress?
2. What could I begin to assert about myself and about God amid my distress?
3. In what way did praying the psalm help me to invest in my sense of well-being and in my relationship with God?
4. How do I imagine my world differently?
5. What was draining about the experience?
6. What was life-giving about the experience?
7. Was the concept of the matrix and its constellations helpful in understanding and using this psalm?

The volume, frequency and format of the participants' responses to these questions were not prescribed. The journaling also incorporated requests which focused on responses to any specific change they noticed as they responded to God, themselves, others and the ritual process itself in terms of thinking, feeling and acting. It also encouraged them to explore any meaning-making they engaged in

---

[13] Dr. Alex Main offered his professional services as a psychologist for any participants who wished to pursue this course.

as part of their experience. The response requests are as follows:

Response:
1. Describe any movement in your thinking about self, God and others.
2. Describe any movement in your feelings towards self, God and others.
3. Describe any effect the breathing, preparation prayer and body movements had on your prayer activity.
4. Describe any new sense of meaning in your experience of distress as you prayed the psalm.

It was hoped that these would provide enough guidance to keep the participants focused on the task without constricting freedom for personal exploration which may clarify any unexpected issues.

The selected psalms of distress

The psalms chosen for this research were 10, 22, 35, 55, 88 and 102. Each of these psalms can be classified as individual psalms of distress and can be viewed through the matrix of lament. However, each one contains particular features which are unique. As a result of this, the participants were exposed to different emphases and nuances within each psalm as they proceed.

The translation of the psalms given to each participant was from the *New Revised Standard Version*. This translation was used as it provides a balance between an accurate reflection of the shape and meaning of the original Hebrew, the nature of the text as poetry and a reflection of present-day English forms. Following is a short description of each psalm and a rationale for its choice as part of the journaling instrument.

Psalm 10

Psalm 10 was chosen as the first psalm for participants to use for prayer for several reasons. It contains all four constellations of the matrix in the order in which they were introduced conceptually (expressing — asserting — investing — imagining) and begins with two questions which are characteristic of many psalms of distress. It is also one of the shorter individual psalms of distress and, therefore, not excessively taxing in terms of how long it takes to pray the complete psalm.

By beginning the process with this psalm the participants began to interact with a psalm of distress containing all the significant elements of the form presented in a straightforward manner before tackling some of the more complex examples. It was hoped that after using Psalm 10 for some time in prayer they would have a clear grasp of the discrete constellations of psalms of distress before engaging with the rest.

There are several significant features in this psalm. Two questions posed at the beginning of the psalm ('Why, O LORD, do you stand far off? Why do you hide yourself in times of trouble?')[14] articulate feelings of isolation and distress *in the form of a question*. The interrogative form immediately places the prayer in the context of a human-divine relationship rather than simply a self-expression of emotion as a result of personal distress.

A second feature is the way in which the text directly quotes the words of the 'enemy.' While this occurs in other psalms of distress it is not present in every one. Psalm 10 offers the opportunity for the person praying to reflect on what it is like to quote the words of an 'enemy.' It also presents an image of what an 'enemy' might look and act like and how these descriptions might help to orient oneself towards the distress one is experiencing. Not only are the enemy's words quoted but an extended description of the enemy's actions and attitudes is also provided in verses 2 to 11 and again in verse 13. This description again contributes to helping the participant to build a picture of what an 'enemy' might be like.

Finally it also incorporates a feature known as imprecation.[15] Again this is evident in some other psalms of distress but not all. It is an element which can form part of the investing constellation and may provide a reference point for personal reflection on the idea of praying for the demise of ones 'enemies.'

The plea, 'Rise up, O LORD; O God, lift up your hand; do not forget the oppressed'[16] creates the clear pivot point for a movement from expressing and asserting to a position of investing. Finally a climax is reached with the imagining constellation contrasting both the perceived powerfulness of God and the importance of the relationship between God and the distressed person.

Psalm 22

Psalm 22 is far more complex in its structure than Psalm 10. It does contain all four constellations but was chosen because it does not flow through each of the constellations sequentially. Rather, it gravitates from one constellation to another, and back, reflecting a more unpredictable response to distress. Thereby, offering a different experience of processing distress through a psalm.

This psalm also provides contrasting reflections on the nature of God and humankind in terms of status and empowerment. For example, after the initial expression of emotion formed again as questions in verse 1 God is described, 'you are holy, enthroned on the praises of Israel.'[17] This is followed by a historical memory and then contrasted with the self-description, 'But I am a worm, and not human; scorned by others, and despised by people.' This psalm appears to be a response to distress emanating from the paradox of a 'powerful' God who is not coming to the aid of the desolated person in distress.

---

[14] V. 1 (NRSV).

[15] This is where the psalmist requests that God act violently towards the enemy.

[16] V. 12 (NRSV).

[17] V. 3 (NRSV).

Interestingly though, this psalm does present an overall movement from the hopelessness of distress, in the first half, to a sense of hope expressed as praise, in the second half. In fact this psalm is possibly the most extreme example of this kind of movement among psalms of distress. In common with Psalm 10, it is the plea found in verses 19 to 21 of this psalm which finally provides the pivot for a movement into the imagining constellation.[18]

The jarring and dramatic shifts in this psalm offer participants the opportunity to pray the dramatic shifts of mood, in response to distress. The shifts also encourage reflection on how they might respond to such a movement in their own engagement with personal distress. Psalm 22 also incorporates rich and graphic imagery to explore the sensitivities of feeling violated by the enemy. This imagery provides an opportunity for emotions to be evoked.

Finally, the first words of this psalm are familiar to many in the Christian tradition as some of the last words of Christ on the cross, 'My God, my God, why have you forsaken me?' This may present another interesting point of reflection for the person praying as they reflect on what these words might mean in light of the Christian faith.

Psalm 35

Again Psalm 35 contains all constellations of the matrix of lament. However, it also has some unique features. It was chosen primarily because it begins with the plea which is part of the asserting constellation. In this way the psalm emphasizes the assertiveness of the person praying before God immediately in contrast to the previous examples.

Psalm 35 also contains a short but not unimportant quoting of God by the psalmist where God is asked to 'say to my soul, "I am your salvation"' (v.3). Again the presumed power of God is implied in such statements and the existence of a relationship between God and the person is affirmed. This, of course, is not unique within the psalms of distress but it is not present in all of them. Consequently, another potential point of reflection may be promoted, focused on how one responds to quoting God's words to God in prayer.

While this psalm begins unusually with a plea this is not the only instance of a plea in the psalm. A second plea can be found in the centre of the psalm and a final one at the close.[19] So, the psalm is framed with the idea of plea rather than simply presenting it at one particular point in the process. Rather than beginning with expressing a sense of hopelessness and ending in a hopeful imagination the plea is revisited in Psalm 35 as a continual focal point.

This psalm also contains considerable amounts of imprecation which emerge

---

[18] Mays, *The Lord Reigns*, 112. He suggests that in these words we find a connection of 'the fate of this afflicted one with the future kingdom of the LORD.' This provides both an eschatological element to the sense of hope here and also the ubiquitous place of individual in the context of the faith community.

[19] Cf. vv.17b and 22b-25.

from the pleas which are offered to God. The emphasis here is not simply on some kind of deliverance from distress but also the significance of the 'enemy' being dealt with decisively by God.[20]

Psalm 55

Psalm 55 also begins with the plea in the same manner as Psalm 35. However, it swiftly launches into a heartfelt and prolonged expression of emotions using descriptive words such as 'troubled,' 'distraught' and 'anguished,' among others. While emotion is expressed often in individual psalms of distress the length of this example is quite unusual. It provides the person praying with an opportunity to linger on some of the emotions associated closely with engaging with distress and reflect on possible responses.

Psalm 55 also offers a lyrical quote of the psalmist expressing a desire of hope to be released from the presenting distress. The words are rich in imagery and evoke hope for the future. Interestingly here, hope is not so much in God's action but, rather, in the action of the one who is distressed. The psalmist says,

> O that I had wings like a dove! I would fly away and be at rest; truly, I would flee far away; I would lodge in the wilderness; I would hurry to find a shelter for myself from the raging wind and tempest.[21]

This psalm ends in rather abrupt fashion with a combination of imprecation (part of the investing constellation) emerging as a vow of trust (part of the imaging constellation). Conflating these two ideas underlines succinctly a confidence in God's ability to deal with the cause of the distress. It also helps to describe the nature of relationship between the distressed person and God, and the supposed fate of the enemy in the hands of this God.

Although all four constellations are represented here in Psalm 55 there is, again, no clear sequence. Rather, a drifting between each constellation is evident throughout the psalm.

Psalm 88

Psalm 88 is unique in that it contains nothing of the imagining constellation. Kraus has suggested that sickness and nearness to death are the issues at hand here.[22] This psalm led Moore to conclude that 'The only possible thread of hope with Psalm 88 is the fact that the psalm does constitute a prayer.'[23] It may also

---

[20] Twice the plea leads to imprecation: From the plea in verses 1-2 into imprecation in verses 3-8 and then again the plea in verses 22b-25 followed by the imprecation in verses 26-27. Each time the imprecations are expressed in the Hebrew jussive form indicating a wish or a desire for God's action on the part of the distressed person.

[21] Vv. 6b-8 (NRSV).

[22] Hans-Joachim Kraus, *Psalms 60-150*, trans. Hilton C. Oswald (Minneapolis: Augsburg, 1989), 192.

[23] R. Kelvin Moore, *The Psalms of Lamentation and the Enigma of Suffering* (Lewiston: Edwin Mellen, 1996), 46.

be that this represents a psalm in progress reflecting on a situation of distress which may change in the future but in the present remains unresolved. Whatever view is taken the relational connection between the distressed person and God in the face of unresolved distress is evident throughout this psalm.

The inclusion of Psalm 88 in the study was based on my view that some experiences of distress may not or, in fact, do not have the possibility of a hopeful resolution. The psalm confronts the person praying with this possibility and yet gives expression to hopelessness within the context of the divine-human relationship. An interesting feature of this psalm is the isolation from the community felt by the one distressed and the belief that this has been caused by God. The psalmist states that, 'You have caused my companions to shun me; you have made me a thing of horror to them. I am shut in so that I cannot escape.'[24] In fact this seems to provide, at least in part, a reason for the accusatory tone of the psalm where God is seen as the primary origin of this distress. In other words, paradoxically, God is viewed as both the 'enemy' and the one holding the power to resolve the distress being experienced. Psalm 88 provides an opportunity for the participants to express personal distress as something which, they might perceive, has emanated directly from God as opposed to many other psalms of distress where an enemy other than God is identified as the source.

Questions are particularly prominent in this psalm. Although they normally form a part of any psalm of distress the volume here is unusual. The psalm presents a rhythm which launches from a question or questions only to return to the same questioning again and again. In this sense the psalm is cyclical in its feel. The form encapsulates an experience of distress which is unique; unresolvable and, therefore, without hope.

Psalm 102

Psalm 102 again begins with a plea and then provides graphic language describing the emotional state of the one distressed.[25] A short affirmation of confidence in verse 12, 'But you, O LORD, are enthroned forever; your name endures for all generations,' provides a pivot into the imagining constellation. Here the position and character of God is viewed in contrast to that of the distressed individual. However, as with the affirmation of confidence, the imagining is expressed firstly as the distressed person speaking *to* God (second person)[26] though shifting quickly to the third person for the rest.[27] This psalm highlights the visceral nature of the relationship with God amid distress.

Psalm 102 also contains a quotation of the 'self' in verse 24 which is quite unique in psalms of distress. Here the person in distress appears to be either re-

---

[24] Cf. v.8 (NRSV).
[25] Vv. 3-11 (NRSV).
[26] Vv. 13-14 (NRSV).
[27] Vv. 15-23 (NRSV).

calling words spoken or prayed at an earlier time or perhaps attempting to emphasize the words being prayed by clearly pointing out that they are spoken and not just thoughts.

As with most of the other individual psalms of distress this psalm contains all the constellations of the matrix of lament. However, again there is no particular sequence. The psalm moves freely from one constellation to another and back. This provides another opportunity to reflect on the potential for distress to be disorienting and disordered in both the experience of it and any response to it.

Summary observations

The participants were not made aware of these features or nuances within each selected psalm as this could create an unwieldy and excessively complex starting point. However, it was hoped that in the prescribed process of praying and reflecting some of these features would influence the participant's reflection on what was occurring for them in the process. Using individual psalms of distress with this variety of features at least allowed for the possibility of engagement with the features identified. It also exposed the participants to praying in ways they may not have experienced and/or reflected on before.

Psychometric tests

Levels of distress

The *Depression Anxiety Stress Scale* (DASS) was used to assess the first identified aspect of psychodynamic change; levels of distress.[28] This psychometric text was chosen as it provides a standardized measure of three significant displays of distress. In addition, it can be administered in a short time and when administered a second time can provide a reasonable basis for comparing levels of depression, anxiety and distress.

Despite the fact that the matrix of lament itself does not incorporate these exact terms it does have embedded in it a general movement in the level of distress being experienced by the distressed person. The DASS provides a measure of both whether change is evident and, if so, to what extent it is evident.

Locus of Control

The second aspect of psychodynamic change identified in the matrix of lament is that of a sense of control, or empowerment. For this study 'control' has been characterized more particularly as 'locus of control.' Rotter's *Locus of Control* scale (LOC) was the psychometric test chosen to examine this aspect of the participant's experience.[29]

The LOC is helpful in evaluating a perceived repositioning of power within the tripartite relationship between self, God and others. This change in empowerment was identified in the matrix of lament. The dynamic can be observed in

---

[28] See appendix seven for details of the scale.
[29] See appendix eight for details of the scale.

the table below:

	Expressing	Asserting	Investing	Imagining
Self	Disempowered	Empowered	Uncertain	Empowered
God	Disempowered	Uncertain	Empowered	Empowered
Other	Empowered	Disempowered	Disempowered	Disempowered

Table 1

The LOC scale specifically measures the individual on a spectrum of internal to external locus of control. The assumption in the matrix of lament, translated into the concepts of internal and external locus of control, suggests that there is a general movement from external locus of control (that is, the other or enemy causing the person's distress is controlling the individual) to an internal locus of control (that is, the person is empowered to control the distress themselves). It is important to note that the matrix of lament suggests that ultimately locus of control is not *exclusively* found within the distressed person themselves but, rather, *in partnership with* God.

Sense of relationship

The third aspect of psychodynamic change identified above is that of the person's sense of relationship. The matrix of lament highlights the relational nature of psalms of distress in terms of a tripartite paradigm. It also flags a potential for change in the sense of the person's relationship with themselves, with God and with the 'enemy' or 'other.' The psychometric test employed to examine this aspect was the *Spiritual Assessment Inventory* (SAI).[30]

Hall and Edwards state that 'The *Spiritual Assessment Inventory* (SAI) is a relationally based measure designed to assess two dimensions of spiritual development: Awareness of God and Quality of Relationship with God.'[31] The inventory 'draws on the theoretical insights of object relations theory' arguing that the development of human relationships is mirrored in the human-divine relationship.[32] They conclude that

> It appears that there is potential in clinical and counseling setting for the use of a relationally based, psychometrically sound measure of spiritual development from a broadly theistic perspective.

---

[30] For a detailed discussion of the tool see Todd W. Hall and Keith J. Edwards, 'The Spiritual Assessment Inventory: A Theistic Model and Measure for Assessing Spiritual Development,' *Journal for the Scientific Study of Religion* 41.2 (2002): 341-57. See appendix nine for details of the scale.

[31] Hall and Edwards, 'The Spiritual Assessment Inventory,' 341-57.

[32] Hall and Edwards, 'The Spiritual Assessment Inventory,' 341.

Clearly the SAI was designed as a tool for assessing spiritual development. However, for this study there seemed to be value in using the SAI to form a 'before' and 'after' picture, particularly of the person's relationship with God, following a concentrated period of engagement with distress. Specifically the SAI measures five particular aspects of relational connection with God.[33] They are:

- Awareness
- Realistic acceptance
- Disappointment
- Grandiosity
- Instability

In different ways each of these measures provides a picture of how the person's sense of their relationship with God might have changed through the process.

Selection of participants and psalms of distress

The participants

The group's ideal size would consist of twelve adults from as broad an age range as possible. A gender balance of six males and six females was desired. The size of the group was predetermined to be this size for two reasons. First, as some of the tasks to be completed would be group work, this number was viewed as an optimum number to function effectively. Second, failure by some to complete the whole process was anticipated. In this case a group of this number provided for some to withdraw and yet still offer a reasonable collection of information for a comparison to take place.

Forming a group of twelve participants of both genders, a broad age range and from varying backgrounds and experience offered an opportunity to supply a valuable body of reflection and response to the proposed process. This would then form the basis for examining any psychodynamic changes which took place for the participants over the course of the process. The participants were sought out through word of mouth and not be selected based on having any particular skill set or experience relevant to this study. This qualification was in place as the study was aimed at examining the efficacy of the process irrespective of a person's specialized skills or knowledge.[34]

---

[33] The SAI also contains a further measurement identified as impression management, which indicates the level of attempts to respond to the questions in ways that the participant might 'expect' the administrator to want.

[34] This if not to suggest of course that training in skills such as reflective prayer, meditation and journaling etc. would not be of benefit as a basis for a process such as the one proposed.

Chapter 7

Results from the Action Research

This chapter will present the data collected from the action research undertaken in this study. As a beginning point I will describe the initial meeting of the group. Following this each participant will be treated as a discrete entity with their experience being reported based on the journaling they provided, information obtained from the final one-on-one interview and results from their pre- and post-psychometric testing. Finally, I will describe the closing group interview and data obtained from that discussion.

Formulation of the group

The final makeup of the group consisted of six males and six females fulfilling the gender balance envisaged. It is interesting to note that there were numerous others who indicated their desire to participate indicating a perceived need for this kind of activity. However, the group remained limited to twelve for the reasons listed above. In receiving indications of interest from various people I discovered that fortuitously they came from a range of Christian traditions. Some were part of groups with a more rigid view of prayer while others were from settings which valued a more *laisséz faire* approach to prayer.[1] None of the participants had specific training or skills in prayer, journaling or any other activity engaged with in this study.

Initial group meeting

All twelve participants attended the initial meeting of the group. Each participant briefly introduced themselves to the whole group. Following this I introduced myself and Dr. Main. Each participant was asked to sign a consent form for their participation in the study and all present agreed to participate.

I then took approximately 30 minutes to describe the rationale behind this study, the model of the matrix of lament and details of the process in which they, as participants, would be involved. Several questions from the group were raised and responded to in order to clarify both the theory and the process of the study.

After these explanations the *Depression, Anxiety and Stress Scale* (DASS), *Locus of Control* (LOC), and the *Spiritual Assessment Inventory* (SAI) psychometric tests were administered (DASS and LOC by Dr. Main and SAI by myself). The initial group meeting then concluded and a few people clarified particular

---

[1] It should also be noted that none of the participants was from religious traditions other than Christianity and none was chosen on the basis of their past experience in prayer and/or reflection activities.

issues before leaving.

In the following section I have provided a summary of the results gleaned from each participant in the study. These results have been collated from the four sources discussed earlier:

1. Personal journal
2. One-on-one interview
3. Pre- and post-psychometric testing
4. Final group interview

The aspects covered by the summary are twofold. First, reporting results from the research instruments, previously identified, which indicate change in the psychodynamic foci of distress, control and relationship and second, participant's responses to the ritual process involved in this study. The results below are a summary of each participant's experience including several vignettes from each participant as examples to illustrate his or her reflections on, and responses to, both the psychodynamic foci and the ritual process.

To preserve the anonymity of the participants I have assigned each participant a fictitious name by which he or she will be identified. It should also be noted that direct quotations from the participant's journal and/or interview are identified by using italics in this chapter.

Participant 1 - John

Journal

John approached the process in a systematic and controlled manner from the timing of his periods of prayer to the reflection and writing up of his observations. He entered the process with an explicit attitude of belief that it would be of benefit to him personally which suggested that he was consciously looking for those aspects which were most helpful. He indicated from his journaling that he wanted to be honest and genuine in his reflections and responses to the process as it unfolded and the journaling supplied ample evidence of this willingness.

Levels of distress

John set out to focus on several distressing experiences from *the past* stating at the beginning of the first week that he had chosen seven specific *points of distress that I want to focus on*. Although his attention was initially focused on experiences of the past he increasingly reflected on these past experiences in connection with present distress. It appears that specific distress from the past caused a growing recognition of generalized distress in John's present experience. This led him to observe *the source or point of my distress is hard to pinpoint, but I think praying this psalm [Psalm 10] and reflecting on it will bring some of that out.* His journal reflections over the following days supported the validity of this observation. As the process unfolded the journaling also indicated that John increasingly began to identify accurately, and mull over, present distress, processing his current experience. As one result of this direction John observed an awareness that *when at the depths I find that there is little self-care in the moment* which prompted him to explore what self-care might look like in response to distress.

As John's attention shifted increasingly from the past to the present he described the efficacy of the process in engaging with present distress as follows: *What is new is the fact that real truth has to be felt, as it is experienced, and 'known' as a present tool if it is to be of any use in the life of faith.* Because of this shift in thinking he also reflected in the third week that *I don't think I felt as much of the pain of distress in praying this time* and a perception that his general feelings of distress had decreased. From this feeling of decreased distress a passion emerged as John continued to find an avenue to express his distress through these psalms. He described this sense of lowered distress as a *peace that transcends my own understanding*. However, before any feelings of *peace*, John's journal suggested an increasing awareness of and ability to name his emotional responses to experience of distress. For example, he stated *I know at times I feel like this... like there [is] a range of emotions or stimuli coming in and I just try to deal with it honestly and rationally— rationality in emotion— now there's an incongruency!*(sic) This observation also belies the early emphasis in John's reflections on focusing on rational thinking rather than emotional expression. However, as the weeks transpired, he appeared to find a more even balance between thinking and feeling his responses to distress. In sum it could be suggested that this did not cause John to avoid expressing his sense of distress or deny its existence. Rather, he embraced it further but with a sense of hope, not hopelessness.

Locus of control

As highlighted earlier the journal was presented in a consistent and ordered format and John's attitudinal approach to the process was clearly voiced and intentional from his perspective. Although from the outset there is a sense in John's journal that he is in control of the process the attitude to experiences of distress was quite the opposite. At one point for example he clearly states, *God is in control. Again I felt this.* This notion of God-control in relation to distress is perhaps best encapsulated in John stating that God, *takes me to the depths, but He is God.* Despite these early affirmations of God being in control the journaling reflection process reveals some significant questions and doubts about the reality of God this for John. Despite the questions and doubts with increasing feelings of loneliness, rejection and the absence of God challenging his perceptions John finds a 'voice' for such issues in the process. In the fourth week he notes that *... it felt as if the Lord had really left me, that his **wrath** did **lie heavy upon me**... I was being truthful about my emotions, and I was so relieved to have such words to use* (emphasis John's). Rather than leading John away from trust in God he found that he was led towards deeper trust in God. In making sense of this experience John concludes that *God is so good to allow this sort of darkness in His Word.* Accompanying these experiences John sometimes mentions physical sensations such as crying, sobbing and quivering of the voice in response to praying the psalms. He recognized these responses as being an appropriate expression of his thoughts and emotions in the situation. In addition John expressed a sense of being *okay* with despair amid distress.

This discovery of trusting God in God's perceived absence also led to a growing recognition of personal responsibility amid distress.[2] Early in the process John reflected a strong belief in what could be described as a 'rescuing god.' John was willing to treat prayer as a mode of handing the problem over to God to resolve saying at one point *God is in control. Again I felt this.* However, as the process of praying continued John increasingly acknowledged the significance of his responses and his actions because of these responses to distress. To this end he noted in week four that *I feel that God is silent regarding the distress and wonder what He thinks of me defending myself like I'd like to.* Interestingly the challenges to God's omnipotence facing John and his struggle to assert some self-control appeared to lead him to an increasing recognition of the importance of partnership between himself and God in engaging with distress.

Sense of relationship

John's journal responses ranged from expressing a very strong awareness of God's presence with statements such as *knowing that God was actually **there*** (emphasis John's) *was the life-giving component I experienced today.* In contrast to this he also voiced a sense of divine absence in his experience with observations such as *I felt this way; that I could say it validly, that at times, many times, God does not answer.* John's journaling became progressively more focused on the emotions related to this sense of God's presence and absence as the process unfolded for him. The emotions identified with these experiences were *disappointment, isolation and sense of injustice.*

John's relationship with himself and his perceived 'enemies' was also freely described and struggled with throughout the process. While he did not describe God as an 'enemy' at any point the sentiment expressed at times suggests this may have been his perception (for example, *his **wrath** did **lie heavy upon me** (emphasis John's)).* There were explicit references to feelings John had of being an enemy to himself (*the self betrays*) and feeling as if other people were his enemies at times. Again the psalms of distress provided a *voice* for this kind of expression. John appeared to resonate with the tripartite relationship identified within psalms of distress. The challenge of imprecation in some of the psalms of distress was a particular challenge to John. However, he seems to have reconciled them with the insight that at times he *feels* destructive attitudes towards someone when he is distressed but that this could be expressed safely through prayer to God.

The process

John's journal stressed his belief in the efficacy of the process in affirming his

---

[2] John noted on numerous occasions both in his journal and his interview that the 'I am ready to begin...' prayer was particularly helpful as re-affirming the safety and security of relationship with God in all experiences of life.

relationship with God. To this end he states in week two that *the prayer, reflection and response process is actually helping me to express myself better* and that *I think this process is actually affirming my faith in God*. However, he also felt that the exclusive focus on distress was perhaps unrealistic. The ritual elements of the process gave structure as well as meaning to the activity. Praying aloud and combining this with body movements often helped John to reinforce what he was praying and feeling in a controlled but not restrictive manner. He also found that he prayed about issues and in ways that he would not normally choose and that this had immense value for his reflection and meaning-making. John concluded that he had *a greater sense of well-being*.

It is evident that throughout the journaling aspect of the process John made consistent attempts at making sense of his personal distress experienced in both the past and the present. Reflection on the content of the psalms of distress together with noticing his emotional and physical responses aided John in making more sense of his experiences of distress. The journal shows significant reflection and suggest that attitudinal change took place at various points in the process for John. Having summarized John's journal reflections we will now examine his responses to the questions posed in the final interview following completion of the process.

Final interview

John found the discipline of praying a psalm each day helpful even though he was not used to this kind of regular use. He did find it taxing towards the end of each week together with the other activities in his daily life but persevered. Praying aloud helped him to *hear the words* in a fresh way and he observed that by doing this they *became mine.*

John found that using psalms of distress as the content over an extended time of praying helped him to *get into it* more fully rather than pass it by or approach it superficially. Repeating the same psalm each day for five days was helpful in this respect. He did find Psalm 88 was a struggle with the absence of the imagining constellation. The lack of imagining was initially troubling for him. Despite this he *pushed through* using it and found that it did cause him to revisit past distress which was unresolved. A lack of resolution for his distress was evident to him *through* the process. John also found the expression vented towards *enemies* to be problematic as he struggled to reconcile this with his Christian world view. However, he did ultimately see the words as a helpful emotional venting.

The ritual was strong extrinsic motivation causing him to continue praying the psalms. While he saw the value in this he also felt that an intrinsic motivation in the longer term would be most valuable. Having said this he did observe that the ritual was helpful to perseverance when the emotional willingness was not there. The ritual also enabled him to look backwards into the past and forwards into the future in relation to personal distress. Overall the ritual was of great assistance. He especially found the 'Now I'm ready to begin...' prayer a helpful beginning point because it offered consistency in the process. It also provided a sense of safety and security in the relationship with self and God as the context in which the psalms of distress were about to be prayed. As well as this John also specifically characterized Psalm 22 as a *safe* way of engaging with past distress.

Recording thoughts and feelings was valuable to John. Although the reflections were very structured John felt that he needed to be more flexible with his responses (that is, answer the questions when he felt they needed answering or not answer them when they seemed irrelevant or had no answer). However, he did reflect that they acted as prompts to his thinking about distress creating a logical approach to the reflection. John also felt that the writing process was valuable for him in expressing and exploring feelings.

From praying the designated psalms of distress John found that the concept of the matrix of lament and its constellations made sense. He said that it took a few days to grasp the idea of the constellations and to see them in the psalms, although the colour-coding was very helpful in this regard. He concluded that the matrix of lament is a helpful way of looking at these psalms. The fact that the process was repeated and focused on one psalm at a time meant that the constellations were reinforced. John indicated that he would continue to pray these psalms but probably alongside other types of psalms as a balance and a truer reflection of real life experience. Used exclusively, John found the psalms of distress very confronting and concluded that perhaps the sole focus on distress was too unreal.[3]

The only external support he had consisted of brief conversations about his experience with his minister and partner. John found their support and understanding helpful in his continuing participation in the process.

Psychometric testing

Below are the results from John's pre- and post-psychometric testing collated in table form:[4]

Depression Anxiety Stress Scale - John

	Before	**After**	**Change**
Depression	Normal	Normal	-
Anxiety	Moderate	Mild	-ve
Stress	Mild	Normal	-ve

Table 2

Locus of Control – John

---

[3] John also noted in passing that perhaps a table of the psalms of distress related to particular types of distress that individuals experience in life would be helpful as a prompter to use these psalms.

[4] The descriptors used in the tables below are standard for each of the instruments utilized. The +ve and -ve markers for each participant in these tables only record movement which appears to be significant in its amount. A +ve for locus of control indicates a movement towards stronger internal locus of control; a –ve indicates a movement towards stronger external locus of control. For charts of the complete scores see appendices ten, eleven and twelve.

	Before	After	Change
Type of control	Internal	Internal	-
Level of control	Moderate	High	+ve

Table 3

Spiritual Assessment Inventory (Relationship) - John

	Before	After	Change
Awareness	Very true	Very true	-
Acceptance	Very true	Very true	-
Disappointment	Moderately true	Slightly true	- ve
Grandiosity	Moderately true	Moderately true	-
Instability	Slightly true	Slightly true	-

Table 4

The decreases in anxiety and stress indicated by the DASS scores above are congruent with John's description of his experience in both his journal reflections and final interview. An increase in John's level of internal locus of control is also a reflection of the experience as John recorded his responses in his journal. However, it should be reiterated that the journal emphasized a shift towards a greater sense of partnership between John and God rather than John taking total control of his situation. This picture is also consistent with the imagining constellation's joint empowerment between the divine and human in the face of distress. The only significant shift in John's SAI results was a decrease in disappointment with God. This decrease could be indicative of John finding a more realistic view of divine action in response to his experiences of personal distress and, so, not feeling as disappointed when divine action appears to be absent.

Participant 2 – Charles

Journal reflections

Charles indicated both verbally and in written form that he began the process with an openness towards God and a willingness to grow and learn from the process. This openness is evident in both the journaling and interview phases of the process. The brevity of his journal entries indicated not only his struggle with writing down his reflections but also his desire to simply *live the experience*, as he put it, rather than attempting to explain it. This desire became more obvious in the final interview.

Levels of distress

The journal entries provided by Charles did not specify exactly what kind of distress he was experiencing during the process or whether he focused on present or past distress. The only description in the first two weeks was of a *key issue in my life*. Despite the lack of details about his distress Charles displayed an increased ability and/or willingness to express his own sense of personal distress through the psalms being prayed. The clearest manifestation of this is in his expression of anger as a response to a sense of not *belonging*. In the days of praying immediately following expression of anger Charles perceived a decrease in his anger and an increase in his ability to express and explore other feelings produced by praying these psalms. However, Charles does not specify what the other emotions might be. It appears as though a significant factor in the increasing expression was his *resonating in the psalm*. Charles increasingly noted in his journal a growing expression of emotion as the weeks transpired. Despite an absence of description for the distress it also appears that while he began the process with a stronger focus on the present this focus moved more towards *past hurts* and the accompanying emotions.

Charles indicated clearly on many occasions that *dwelling* with distress through praying psalms of distress became a significant experience for him. He felt that this *dwelling* allowed for a greater authenticity in expressing what he was feeling and the opportunity to re-define the experience through a process of self-reflection. This indicated that, for Charles, *the process* was significant in promoting his engagement with personal distress rather than avoidance or denial. One outcome of this was finding himself expressing thoughts and emotions which were at times challenging for him causing him a level of uneasiness.

Despite the reflection which took place for Charles there is little written evidence to directly support a movement from reflection to meaning-making. In other words, his journal reflections tended to be more descriptive than analytical in nature. Despite this, he strongly affirmed that the process had promoted fresh understanding of the distress he was experiencing. His hesitancy to analyze his experience contrasted with his desire to *live the experience* remained unexplained and unexplored as a potential basis for meaning-making.

Locus of control

Charles seemed initially willing to allow the activity to take its course. However, as the weeks transpired his journal indicated a greater ownership of the process and the direction he wanted to take in terms of what he reflected on and how he reflected on it. He described his experience as one of feeling *in the groove* in later weeks.

The most specific and obvious example of sensing a level of self-control in the process is recorded in the fourth week where Charles observed that he *embraced prayer more as an internal struggle*. This kind of observation indicates that he had become more realistic about his distress but at the same time has discovered a willingness to *embrace* it as part of his experience.

In summary, Charles did not perceive God as one who rescues a person from a situation of distress but rather as a god who is *with* the person in that distress through relationship. It is these two factors that seem to have provided the continuing impetus for Charles to continue to pray these psalms and find solace in their use.

Sense of relationship

The initial journal entries in the first two weeks indicated that Charles was uncertain how to connect his sense of relationship with God and expressing personal distress as he prayed psalms of distress. However, the journal entries of the last two weeks indicated that some resolution to this had been reached in the form of a *focus on re-birth* which Charles noted as a fresh perspective on the divine-human relationship. As a result he found the ability to express a broader range of emotions, observing and describing how these impinged on his relationship with God. Interestingly he did not address the issue of his relationship with others or perceived enemies. This may have been because the distress focused on was personal to him or perhaps he was not aware of the potential rôle of others in experiences of personal distress.

The process

Charles' appreciation of the ritual was clear in his journal reflections. It appears that the ritual gave structure, a sense of safety and permission for Charles to express his sense of personal distress. He described the ritual as helping him to *recognize, embrace* and *process* his issues of personal distress. He also found that the body movements mirrored his thinking and emotions helping him to be more expressive than he might otherwise have been. His comments highlighted the potential value of *acting out* a prayerful response to distress rather than simply reading the text. Charles did, at various points, also emphasize the value he found in speaking the words aloud.

Final interview

Charles reflected that he found the discipline of praying one psalm a day helpful but not unusual. He stated that being from a Roman Catholic background he was familiar with the daily office. Despite this familiarity he found that the process revived an old discipline which he has not practised for some time. Charles also found that the practice of praying the psalms aloud was valuable. He said that he felt *empowered* and that it gave him a *voice of his own*. He also felt that praying aloud helped him to *re-define* the relationship between God and *creature*.

Charles observed that the psalms of distress covered much content. While he could see the connection in content between the psalms used each week he felt that Psalm 35 in the third week was less powerful and more mundane. Generally he felt that following the content at times caused him to feel more *childlike* and *simple*. That is, he followed it because it was required. However, he did not see this as a negative aspect of the process and continued to explain that he found the content helpful to express the reality of life experience without hiding behind a façade. Use of psalms of distress helped him to *walk down* into the depths and in *letting go* of distress from daily life.

Charles also found that the ritual helped his experience of expressing distress through psalms of distress. The body movements were particularly powerful for him because they moved him into a *different sphere* of dramatizing the response to distress by involving the whole person. He felt that he had physically entered a conversation rather than it being *simply a said prayer* and that nothing in the rigidity of the ritual became a hindrance for him.

Journaling was the most difficult part of the process for Charles. He observed that he struggled to move from the experience to the idea of *thinking about it*. Often, as mentioned above, Charles felt that he wanted to just *live with the experience* (the process) and not try to explain it. In some ways he found that an attempt to put words to the experience detracted from the process. Having observed this he did concede that the focus questions provided for the journal did help him to reflect on existential questions of *Who am I? Who is God? Is there a purpose in distress?* It also enabled him to focus on his feelings but Charles still expressed a desire just to experience them rather than to explain them in words. Ultimately he did agree that the journaling did help him to express his feelings in writing but he felt rather uncomfortable with this. He added that the process as a whole led him to silent contemplation of what had just taken place.

The matrix of lament and its constellations made sense to Charles. He felt that they were clearly evident in each of the psalms and that they fairly reflected the form of the psalms of distress. He also added that, in his view, the matrix and its constellations mirrored the shape of typical human response to distress. Charles felt that it enabled him to *line up issues in life with the psalms' content*. He also noted that it challenged the *honesty* of his prayer in expressing his feelings to God. He said that he would like to continue to pray these psalms and did not see any particular difficulty in praying them in isolation from other psalms.[5] He also felt that the psalms of distress really get to the foundations of what life is really like.

Charles said that he had support from his partner who also wanted to enter the process after discovering what was involved. Charles appreciated this but felt that this was something he needed to explore on his own. He did find that he was able to share some of his experiences with her during the process.

Psychometric testing

The tables below summarize Charles' pre- and post-psychometric test results:

Depression Anxiety Stress Scale - Charles

	Before	**After**	**Change**
Depression	Moderate	Normal	-ve
Anxiety	Extremely severe	Mild	-ve
Stress	Severe	Normal	-ve

Table 5

---

[5] Charles added at this point that while he found praying only the palms of distress helpful he also thought that praying them alongside the other psalms in the Psalter would be of great value.

Locus of Control – Charles

	Before	After	Change
Type of control	Internal/External	Internal	Internal
Level of control	Balanced	High	+ve

Table 6

Spiritual Assessment Inventory (Relationship) - Charles

	Before	After	Change
Awareness	Substantially true	Substantially true	+ve
Acceptance	Substantially true	Very true	+ve
Disappointment	NR	Substantially true	NR
Grandiosity	Slightly true	Slightly true	-
Instability	Slightly true	Slightly true	-

Table 7

The decreases in depression, anxiety and stress indicated on Charles' DASS results are congruent with his journal reflections. This is particularly evident in his processing of anger as an initial response at the beginning of the activity. The increase in internal locus of control is again congruent with journal reflections and the final interview where he indicated a clearer sense of personal responsibility in response to distress. However, it must be reiterated that Charles maintained a strong emphasis on *living the experience* rather than being too intentional in directing it. By expressing it this way Charles appears to have become more assertive in his expression towards God but at the same time maintaining a willingness to be open to external influences (that is, God). Other aspects of change for Charles appear to have been an increase in an awareness of God and an accompanying more realistic acceptance of his situation. Again these changes are congruent with both his journal and final interview reflections on the process.

Participant 3 – Anton

Journal reflections

Anton presented both in his journal and in person as someone who was willing and open to learn and grow through the experience of taking part in the study. His journal was set out clearly with reflections on each day of the process ending in the third week. The journal entries were both descriptive of what he observed in the psalms as he prayed them and how he attempted to make sense of the content for himself.

Levels of distress

It was evident on reading through Anton's journal entries that he appeared to become more distressed as he reflected on his personal situation describing his observations early on as *a shock*. These feelings particularly manifested themselves with the realization that *I found myself on the side of the oppressor*. While Anton did not elaborate on the specific circumstances of the situations they were self-evidently real enough experiences in his present experience to provoke the response just described. It appears that, as Anton gained an increased awareness about his distress, his feelings of dis-ease were exacerbated. In spite of this early reaction to praying the first psalms Anton continued in the process. He reflected on his continuing in the process stating that *God is not scared away* and this continuance led to a broadening of Anton's expression as he continued to reflect and journal through the process.

Despite noting increased distress (see above) this did not appear to be an altogether negative experience for Anton. Once the issue of self-identification with the *oppressor* was reflected on it led to an increase in Anton's honesty with God. However, this increase in honesty with God became problematic for Anton as he appears to have had a growing desire for such expression but with an accompanying ambivalence about its appropriateness. The tone of Anton's journal reflections suggests that this ambivalence was never fully resolved. Regardless of any ambivalence and in spite of an apparent increase in his level of stress Anton continued to broaden his expression in praying the psalms. He clearly pointed out in the final interview that the process did engender in him a greater honesty between himself and with God. He also concluded that it was a valuable growth for him. To this end he noted as early as the second week that he could *express the isolation I feel and the experience of suffering I am feeling* and that he was discovering a *growing understanding of the love that God has for people*. In reflecting on his own feelings of dis-ease at what the process was revealing about himself Anton also described his experience of God as one *who reaches into the lives of the afflicted*.

Locus of control

Although Anton did not express his response to his discoveries about himself in 'control' terms it is evident from his journal entries that the feelings he experienced became increasingly uncomfortable and also seemingly uncontrollable. He also saw what he characterized as 'powerlessness' in others and found himself reflecting on taking advantage of others' weakness as *the oppressor*. Rather ironically Anton then found himself feeling powerless in himself before God in prayer. As one response to the situation Anton expressed his perceived need for forgiveness from God for his attitudes and actions. By doing so his reflections suggest that he was doing two things. First, he was taking personal responsibility for what he perceived as 'sin.' Second he acknowledged God's part in the process of dealing with this distress. He did this by giving control of the situation over to God to offer forgiveness and, presumably, relief from the distress.

The theme of distress being engaged with by a process of confession and forgiveness which persists in Anton's journal reflections for some time is unique to his experience within the group. Towards the end of the first week Anton states that despite his situation and his feelings *God is king*. This reflection seems to reinforce Anton's perception that despite what anyone does or says, ultimately God is in control of the situation. So for Anton there was a strong affirmation of

God's control throughout his journal reflections but also a growing recognition of personal culpability and responsibility for him to respond proactively to his experiences of distress.

Sense of relationship

Some observations can also be made about Anton's perception of his relationship with God. A sense of low self-worth emerged as Anton moved into the second week. This was contrasted with a high view of God's worth. Anton characterized himself as a *worm* and *worthless* at one point. However, he did not see his relationship damaged because of this low self-worth. In fact expressing this lack of self-worth through the psalms of distress seems to have led Anton to greater confidence in God's presence and worth. Anton does not grapple with this sense of low self-worth in his journaling. He appeared to be resigned to such a view of himself and found consolation in his high view of God's worth.

Anton found comfort in his relationship with God amid personal distress. As highlighted previously, he used the word *rescue* in his journal to describe God's action but clearly does not see this as God simply removing the distress. On the contrary he sees his own rôle in dealing with distress by working positively in the relationships he has with others.

Although Anton does not directly address the idea of those he may perceive as his 'enemies,' his expression of injustice enacted against him implies their influence. However, his journal reflections, at times, also suggest a perception of the 'self' as a kind of 'enemy.' The 'self,' being characterized as an 'enemy,' appears to create significantly more anxiety for Anton than any 'external enemy.'

The process

Anton reported that the matrix of lament aided him by providing a helpful framework for viewing his distress. Grasping the principal behind the practice may have resonated with his high level of internal locus of control. Because of this understanding Anton appeared to feel safe in expressing thinking and emotions that otherwise seem to have remained unexpressed. He found this kind of engagement with distress through prayer and a renewed sense of God's presence as empowering for his self-expression and in reassessing his relationships with God and those around him.

Final interview

Anton reported that he found the discipline of praying a psalm each day to be important for him as he felt himself lacking in this area. He also added that the activity being prescribed meant that he participated regularly because it was required. Anton noted that fixing a certain time each day was more difficult for him although this was not required in the process instructions. However, he felt there was value in making a set time. Praying aloud as opposed to praying silently was not something with which he was familiar and he did not find it a help or a hindrance.

Anton *loved the content of the lament psalms*. He found that they accurately reflected his experience and feelings and found himself *shocked and challenged* at times by what he was praying and, therefore, thinking and feeling. He also found himself *often on the side of the oppressor* and this challenged his *view of [his] relationship with others.* The form of psalms of distress was both *challenging* and *redefining* for him in terms of how his relationships with God and others could be expressed.

Anton was comfortable with the rigidity of following the same ritual each day. Again he emphasized that it was a helpful discipline. The opening part of the ritual, breathing and the 'I am ready to begin…' prayer, was great. Because of this he felt focused and ready for the task at hand. He stated that he did not find the hand movements helpful. He felt that the movements prescribed did not necessarily reflect the content for him but said that he *would like to develop his own.*

Anton enjoyed the journaling immensely as he had found with this process in the past. However, he said that he *discovered a dark side to myself* in this process and felt vulnerable putting the thoughts and feelings into words. The questions were very helpful and he found that this caused both *reflection* and *change* for him. He did feel that the journaling was a place for the effective expression of emotion and found a resonance with what was expressed in the psalms.

The nature of the matrix was clear to him. Although he agreed with my identification of the constellations he again stressed that he *would use other hand movements* to reflect these. He felt that the matrix was *definitely a helpful way of looking at the structure of lament psalms.* He also said that it *structured his own reflections and how I contextualize the psalm to be about me.* He added that he *would definitely use the lament psalms again.*

Anton indicated that he would prefer to pray these psalms in context with others in the Psalter and would encourage others to do the same. He felt that this more wholistic approach would encourage others to engage with psalms of distress and that the Psalter included all aspects of life in a helpful way. He did not intentionally seek support from others during his involvement in the process. He felt that this was normal for him and did it because he felt the process was a solo effort in reflection.

Psychometric testing

The tables below are summarized results of Anton's pre- and post-psychometric testing:

Depression Anxiety Stress Scale - Anton

	Before	After	Change
Depression	Mild	Normal	-ve
Anxiety	Normal	Normal	-
Stress	Normal	Mild	+ve

Table 8

Locus of Control – Anton

	Before	After	Change
Type of control	Internal	Internal	-
Level of control	High	High	-

Table 9

Spiritual Assessment Inventory (Relationship) - Anton

	Before	After	Change
Awareness	Moderately true	Moderately true	-
Acceptance	Very true	Substantially true	-ve
Disappointment	Substantially true	Very true	+ve
Grandiosity	Slightly true	Moderately true	+ve
Instability	Slightly true	Slightly true	-

Table 10

The decrease in Anton's level of depression may be a result of his discovery of a pathway through dealing with his feelings of being an *oppressor*. These feelings, if ignored or denied, may have been internalized leading to an increased level in this aspect of his experience. The accompanying increase in stress reflects the discoveries made about the 'self' by Anton in the first week of the process. Anton's high internal locus of control did not alter but appears to reflect his growing desire to take some form of action once issues were identified (for example, oppression). Despite the high internal level of locus of control Anton still maintains a recognition of what he perceived only God can do.

There does not appear to be any congruence between the decrease in Anton's level of realistic acceptance and his journal reflections. However, the increase in disappointment may be indicative of his growing recognition that God may not rescue him. In reflecting on the idea of divine *rescue* at one point in his journal Anton redefines it in terms of discovering a direction in which to move in response to distress rather than seeking a removal of the distress. The increase in grandiosity may reflect Anton's increased willingness to be more open and honest with God in prayer.

Participant 4 - Jim

Journal reflections

Although Jim entered the process with a willingness to participate this seemed to be overshadowed by a concern about expectations stating that *I'm not sure what to feel*. As his reflections unfolded it appears as though this ambivalence gave way to a belief that he had to feel distressed even if he did not. During the second week when he either did not feel distressed, or did not want to face his distress, Jim decided to withdraw.

Jim's journal reflections were mainly focused on his reactions to praying the psalm each day. While there was a decreasing focus on the actual content, as the days passed, he did address the relationship between the matrix's constellations and the psalm being prayed. By doing this he found the model itself helpful. The journal also contained Jim's reactions to the content as he prayed the psalms and reflections showing attempts to make meaning out of the experience.

Levels of distress

Discussions with Jim before his withdrawal indicated that he felt the process itself increased his experience of stress and anxiety. Rather ironically though, Jim also indicated that he wanted to withdraw because he was no longer feeling distressed. The latter was reinforced in his final interview. Jim's journal reflections recorded both the feeling of having no distress on which to reflect **and** the feelings of being distressed by the process itself.

Although the final interview responses are discussed below it is significant to add at this point that during the interview, Jim elaborated on his experience saying that the process was prompting him to revisit past distress. He noted that the revisiting was elicited by the process even though he felt that he had already *dealt with it*. It also led to the conclusion that *to dwell on lament feelings is unnatural for me*. These comments, combined with another observation in the final interview that Jim felt more at ease focusing on other peoples' distress in a vicarious sense, may indicate an avoidance mechanism for dealing with deeper intrapsychic levels of personal distress. It could be that this process was functioning on two concurrent levels for Jim. At a more immediate level he was able to voice and engage with the current presenting specific distress well leading to his observation that he was not feeling distressed any longer. However, at a deeper level the process of praying psalms of distress resonated with past experiences of distress, stimulating reflection on events that Jim either did not need to, or did not want to, revisit. It was this deeper stimulation that appears to have contributed to his early withdrawal from the process.

Locus of control

From both Jim's journal entries and the final interview it is evident that he felt a personal empowerment in being able to voice his thoughts and feelings through praying these psalms. This empowerment had, apparently, not been his experience in the past. The notion of God's 'control' in the situation was an issue about which Jim was ambivalent. A plea such as *remove the horror in my heart* seems to be more a wishful desire than a believed possibility. Jim appeared to want God to be in control but did not seem to experience divine control as reality. Rather, ironically this ambivalence about God's control in Jim's situation of distress was punctuated with a powerful recounting of a personal encounter with God exercising power. Coupling this with Jim's high level of internal locus of control it seems that he struggled with the theology of psalms of distress where they emphasize the omnipotence of God. Jim indicated that he did not see God's omnipotence himself and, perhaps because of this, he innately desired to take control of the situation himself. In a sense he did this as he acknowledged at one point that he *wept and forgave*.

Relationship with God

Throughout his journal Jim also struggled with the concept of God's presence. He seemed to resonate strongly at times with the psalmist's sense of abandonment and isolation from God observing that he felt *very distant from this One*. In the latter stages of the journal his reflections actually became prayers where he began to speak *to* God about his thoughts and feelings. However, if the two levels of reflection on past **and** present distress suggested above are in operation, seemingly God's presence was more obvious to him, only in the immediate situation of distress. God's presence in Jim's past experience of distress appears to have been more problematic prompting him to avoid revisiting the past.

Clearly Jim began praying the designated psalms feeling as if he were the 'enemy,' or the one in the wrong. That is, he perceived himself to be an 'enemy' of God reflecting on the question, '*Why does my soul feel so dark?*' It could also have been that he felt alienated from God, others *and* even from himself. The distress at his perceived need to forgive, recorded in his journal reflections, may have been one manifestation of this perceived alienation. A further example of the 'self' as enemy was evident in the statement *one who supposedly knows God and is close to God* as a self-description.

While never stated explicitly in his journal reflections, Jim also appeared to view God as a kind of 'enemy' at times in his experience of distress. He alluded to the idea as he explained his struggle with a sense of God's presence. The tension here may have been between a god who he felt 'ought' to make God's presence felt and an individual (Jim) who feels that it was at least partly his responsibility to sense God's presence.[6]

Final interview

Jim said that he did not find praying the psalms of distress each day difficult for the first week. However, it became more taxing in the following week leading him to end the process early. He did find that praying the same psalm each day led him to focus on a different aspect of the psalm and that this was helpful. He also indicated that he found some connection with the words as he prayed them aloud. They became his words. He also felt that by praying aloud the significance of the words would be more likely to be taken in.

The content was easier for Jim to use in the first week but also became more difficult in the second. He reaffirmed his journal reflection that the constant focus on distress was taxing for him emotionally. He felt that the psalms were *not compatible* with where he was currently in life but that they caused him great distress because of *having a lot of distress in the past*. He found revisiting this distress difficult and painful but also said that he felt he had *told the story so many times* and *walked through it...* considering this to be a successful process in the past. In the first week he felt that the psalms connected with his immediate distress but when it started moving him back in time the encounter became too difficult. His

---

[6] That is, perhaps, indicative of a high level of internal locus of control.

word for dealing with the past *again* was that he felt it was *fake* because he had already *dealt with it.*

The ritual aspect was not too rigid and gave a shape to the experience for Jim. He felt that it kept him focused. The opening prayer was helpful, giving him confidence going into praying psalms of distress. The hand movements were helpful as he felt the *acting out* of the constellations helped with expression. He stated that the hand movement for the 'imagining' element was most helpful of all. Jim found journaling to be useful and also a process with which he was familiar. The questions were helpful as he preferred responding to specific requests but in the end found them helpful more as a *jumping off point*. He also indicated that he was able to freely express his feelings through the journaling process.

Jim understood the nature of the matrix and its constellations. He felt that the form gives a person *permission to speak*. He would use the psalms of distress to reflect on personal distress as it arose because he did find it a helpful way to view personal distress and to express it. Subsequently, he had returned to these psalms in the two weeks before the interview again. He found it helpful to enable him to connect with *other peoples'* experience of distress facing issues such as poverty and felt much more connected to the psalms when doing this. Jim pointed out that he would find it more helpful to pray psalms of distress in context with other types of psalms to find a balance. He did not seek support from others intentionally except for a short discussion with his partner but believed that doing this could have compromised the process in some way.

Psychometric testing

Below are the collated results of Jim's pre- and post-psychometric testing in table form:

Depression Anxiety Stress Scale - Jim

	Before	**After**	**Change**
Depression	Low	Low	-
Anxiety	Low	Low	-
Stress	Low	Low	-

Table 11

Locus of Control – Jim

	Before	**After**	**Change**
Type of control	Internal	Internal	-
Level of control	High	High	-

Table 12

Spiritual Assessment Inventory (Relationship) - Jim

	Before	**After**	**Change**
Awareness	Substantially true	Very true	+ve
Acceptance	Moderately true	Substantially true	+ve
Disappointment	Moderately true	Moderately true	-
Grandiosity	Slightly true	Slightly true	-

| Instability | Moderately true | Slightly true | -ve |

Table 13

Interestingly the DASS results do not reflect the journal reflections Jim recorded. In both the journal and the final interview it was evident that he experienced increased levels of both stress and anxiety as he worked through the process to the point of withdrawing. There is no clear indication of why this incongruence was present. The high level of internal locus of control appears to have been part of the struggle for Jim in praying the psalms of distress and engaging with his personal distress. While he pointed out that he wanted to sense God's presence and God's activity in his life a tension seems to emerge as he attempted to take control in his own hands. It may be that he struggled to discern between what his responsibility was and what God's rôle was in engaging with distress.

The greater awareness indicated in the SAI is borne out in Jim's journal reflections. It is congruent with his attempts to view God as being present even when his feelings indicated otherwise. Realistic acceptance also increased, again congruent with a growing sense that distress was present in Jim's experience. Yet, as highlighted above, this acceptance only appeared to progress so far before the avenue of reflection on distress was closed. This seemed particularly pertinent to reflection on past distress. The decrease in instability is difficult to explain because Jim's experience as reflected on in his journal and interview suggest otherwise.

Participant 5 – Peter

Journal reflections

Peter indicated that, as the process began, he was enthusiastic about what might occur. This enthusiasm was also obvious in his journal entries throughout the first week and the feedback from the final interview. However, he indicated an increasing struggle with the writing process as part of his reflection, feeling troubled that he *had to commit* his reflections to paper. This aspect of the process became an increasingly difficult challenge.

Levels of distress

In the second week Peter identified the process itself as becoming distressing. It is interesting to note the observation in his final interview that the process *put him in discomfort*. In contrast to this his journal showed that he felt some resonance with the words of the psalms. The content, then, appears to have led Peter to a position of feeling helped in engaging with his distress. However, the actual process seemed to compromise any value he had discovered. This in turn led to his withdrawal from the process altogether.

Peter's observation in the final interview about his tendency to *internalize* was interesting given the above scenario. The completed journaling suggested the beginnings of articulating some significant thoughts and feelings about his personal distress. For example, early on Peter says *there is a chasm between me and God* and he speaks of the *hurt... inflicted by others*. The expression of such thoughts and emotions emerged from praying the designated psalm of distress. Therefore, it could be that using the psalms of distress actually caused Peter to externalize thoughts and feelings that he might normally, by his own admission, internalize. On the one hand the validation and safety of externalizing these thoughts and feelings through psalms of distress appeared to be a helpful experience for him. However on the other hand, for a person who is more practised at internalizing thoughts and feelings, the externalizing process of prayer could quite easily become distressing in itself. This seems to have occurred for Peter.

From these observations it appears that Peter's level of distress did in fact increase throughout the course of his involvement in the process. However, the catalyst for his distress was not so much reflection on personal experiences of distress but the process of externalizing something which he had typically tended to internalize. He was not able, at this point in the process, to reflect on his distress at the process and what this might be suggesting about his way of processing distress. A deeper reflection on the dynamics at work for Peter in this internalizing/externalizing process may have led him to engage with the distress caused by the process itself. This could then have engendered deeper reflection on the experiences which have caused him personal distress.

The difficulties Peter experienced resulted from his view that the process created a contrived experience of distress. He did not appear to be aware that his distress at the process may have indicated something of significance happening for him at a deeper level of intrapsychic processing.

Locus of control

Peter began with the view that he needed to be the one to take initiatory action in the divine-human relationship and this view seemed to consolidate throughout the process. Taking personal responsibility is evident in a prayer for freedom from *guilt and shame* with him concluding that *it [removal of guilt and shame] can be so*. The removal of sin and guilt that Peter focused on was based around his action in seeking forgiveness and the divine response of forgiveness. There is not a strong sense of God as an initiator in taking control of his distress. Rather, as described above, Peter acts and God responds as Peter expects God to respond. At one point Peter makes the observation: *If I just have the courage to turn back to him...* which suggests his sense of personal responsibility. Although this taking of personal responsibility is clearly evident in his journaling there is also a sense of divine-human partnership.

Relationship with God

The journal entries, although brief, indicated a significant level of anxiety for Peter about the nature of his relationship with God. Observations such as, *there is a chasm between me and God* reflects this anxiety which was evident at the forefront of his experience from the first day of praying the psalms of distress. From the journal entries which followed there seemed to be a continuing sense of distress around the idea of what relationship with God might look like and feel like for Peter. Just as he took personal responsibility for his distress, so he took personal responsibility for his sense of isolation from God. He sees it as something which had been caused by his own action. At one point in the first week he asks, *Is God really far away or have I just turned my back on Him?* Peter's reflections rarely alluded to God's action in either abandoning him or doing something to re-establish a damaged relationship. The responsibility for response, in Peter's view, was situated squarely with Peter himself.

Rather than reflecting on what God's part might be in such a process of reconciliation Peter preferred to state what he sensed God was like. In other words, he attempted to counter his feelings with 'facts' that he believes about God. For example, Peter affirmed that *the Lord is truly great* and that he envisages a *future with HOPE (emphasis Peter's)*. However, this description in his journal was never expressed in terms of the divine-human relationship. Rather it seems to affirm the status of God as being powerful. Because of this, Peter seemed to be more at ease reflecting on past distress in terms of his *sin* and subsequently seeking *forgiveness*. He also focused on a future when *he* will be able to relate to God appropriately. Again, **Peter's action** was the emphasis here rather than God's.

Peter's self-description of *numbness* towards the middle of the first week may also indicate a blockage in his ability or willingness to reflect on the feelings produced by this experience of isolation. At times he preferred to counter feelings of isolation with observations that he *feels the mightiness of the living God*. Although observations such as this are no doubt heartfelt they appear to be hopes rather than reality in the context of Peter's broader reflection on his sense of relationship with God. As a result he appeared to view the isolation as being his fault and, therefore, his need to do something to rectify the situation. This is also reflected as he then began to think about distress in his personal relationships with others. Peter's emphasis on personal volition remained very strong. This manifested in attitudes of self-blame when Peter evaluated the relationship he has with God and people around him. Praying these psalms seemed to promote Peter's expression of these issues through participation in prayer and self-reflection. However, he failed to move beyond this to make sense out of the experience.

Despite the initial experiences of isolation from God, both felt and expressed by Peter early in his journal, a growing sense of connection with God is increasingly evident as the process continued. However, he viewed this process of connection with God (through psalms of distress) as problematic. The tension seems to have emerged because of the discomfort he felt at expressing himself so openly in prayer to God. As a result, his feelings of isolation, and his increasing desire to express himself honestly in prayer, created an uneasy coexistence. However, Peter did find a pathway for expressing his sense of isolation *within* the relationship rather than *apart from* the relationship.

Final interview

Peter was not familiar with praying these particular types of psalms or praying a psalm once a day. However, he found the process enjoyable. Praying them aloud was helpful in that it *made it more like a physical conversation.* Interestingly, he indicated that he continued to pray the psalms even though he stopped the formal process prematurely.

However, Peter felt that the content of psalms of distress was difficult to cope with. He felt that it *put [him] in a position of feeling heavy.* He also used the term *depressed* but then corrected himself adding that he felt it difficult to *put [himself] in the psalmist's shoes.* It appears that he felt it was inauthentic to voice the content of psalms of distress when he did not think he was feeling distressed. Having stated that, Peter did observe a resonance at some points with the feelings expressed in these psalms. As an example of this he described a time when he found himself in tears as he prayed one of the psalms. However, from that point he found it increasingly difficult to cope with the constant revisiting of distress.

The prayer to begin the ritual was *very helpful.* For Peter it set the scene and helped him to position himself before God and self in praying psalms of distress. Use of hand movements was also unique for him but, again, *very helpful.* He noted that the body movement felt very structured at first but then found that it *enhanced* the meaning of the psalms as he continued to use them in this manner. Peter found that after some time the movements became quite natural and helped him to enter the prayer in a more wholistic way. He added that he began to use movements in other times of prayer as well.

Journaling was the most difficult aspect of the process for Peter as he does not see himself as a writer. He felt that as a musician he could best express himself through song-writing and playing music. However, he had not done so with distress up to this point. He felt that the questions for the journal did help him to focus but he said that he tended to view questions as a *question and answer type process* rather than prompts, finding them rather restricting. Overall Peter observed that he *internalizes* the reflections and that journaling *got in the way.*

Peter indicated that he clearly understood the idea of the matrix of lament and its constellations. He felt that the model opened the content and significance of the psalms of distress up to him in a new way. He also found the matrix to be a helpful lens through which to view personal distress. However, he reiterated that the constant focus on distress during the process was problematic for him. Peter felt that a mix of psalm types for prayer would have been more balanced and *in tune with real life.* Peter shared his journey in the experience with one other person and found this to be very helpful in processing the material.

Psychometric testing

The tables below represent a collation of the results from Peter's pre- and post-psychometric testing in the form of tables:

Depression Anxiety Stress Scale - Peter

	Before	**After**	**Change**
Depression	Low/normal	Low/normal	-
Anxiety	Low/normal	Low/normal	-

| Stress | Low/normal | Low/normal | - |

Table 14

Locus of Control – Peter

	Before	**After**	**Change**
Type of control	Internal	Internal	-
Level of control	Moderate	Moderate	+ve

Table 15

Spiritual Assessment Inventory (Relationship) - Peter

	Before	**After**	**Change**
Awareness	Substantially true	Very true	+ve
Acceptance	Very true	Very true	-
Disappointment	Moderately true	Moderately true	-
Grandiosity	Not at all	Not at all	-
Instability	Moderately true	Moderately true	-

Table 16

It can be observed in the tables above that very little change was indicated in Peter's psychometric testing. However, there are a couple of significant exceptions. First, the increase in internal locus of control is noticeable. As shown in the summary above, Peter's desire to take personal responsibility for his distress and sense of isolation from God is evident at various points in his reflections. It may be that the process actually caused him to place a greater emphasis on this than previously which would be congruent with the increase in internal locus of control. Second, the increase in awareness of God indicated in the SAI again is congruent with his journal reflections at various points which reflect these sentiments. Perhaps rather paradoxically it appears as though Peter perceived isolation **from** God and yet, at the same time, a growing awareness **of** God.

Interestingly the DASS did not indicate any change in Peter's level of anxiety or stress. It appears that increase stress and anxiety were initial responses to the process at the time which had subsided to some degree by the time the post-psychometric testing took place.

Participant 6 – Samuel

Journal reflections

Samuel engaged in the journaling aspect of the process indicating that he felt somewhat lost in not being able to identify specific distress in his lived experience. Despite these concerns he continued to utilize the journal to record his responses and reactions while praying the psalms of distress and, subsequently, recorded some significant discoveries.

Levels of distress

Early on Samuel concluded that *I really don't know of much distress in my life at the moment* and observed that *I am either blessed or in denial*. It seems that the major struggle for him at this point was the fact that psalms of distress have no element of denial (as he noted in his final interview). Therefore, he was *caused* to look for his personal distress by praying these psalms each day. As a result the journal entries increasingly displayed an engagement with personal distress from the past and the present. As he continued to *struggle* to find distress it gradually became more obvious. The first week showed a progression from struggling to find distress to *we all have li'l struggles* and then to describing a situation of *dread*. This reflected a gradual discovery of and manifestation of personal distress. Samuel pointed out that the process helped him to *remember* experiences of personal distress rather than ignoring or denying them which is what he had tended to do in the past.

Samuel's *awareness* of distress seemed to increase through the process as he reflected on, and became more aware of, his experiences of personal distress both past and present. The reflective process, in prompting memory, also opened an opportunity for meaning-making to take place. Some evidence of meaning-making was recorded in his journal reflections on his experience. For example, Samuel described one past experience in terms of *surviving* and as he reflected in his experience focused on why he felt empowered at that time. This led to a reflection on the significance of the divine-human relationship in situations of distress. As the awareness of personal distress increased it was balanced by Samuel's observance of the imagining constellation saying *I felt empowered every time I read this aloud*. Again, meaning-making was evident as Samuel discovered a sense of hope in a seemingly hopeless situation. As a result his *level* of stress did not appear to increase.

Locus of control

Samuel's journal reflections suggest an increasing willingness to take on the opportunity to express his sense of personal distress. While this sense of personal responsibility for voicing distress is evident, the engagement with distress is viewed in terms of divine-human teamwork. By using the term *team* Samuel observed that distress is best met with God. Samuel did not sense he was alone; God was an empowering presence who would *fight with me* and the distress was not *too big* for the *team* to overcome. Despite characterizing God's presence as empowering Samuel did not abrogate his personal responsibility for voicing his distress within the divine-human relationship. Rather, he came to clearly view articulation as important and empowerment in terms of interdependence. This reflects the imagining constellation's empowerment with the 'self' **and** God. This discovery of interdependence seems to have come about in part because of the frequent clash between what Samuel 'knows' and what he 'feels' amid distress. Growth was evident in Samuel's journal reflections as he reconciled sometimes paradoxical thinking and feeling to a point of being at ease with both, even if a paradox remained.

Sense of relationship

Samuel did not express any feelings of isolation from God in his reflections. The issue was more a question of how that presence was shown in times of personal distress. He reconciled the belief that God was present with the feeling that God was not present by concluding that both perceptions can co-exist, from a human perspective. Samuel found great freedom and validation in being able to express this paradox **in** relationship **through** prayer. It seems that the vocalizing of this paradox through the psalms of distress was particularly meaningful for him. One way Samuel described his experience was in *being able to see beyond the issue* while granting that the paradox was not easy to fully accept. As a general observation Samuel appears to be a person who moved from a position of denying personal distress to the point of acknowledging its presence and beginning a process of engagement and integration.

Final interview

Samuel found the discipline of praying a psalm each day helpful even though he had not experienced this kind of prayer before. He indicated that the practice of praying the psalms aloud was *weird* at first but then he felt that it helped him to engage his heart in the process, to *slow down* and *connect with the words*. The combination here of written psalms and oral prayer was helpful.

The content of the designated psalms, as an expression of distress, was not unique to Samuel. He felt that in his pre-Christian experience he was engaged in a process of honest expression of distress. However, his distress was not necessarily expressed to God then. He did feel that the psalms of distress *gave permission* for this kind of expression to God, which provided a new perspective to his faith experience. He felt that the process was a very positive experience and found it rather strange that some Christians may see the content of these psalms as difficult to express personally.

Samuel struggled with the rigidity of the ritual. He *knew* this would be the case as he does not think that he is a disciplined person. In fact he said that this was one reason why he decided to enter the process. As well as this, he pointed out that normally he does not value ritual. He said that he would rather *just get into it*. The pre-prayer material was not particularly useful but the hand movements did help to reinforce the constellations of the matrix of lament. He found that the tone of his voice noticeably changed when combined with lifting hands and praying aloud in the imagining constellation of the psalms. Overall the ritual did not take away from the experience but he found that he felt it required a deep *mental effort* at times to keep going.

Journaling was *interesting* for Samuel on the first couple of days. He found it quite *boring* responding to the same questions each time and found that sometimes he simply *didn't have stuff* and *wondered what to do*. In response to this he was simply honest in how he felt at the time. Despite this, the questions were helpful in providing a beginning point for reflection. He *felt stifled* in expressing his feelings through writing because he did not see himself as a writer and had not journaled for some time. He preferred to walk and process the psalms as he did this activity.

Samuel did feel that he clearly understood the nature of the matrix of lament and the constellations in it. This helped to *clarify* what he was encountering in the psalms of distress as he prayed them. He also noticed that, for him, the matrix constellations represented a reflection of real life experience of people's engagement with distress. He observed that *denial* was not encountered in these psalms and that he would continue to pray these psalms as a way of facing distress because he felt now that he saw them as a *true* reflection of engaging with distress for a person of faith. He also felt that combining psalms of distress with other types of psalms would be helpful noting that *praise was not so much of a problem*. He did not seek support from others preferring to view the process as something he wanted to complete on his own.

Psychometric testing

Below are Samuel's collated pre- and post-psychometric test results in table form:

Depression Anxiety Stress Scale - Samuel

	Before	After	Change
Depression	Normal	Normal	-
Anxiety	Normal	Normal	-
Stress	Normal	Normal	-

Table 17

Locus of Control – Samuel

	Before	After	Change
Type of control	Internal	Internal	-
Level of control	Low	High	+ve

Table 18

Spiritual Assessment Inventory (Relationship) - Samuel

	Before	After	Change
Awareness	Substantially true	Substantially true	-
Acceptance	Very true	Very true	+ve
Disappointment	Moderately true	Substantially true	+ve
Grandiosity	Not at all	Not at all	-
Instability	Not at all	Slightly true	+ve

Table 19

Samuel's increase in internal locus of control is congruent with an emerging desire, reflected on in his journal, both to voice and grapple with his experiences of personal distress. To begin with Samuel expressed his experience of distress as non-existent or perhaps slight and no desire to explore distress which he did not feel was present in his life experience. However, praying the psalms seemed to cause a reflective process to begin which opened him up to the reality of personal distress and encouraged him to take some level of personal control in voicing that distress.

The SAI measure of greater realistic acceptance is congruent with Samuel's growing awareness of distress and its implications for his thinking and emotions. It appears to be a movement against the initial denial of distress evident in Samuel's journal reflections. Perhaps because of this acceptance the SAI also suggested an increased disappointment with God. This disappointment with God is not plainly evident in his journal reflections but could be inferred from the content at times. The accompanying increase in instability does not come as a surprise. At the beginning of the process Samuel's denial of distress appears to have caused him to feel quite stable, or at least present himself that way. However, as the process opened up his experiences of distress he appears to have experienced an increased level of instability. This is, perhaps, not surprising as Samuel was challenged to articulate the voice of distress and embrace the real struggles of his life experience.

Participant 7 – Joan

Journal reflections

Joan's journal reflections indicated a balance between identifying her thoughts and feelings and various attempts to engage in meaning-making from those reflections. She had little difficulty identifying distress to begin the process. It is interesting to note that, while not giving extensive details, it appears as though the distress of abandonment is one of long-term significance for her which had been largely unresolved in her mind. It was only later in the process that she moved to more immediate distress. Engagement with her experience of abandonment seemed to contribute positively to her ability to deal with the immediate distress she faced in the latter weeks of the process.

Levels of distress

Joan's journal reflections revealed an increasing willingness to continue engaging with her distress even though this sometimes appeared to exacerbate her sense of distress for a time. Early in the process she observed that *the way the pain was brought to the surface was very powerful*. However, continued perseverance led to Joan grasping a greater sense of meaning in her distress and a greater capacity to work through the distress rather than slipping into denial. Some of this meaning-making aided her in discovering a greater understanding of the divine role in distress. For example, on reflection Joan takes the view that *God did and does see* and that *God does care for the wounded* when distress is experienced. As well as this, she also made greater sense of her own responses at times. At one point she asks of herself, *Have I discovered any new sense of meaning in my distress?* What follows is a thoughtful reflection on Psalm 35 and an intentional connection between the words of the psalm and her present experience of distress.

It became obvious in her journal reflections that there were significant issues of distress she was facing. It is unclear why this might have been so. However,

Joan's reflections suggest a decrease in her feelings of distress because of the praying process. Joan describes her ability to *relinquish* her distress.[7] By describing her feelings around this relinquishment she observed that *I have a peace that I didn't have before*. It is interesting to note that before this decrease in feelings of distress there was a marked increase in Joan's awareness of her distress. For Joan it appears that the first step towards a decrease in feelings of distress was an intentional labelling or articulation of the distress.

Joan's journal reflections also suggest that she increasingly discovered the voice of the psalmist *becoming one's own voice* and that this resonated with her feelings of distress. The practice of praying aloud provided a helpful pathway for the discovery of a 'voice' to occur. She also indicated that repeating the ritual process also aided her awareness of what was happening for her in the process as she did not need to focus on what she was doing rather than on what was happening.

Locus of control

A major theme of Joan's journal reflections was the observation that *God is in control* and that *God does see and know*. To begin with these ideas seemed to be expressed as more of a hope as she prayed the psalms and reflected on her distress. However, as the weeks transpired, this hope appeared to become more of a firm conviction for Joan. In describing her experience Joan characterized it as a *rebalancing* of her perception of what it means to have self-control in the face of personal distress and what divine control might look like.

In the last week of the process Joan stated, *I am so small in the face of almighty God and yet he chooses to hear my prayer*. This observation appears to reinforce the idea of God being the one in control and Joan handing over her distress to God who is perceived as the one able to deliver her from her difficulty. However, it also reflected her understanding of her rôle as the one voicing distress through prayer.

As a work in progress she referred to two particular issues of distress which she had already *handed over* to God. It appears as though Joan had worked through a process which began with a belief of personal powerlessness, hoping God could do something, followed by a movement towards believing God would in fact do something. From this point she then found an empowered partnership **with** God in working jointly towards resolution. Joan herself did not explicitly indicate that she had discovered this sense of partnership with God. However, this could be inferred from her journal reflections.

Sense of relationship

Joan's sense of relationship with God, at the beginning of the process, displayed feelings of abandonment and the paradox which existed for her between what

---

[7] It should be noted that in the context of her journaling the concept of relinquishment did not indicate an abrogation of personal responsibility but, rather, recognition that some things cannot be altered by human response.

she thought theologically and what she felt existentially. At this point she described her experience as feeling *resentment* and *almost drowning.* The challenge for Joan appeared to be her ability to grapple with this and find some sense of resolution. As her journal reflections continued the contrast of thoughts and feelings remained the major focus as Joan grappled with distress. However, praying the psalms of distress seemed to reinforce for her the significance of God's presence *in* her distress seeing them as *affirmations of what I know to be true; that God does see and know....* She came to a fresh realization of the immanence of God in her situation. During the experience of praying the psalms Joan also recognized that the paradoxes between her thinking and her emotions still existed and that ultimate resolution to her distress may not become a reality. However, she reported that she had a sense of movement towards hope for the future observing in the last week that *...the issues of lament have been drained of their urgency and power.*

Joan's attention in praying the psalms of distress shifted gradually from a focus on the expressing and asserting constellations to emphasizing the investing and imagining constellations. This suggests that towards the end of the process she found a balance between all four constellations and discovered a well-rounded articulation of both distress and hope. Her final journal reflection is ironic in observing that she now found herself able to *relinquish* her experience of distress. The reported ability to relinquish seems to have come about as she has firmly grasped the process of the matrix of lament as her own and allowed the voice of the psalmist to become her own voice.

Final interview

Joan found the discipline of praying psalms of distress very helpful. She said that it *led [her] to expression* and was surprised that there was *so much stuff.* She did find it rather *odd to be lamenting* in this way (a prescribed way). In her normal practice of praying she does vary between praying quietly and aloud. However, Joan found that in praying these psalms aloud she was able to *participate meaningfully* in the psalms. She also noted that praying aloud *slowed [her] down* from her normal pace of reading and/or praying and helped her to feel that the psalms were her own.

In the first week Joan felt that the psalm was *written for me.* She struggled with the issue of 'enemies' and what it meant if, as a Christian, she wanted a destructive thing to actually happen to her 'enemy.' However, she rationalized this by saying that it is prayer and it is poetry and so it is a venting of emotion rather than a description of reality. In the last couple of weeks Joan did not find the content as relevant as she concluded, *I'm done,* in regard to distress. It was not that she felt she would never be distressed again but the concentrated focus meant that for the moment she had gone as far as necessary. She noted that Psalm 88 was a struggle to pray but *awesome* as she recognized distress in her life that had not been, and may never be, resolved. She was looking for the imagining constellation and was challenged by the fact that she could not find it!

Results from the Action Research

Joan found the ritual helpful but noted that it could become meaningless if the same all the time. She described her personal approach to life and prayer as fairly casual but did not find the prescription of the process unhelpful. She found the preparation time was *very* meaningful. It helped her to centre herself and acknowledge the fragility of life but also the security and safety in knowing *her place and God's place in the universe.*

Journaling is something with which Joan said she was familiar and did periodically. It was helpful for her to record her thoughts and feelings and caused her to focus on how she experienced the psalms and what they meant to her. She felt a freedom to express her feelings through the journal but did say that she was not always able to find words clearly to describe precisely what she was feeling.

Joan found the lens of the matrix a very helpful way to view psalms of distress and clearly understood it. She felt that the ordering/revisiting/repeating of various elements in different psalms reflected the *ebb and flow* (*wave effect* is another term she used) nature of the experience of distress very well. For Joan, this created resonance with ordinary human experience. Because of this Joan experienced a sense of *validation.* She said that she would not use psalms of distress every day or even every week but certainly in a time of distress.

She then added that praying psalms of distress exclusively and being *in the depths* is difficult if that is the sole focus. However, when used in combination with other psalm types the balance would be valuable. She also added that she found *praying what we don't feel* a useful activity. She shared her journey with a couple of people during the time and found that comforting.

As a final comment Joan observed that psalms of distress challenged her ideas about God's omnipotence and omnipresence (divine sovereignty) amid distress. She had not yet fully resolved her views on these theological issues.

Psychometric testing

Joan's results from her pre- and post-psychometric testing are represented in the tables provided below:

Depression Anxiety Stress Scale - Joan

	Before	After	Change
Depression	Normal	Normal	-
Anxiety	Normal	Normal	-
Stress	Normal	Normal	-

Table 20

Locus of Control – Joan

	Before	After	Change
Type of control	Internal	Internal	-
Level of control	Low	Medium	+ve

Table 21

Spiritual Assessment Inventory (Relationship) - Joan

	Before	After	Change

Awareness	Very true	Very true	+ve
Acceptance	Substantially true	Very true	+ve
Disappointment	Slightly true	Slightly true	-
Grandiosity	Not at all	Slightly true	+ve
Instability	Not at all	Not at all	-

Table 22

The increase in Joan's internal locus of control is congruent with her journal reflections. While she appeared to have a strong sense of 'ownership' of her distress rather than ignorance or denial she increasingly takes hold of her responsibility to articulate her distress and her desire for resolution to that distress.

Joan's journaling is congruent in many places with the SAI's indication of an increasing awareness of God's presence in her situation of distress. While she presented in both her journaling and her final interview as a person who had a healthy level of realistic acceptance of her distress the increase indicated by the final SAI is not surprising. Again this is congruent with her reflections. The slight increase in grandiosity may be reflective of her increased internal locus of control and also be indicative of a greater willingness to confront God with her thoughts and feelings. This appears to be particularly so in regard to the theological paradox of distress which Joan experienced as described above.

Participant 8 – Sandra

Journal reflections

It is evident from the format of the Sandra's journal that she approached the prayer and reflection in a systematic and consistent manner. Because of this it seems that in the first two weeks her responses were confined to a question and answer process. However, following second week, the responses became much more embellished in describing her thinking, feelings and experience. The content also broadened mainly through Sandra expressing her responses to the reflection questions with her own prayer to God. This provided greater insight into her experience of praying the designated psalms. It seems from this that what Sandra initially perceived to be a restricting structure (that is, in terms of the reflection questions provided) actually provided a starting point for much broader reflection.

Levels of distress

Sandra's journaling indicated that the process had promoted an engagement with experiences of personal distress in both the present and the past. This in turn appears to have led to an increased ability for her to make some sense of the distress. In Sandra's case there is evidence throughout her journaling of her attempts to make meaning. One example of this is found in the third week where Sandra comments, *I felt a degree of pain of the inner child and then the love of that child by God... I felt encouraged that my future decisions and communication with others will be more from a place of strength in God.*

Sandra expressed throughout her journaling a clear understanding of the matrix of lament as a model indicating that it helped her to see a framework for her experience of distress without being restrictive. The same could be said of the ritual which she also found to be mostly an encouragement to reflect. As with several other participants Sandra also noted the significance of the prayer, 'I am ready to begin....' She indicated that this prayer provided a sense of safety and security in her relationship with God as the process began each day. It is evident from the frequent use of terms such as *safety* and *security* that these were important issues for Sandra. Her journal reflections also indicated that the process provided a pathway for a freedom in expressing her thinking and emotions.

Sandra's journaling began with identifying several experiences of distress. As she engaged with distress she seems to have begun to express her disappointment with God in a more overt manner. Accompanying this feeling was the perceived need for her to defend herself. Sandra observed in week 1 that *I felt like I needed to look after myself, to stand up and do what I could in my... situation.* However, expressing imprecation within the psalms as an example of standing up for herself became a challenge to her theology. Interestingly, in the final interview Sandra described this challenge as causing a *blockage which became an avenue.*

Despite the challenges discovered in the first couple of weeks Sandra observed in the third week that *the psalm enabled me to express pain, hurt, regret and release unresolved issues of the past.* As she attempted to make sense of this experience Sandra appeared to come to the realization that while resolution may not be possible, engagement is painful but nonetheless valuable in shaping her as a person. Because of the engagement she recognized that *I have more peaceful thoughts towards myself, God and others* which reveals itself as a *deeper trust [in God] and delight.* These observations are in marked contrast to the early weeks where Sandra's emotional state appeared to be conflicted.

Locus of control

Sandra's journaling indicated that the content expressed in the psalms of distress resonated with an inner desire she had to be more expressive. They encouraged her to take a more assertive approach towards God. Statements such as *I felt like I needed to look after myself...* reflect this assertiveness. It is evident as the journal unfolds that her assertiveness before God continued to become stronger to the point where her reflection and responses actually become her own prayers. These prayers combine expressing distress, attempts and making meaning of the events and also recognition of where she had the ability to take some action on her part as a response to the situation. By the third week Sandra articulated a *greater sense of self-control for the future* as a result of voicing her experience of distress through prayer.

In the first week of prayer Sandra's reflections indicated a desire for God to rescue her from the distress she is experiencing and yet a sense that *God [was] standing far off.* As the second week began and the following weeks unfolded a growing sense of her own responsibility to deal with her distress together with an increased reliance on God became evident. This culminated with Sandra reflecting on what it meant to be reliant on God and, at the same time, proactive in doing what one can do to work through the experience. As Sandra reflected on this idea she stated, *I recognized that I had a degree of responsibility for my thoughts and how I perceived the events of life* and also, *I expressed to myself it was ok to sit in the mud because God is God and He is bigger than any other circumstances, any feeling of loss.* So, while initially Sandra polarized strongly between God in total control and total self-control there seemed to be a growth towards recognizing and finding a balance of the two.

Sense of relationship

Earlier in the process Sandra expressed feelings of isolation and alienation from God in her distress saying, *I saw God standing afar off like an overseer.* However, as the weeks proceeded a stronger connection with God became evident. Most notably this stronger connection is found in the formulation of prayer responses to the reflection questions. One example of this is found in the following journal reflection:

> *I felt a real connection with myself, God and others and how I related to people. God helped expose deep hidden hurts and needs that were unmet and co-dependent coping habits that had formed and there was a beginning of healing and release.*

A general theme of Sandra's journaling was the prominence of relationships. While the focus on her relationship with God was significant it was also evident that Sandra placed great value on her relationship with herself and others. The process of engaging with her experience of distress through these psalms appears to have been a helpful tool for self-reflection. Sandra became aware of a broader range of emotions and thoughts within herself directly because of praying the designated psalms. As well as this she also reflected on how she viewed others in her life. This was particularly so in the case of those she perceived as 'enemies' who were in some sense causing her distress. It seems that praying these psalms aided Sandra in being able to view her distress more from the perspective of God and others. This in turn led to a deeper level of self-reflection and awareness of what was happening for her in the process.

Final interview

Sandra found the discipline of praying a psalm each day as helpful. A different aspect of the psalm tended to *stand out at different times* for her and the repetitive process gave this the space to happen. She also found the practice of praying aloud not unusual and engaged with the process completely. The psalms helped her to be able to hear herself more and be personally involved with the words on the page. The major question she had to begin with was, *How can I say that to*

God aloud? Although she could not necessarily give a clear answer to this question by the end of the process she found great value in the practice and it became increasingly comfortable.

Sandra had some questions about the content at various points. She found that she could not return easily to Psalm 22 recognizing that she was in fact angry with God, let down by God and blocked in expressing this. However, she found on returning to it that the psalm in fact became an avenue for expressing these emotions.[8] Sandra also found that using these psalms as prayer brought to mind a whole range of situations, accessed the past, and helped her to think a lot about God and 'others' in her own situation. She also felt that using these psalms helped to make more sense of life and the ability to process the distress *privately*. These psalms provided the *freedom to say what we feel*.

Sandra *loved* the 'I am ready to begin…' prayer at the beginning. However, the hand movements *took away from the experience* and she did not always find that she agreed with the colour-coding of the psalms. Because of this she found at times she was *thinking* about the process rather than *feeling* it and prayer became *more intellectual than emotional*. She also suggested that finding one's own movements would have been more helpful for her but did find the ones prescribed useful in reinforcing her experience.

Answering the questions became a hindrance for Sandra as she tried to process what was happening. However, she did say that she would often recall particular questions and her responses at other times during the day and *mull them over*. Despite her reservations Sandra did find the structure of the questions useful at times to keep on track. As well as the prescribed questions Sandra also found it helpful to ask, *Who am I in the psalm?* She found that her response to this question helped her to focus more on the content. Sandra also felt that the journaling was a bit too rigid but the required commitment to writing brought a closure to the process for her.

Sandra found that the matrix and its constellations was a helpful way of looking at the content and structure of these psalms. She also felt that it reflected the normative human response to distress. However, she did feel that the red and green was muddled at times, in her view, and not always clearly distinguished. The matrix aided Sandra in realizing that she had been *internalizing for so long...* and found it helpful to *see it and deal with it* through using these psalms. On this basis she agreed that she would continue to use these psalms as a way of engaging with personal distress. However, Sandra pointed out that she would find it more helpful to pray these psalms in context with other psalm types as she *sometimes didn't want to go there*. She also realized through these psalms that there was more work to be done on some events of the past. Overall she felt that her sense of relationship with God varied over the time but that she sensed a greater 'control' in her distress. Sandra also added that she sought support from her partner

---

[8] Sandra also noted that knowing the author and the receivers would help to contextualize the psalms for her a little better.

by sharing some of her journey with him.

Psychometric testing

Below are tables which summarize the pre- and post-psychometric test results of Sandra:

Depression Anxiety Stress Scale - Sandra

	Before	After	Change
Depression	Normal	Normal	-
Anxiety	Normal	Normal	-
Stress	Normal	Normal	-

Table 23

Locus of Control – Sandra

	Before	After	Change
Type of control	Internal	Internal	-
Level of control	Moderate	Moderate	-

Table 24

Spiritual Assessment Inventory (Relationship) - Sandra

	Before	After	Change
Awareness	Very true	Very true	+ve
Acceptance	Very true	Very true	-ve
Disappointment	Substantially true	Very true	+ve
Grandiosity	Moderately true	Slightly true	-ve
Instability	Slightly true	Moderately true	+ve

Table 25

While Sandra's DASS scores showed normal levels of depression, anxiety and stress this was not congruent with her journal reflections which recorded significant expressions of both anxiety and stress. The constant result in locus of control again does not reflect the movement evident within Sandra's journaling and her comments in the final interview. The journal reflections and interview suggest that she became more assertive in taking control of her situations of distress and responses to them.

While there is movement in each category of the SAI the most significant moves were disappointment with God and grandiosity. Sandra appears to have become substantially more disappointed as she concluded that God would not rescue her from her distress. This realization also possibly contributed to the increase in instability. The large decrease in grandiosity is difficult to explain. It does not appear to be consistent with Sandra's journaling which signals an increased assertiveness in prayer.

Results from the Action Research

Participant 9 – Julie

Journal reflections

It seems from the style of the journal entries and the approach taken early in the first week that Julie was attempting to take a detached and more 'objective' approach to the process. It also seems that there was a barrier for her at first in coming to terms with the content of these psalms expressed directly to God in prayer.

Levels of distress

Julie had little difficulty in recognizing specific distress in her life situation. She displayed a willingness to engage with the distress and voice both thoughts and feelings around the experiences. In praying the psalms she found that they resonated with her experiences and provided a language for expressing her own story of distress.

When Julie identified, and focused on, a particular situation of distress while praying the designated psalm, she appears to have become anxious as she questioned the appropriateness of such an expression. This anxiety was exacerbated for her by the praying aloud of the psalm. While it became an obstacle for her early on it seems to have been overcome and she continued with the process. As a result the second week contained much more reflection on the emotional response for Julie to both her distress and the psalm being prayed.

Throughout the process of praying the designated psalms Julie did not indicate a resolution to her distress. However, she did emphasize the importance of being able to tell the story of her distress through prayer in the presence of God as a significant part of the process for her. This was evident in both her journaling and the final interview. An example of this 'storytelling' is recorded in the third week where Julie recounts: *I paraphrased the... situation into the psalm and found it helpful to do so.* This example also suggests an integration of personal experience with the text as a retelling of ones story to God, through prayer. As a final reflection on the process overall Julie indicated that *I found the level of personal stress reduced* by the end of the process.

Locus of control

While Julie affirmed God's control with reflections such as I am *reassured that God is in control of my world* this did not appear to soothe her feelings of distress. Although she did not voice questions about the nature of God's control in her situation they appear to underlie some of her thinking around distress. It was not until the last week that some explicit references were made to doubts about God's action or inaction. Julie observed that *I have often felt hollow, that God has turned from hearing me* but then immediately qualified this by stating *but... He has not let me go completely.* From this struggle Julie began to reflect on what it meant to believe that God was actually in control of the situation.

In terms of the 'self' Julie showed a willingness to be assertive in quite descriptive ways about her distress in the form of a prayer. Even a cursory scan of her journal entries reveals strong assertions about how she responds to God in her distress. She uses statements such as *I talk..., I look for..., I will continue et al* to express her taking of personal responsibility to respond to distress. At the same time Julie recognized the significance of divine response for her saying that *He does not always specifically do something, we must wait and trust.* The two aspects of self-assertion and recognition of divine response appear to provide Julie with a pathway forwards in engaging her experiences of personal distress.

Sense of relationship

Julie struggled with the supposed presence of God (*I felt as if God was hearing me and would continue to uphold me*) and yet the accompanying feelings of God's absence at times. As a result she began to focus more on her situations of distress in relational terms noting at one point that *my relationship with God is my strength.* In the third week Julie reflected on Psalm 35 as a *reassurance of God's presence* with a focus on the divine-human relationship alongside the struggle with her perceived 'enemies.' The high level of internal locus of control for Julie appears to have presented her with the dilemma of who *is* actually in control, if anyone, and what her responsibility was in the situation.

A significant shift took place in the third week where Julie appeared to move from a situation of **believing** in God's presence to her to **sensing** God's presence. The language change, noted earlier, from describing God as being *there* to God being *here* suggests this. It is from this point on that she seemed to gain a greater acceptance of the present reality compared with a future hope. Julie described this as *getting some things in more perspective.*

Julie also identified the issue of trust as a key issue in her experience of distress. While she reflected on this in terms of human relationships and a lack of trust which brings feelings of being *unsafe* there is no mention of the same in the divine-human relationship. However, it does seem that as Julie continued through the process of praying these psalms, her trust in God accepting her expression of distress grew. This resulted in her describing God as a *companion* and distress as something to be faced together. This companionship mirrored the empowerment of both God and the distressed person found in the imagining constellation of the matrix of lament.

While Julie's journal contained much description of how she thought and felt there was an absence of any extensive attempts to make sense out of her reflections. It would seem that it could be a worthwhile experience for Julie to go back to her journal entries at some point and reflect on what was happening for her at various points in her experience. This could prompt further reflection on why she responded in the way she did.

Final interview

Julie indicated had she had not practised praying a psalm a day, or praying psalms at all, before but did not find the practice difficult. In fact she found that it helped being set out in systematic manner. Julie said that she did not normally pray aloud and found that an interesting experience. This aspect of the practice meant that the psalms *made me hear myself* and that they were *more personalized* as a result. She also found a greater connection with friends who are in distress as she paraphrased both her own, and others', situations into the psalm. Adding to this idea of paraphrase Julie firmly stated that we today *have a different perspective since the cross*. She was unable to articulate exactly what this meant for her. However, she still found *deep resonance* with the content. Julie indicated that with some psalms she connected with very strongly while others this was not so. As examples she observed that she could not connect at all with Psalm 10 and Psalm 88. She said that the content did not resonate with her experience and that she felt like praying these psalms was *vane babbling* rather than authentic prayer.

The hand movements helped to reinforce the concept of the matrix and its constellations but she did find it made the activity a bit stilted and uncomfortable overall. However, Julie added that she did not feel this took anything away from what was happening for her. If anything it added to the experience. Again she could not articulate exactly what this might have been. The opening prayer did not say enough for her and so she paraphrased it and added more at the end to reflect her own perspective. The ritual itself gave further meaning to the psalms of distress and the sense for Julie of it being a group activity even though she was doing it alone.

Julie has not familiar with journaling as a form of reflection before beginning this process. She found this requirement difficult contrasting her need to record 'facts' in her work but not feelings through a similar process. Julie did ask a friend for some guidance in journaling and then felt more comfortable with the process. Even though she found the questions helpful she still found herself *wondering what was being looked for*. Despite her difficulty with the practice of journaling she considered it to be a valuable way of recording and reflecting on thoughts and feelings.

Julie clearly understood the concept of the matrix and felt that it fairly represented the structure and function of these psalms. However, the explanation in the first group session was necessary for her to understand it. She did find it a helpful way to look at these psalms and felt that the constellations were quite clear in the psalms used. The colour-coding was also very useful. She said that she would continue to use the psalms of distress to reflect on her distress but thought that used together with other psalms the overall experience would provide a more balanced and reflective view of life experience. She did not share her thoughts or feelings with anyone during the experience except to ask her friend for some journaling techniques. Julie also noted that there are only a few people with whom she shares deeply about distress in life.

Psychometric testing

Julie's pre- and post-psychometric testing has been collated into the tables below:

Depression Anxiety Stress Scale - Julie

	Before	After	Change
Depression	Mild	Normal	-ve
Anxiety	Mild	Mild	-
Stress	Mild	Normal	-ve

Table 26

Locus of Control – Julie

	Before	After	Change
Type of control	Internal	Internal	-
Level of control	High	High	-

Table 27

Spiritual Assessment Inventory (Relationship) - Julie

	Before	After	Change
Awareness	Very true	Very true	-
Acceptance	Very true	Substantially true	-ve
Disappointment	Slightly true	Slightly true	-ve
Grandiosity	Slightly true	Slightly true	+ve
Instability	Moderately true	Slightly true	-ve

Table 28

The decrease in depression and anxiety in Julie's DASS results are congruent with the journal reflections and final interview. While it appears that several situations of personal distress were prominent in her reflection the process encouraged an articulation of what Julie was thinking and feeling. One significant aspect of this articulation was the opportunity to weave her personal story with the story of the psalm as an expression of prayer. This method of combining personal story with text was helpful according to Julie herself and may have contributed to the decline in depression and anxiety.

The high internal locus of control is congruent with Julie's approach to writing the journal and her frequent reflections on the course of action she could take in response to personal distress. Interestingly though, divine response is not ruled out. Rather, Julie's strong internal locus of control appears to be more indicative of the **type of response** she has towards God. It does not appear to be indicative of a belief that divine action is unnecessary.

The lack of change in awareness of God in the SAI is not surprising as Julie demonstrated this quality throughout her journaling. The decreases in instability and disappointment with God are indicative of her 'coming to grips' with her experiences of personal distress and the role her relationship with God plays in these experiences. The slight rise in grandiosity may indicate a stronger sense of being able to assert herself in prayer. Finally, the decrease in realistic acceptance does not appear to be congruent with Julie's journaling. The results indicate a marked drop in this aspect but would need to be explored with the participant herself to find further explanation.

Participant 10 – Tanya

Journal reflections

Tanya seemed to respond well at first to the requirements of the process. Even though she was initially a little confused about the matrix of lament and lacked some understanding she was determined to go through the ritual. Despite admitting that she was not familiar with journaling about her thoughts and feelings she expressed both of these aspects of her experience very clearly at various points. She also identified particular emotions which arose for her as she prayed the designated psalm and tended to reflect on her thoughts and feelings by asking significant questions. These questions prompt her to further reflection and sometimes the beginnings of making meaning out of her experience.

Levels of distress

A significant point of reflection was the paradox Tanya perceived between her continuing, often unresolved, experiences of distress and a god, who she believed strongly, was in control of the situation. At one point she articulated this attitude saying, *I'm sticking with God... It's much better to be on God's side of the fence.* Praying these psalms did not resolve the problem for Tanya but appeared to have aided her in expressing her thinking and feelings. Emerging from her questions about God's control Tanya felt the process ...*allowed me to express my anger and frustration... it gave me permission.* This type of reflection led to *weeping* which Tanya described as a *stress relief valve* suggesting that her feelings of distress were reduced because of the process.

Tanya became increasingly focused on the breathing and the ritual as a calming influence as she engaged with distress by praying the psalms. It seems that the *disorder* which she identified so readily in her *world* was brought into some sense of order by the ritual being followed. Significantly she offered a reflection on a specific situation of distress where she reacted differently to the past and *felt calm* as a result. Tanya attributed this to her participation in the process of praying psalms of distress.

As the first week proceeded, the concept of Tanya confronting her distress *with* God continued to grow. She viewed this as *taking sides with God* and expressions such as *refuse to become a victim* indicated a level of empowerment not expressed earlier in the week. However, with this Tanya also reflects that the process was causing an increase in distress for her. While her reflections were insightful and appeared to be influencing her thinking about God, self and others, the level of anxiety was rising. It remains unclear whether this anxiety was caused by psalms of distress or the events of the period. However, praying the psalms offered an avenue for focusing on anxiety. This focus is what appeared to have been overwhelming for Tanya.

Struggling to see the point of the questions and only wanting to focus on the imagining constellation was in contrast to a journal that seemed to express the opposite. It should be considered that she appeared to be in a very anxious state at the final interview and this may well have influenced some of her responses.

Locus of control

Tanya affirmed her sense that God is in control of her situation and a 'wondering' about God's possible response to her situations of distress. At one point she noted, *perhaps God was even listening to my 'flitting' thoughts.* Late in the second week this 'wondering' became more of a conviction. Tanya stated that she felt *assurance that God knows about my concerns and that if anything can be done, He will prompt me and He will help me.* Inherent in this reflection is a recognition of balance between divine action and the action of the individual in response to distress.

Sense of relationship

Tanya viewed her relationship with God as critical to her engagement with distress. She was reluctant to entertain the idea of blaming God for her predicament or for God's seeming lack of response. Her preference is to fix blame on herself. In the first week she reflected *I blame myself for not listening and for not trusting[God]...* In contrast to her own perceived inadequacies she then affirms that she can *trust Him[God] with everything... even my heart.*

Finally, it also became clear within Tanya's journal, and was confirmed during the final interview, that praying with psalms of distress precipitated a paradox for Tanya between trusting in God and yet not experiencing divine intervention in her situation. As well as this, the process appeared at times to provide a 'trigger' for reminders of various past and present distresses. This 'trigger' seems to have overwhelmed Tanya to the point where she felt she needed to withdraw.

Final interview

Tanya stated that she did not find the discipline of praying these psalms difficult in itself although she was not used to this kind or process. She did find praying the psalms aloud caused her to be *more passionate* in her expression of distress than if they had been silent prayers.

This interview was in some ways at odds with Tanya's journaling. On reflection Tanya was much less favourably disposed towards the process. She pointed out that she found the content of these psalms to be *depressing* and *disheartening.* The *praise* portion of these psalms was *way out of proportion* to the rest of the psalm which she felt lingered far too much on *the negative.* As a result she found the content of these psalms increasingly difficult to cope with and felt that her level of distress became higher a she prayed them.[9] She said that the process, *made it worse.*

The ritual preparation was helpful for her and she noted that the breathing was particularly useful because it *slowed her down* and focused her attention on the task ahead. However, the opening prayer was not helpful in putting her at ease

---

[9] At this point in the interview she became visibly upset and she began to cry.

Results from the Action Research

or preparing her to enter praying the psalms. Physically she found the hand actions difficult to maintain and indicated that the only constellation where she felt a positive response was lifting hands for the imagining constellation. She felt *more uplifted* than at any other time in the process.

Journaling was not easy for Tanya. She was not used to writing much and was also not used to expressing her feelings in this way. She found the questions too repetitious and *couldn't see the point*. Despite this, Tanya did add that she was able to express her feelings to some degree through writing in response to praying.

With the initial explanation of the matrix and its constellations Tanya said that she did not understand what it was about. The colour-coding was, however, helpful and she did begin to see the pattern and structure after a few days. She was uncertain about how helpful this was at looking at personal distress. Tanya indicated that she would use praise psalms instead of psalms of distress in a continuing way to deal with personal distress. Having said this she did add that using psalms of distress *with* other types and not focusing on the same psalm every day would be helpful. She did not seek support from others at all.

Psychometric testing

The tables below represent the pre- and post-psychometric testing of Tanya in summary form:

Depression Anxiety Stress Scale - Tanya

	Before	After	Change
Depression	Normal	Normal	-
Anxiety	Mild	Severe	+ve
Stress	Moderate	Mild	-ve

Table 29

Locus of Control – Tanya

	Before	After	Change
Type of control	Internal	Internal	-
Level of control	Low	High	+ve

Table 30

Spiritual Assessment Inventory (Relationship) - Tanya

	Before	After	Change
Awareness	Moderately true	Slightly true	-ve
Acceptance	Substantially true	Substantially true	-
Disappointment	Very true	Substantially true	-ve
Grandiosity	Slightly true	Slightly true	-
Instability	Moderately true	Slightly true	-ve

Table 31

The results from the psychometric testing are largely congruent with Tanya's journal reflections and her final interview. The decrease in stress is interesting.

It seems to show that the process was helpful for Tanya in voicing her experiences of distress. However, there was an accompanying increase in anxiety which was also evident in the final interview. This may suggest that Tanya would have benefited from intentional support through the process to help her work through her anxieties at the time.

The increase in internal locus of control is also congruent with the journaling and final interview. The process appears to have encouraged Tanya to take more personal ownership for voicing her distress. The first week of her journaling showed that she was assertively observing and reflecting on her thoughts and feelings. However, the resulting anxiety mitigated against this process continuing. The final SAI results do not appear to be congruent with Tanya's journaling or her final interview. However, there is some evidence in her journal to suggest that she did feel less disappointment with God in some situations of specific distress. She also may have felt less instability because she could begin to see a way forwards and some hope for the future.

Participant 11 – Fran

Journal reflections

Fran appears to have entered the process with an open mind and a willingness to both identify and engage with past and present distress. Despite the fact that the practice of ritualizing prayer and reflecting on prayer was not something very familiar to her both the journal entries and her final interview indicated that she found the experience beneficial on the whole. It also became evident reading through her journal and interviewing her that she is a person who had done work to process these experiences before entering this study.

Perhaps indicative of her initial low level of internal locus of control Fran followed the suggested pattern of prayer, reflection and response systematically. As the weeks unfolded she began to alter the ritual at times to fit with her situation and to complement the words of the psalms with her own. The change evident here suggests that the structure of the ritual provided Fran with the impetus to engage with it and then continue to become creative through it as she personalized the process. The increase in internal locus of control supports a movement such as this.

Levels of distress

Despite the fact that there were several points where Fran noted that the process exacerbated her experience of distress it ultimately seemed to lead her to a place of greater calm and deeper contemplation. One reflection on this appeared at the end of week three with Fran stating: *Clearly a movement between yesterday and today— emotions much calmer today even though the situation remains unchanged.* This, in turn, resulted in her finding a fresh perspective on her distress as she sought to make sense of her experience. In particular a response of anger towards God was evident for Fran at various times. One reflection on this was her observation that *huge anger rose up at his <u>lack</u> of care and protection of me* *(emphasis Fran's)*. As a part of this process she was often able to identify several specific emotional responses, such as *helplessness,* in response to the content of the psalm being prayed and the situation of distress on which she was focusing. In both her journal and the final interview Fran pointed out that the process was a major factor in her sensing a lower level of distress.

It should be noted that at no point did Fran identify a distressing situation as being resolved. The result of the reflection process appears to have aided her in coping with the situation more effectively. Supporting this observation Fran noted that the imagining constellation became more prominent and meaningful in her praying as she moved through each week. To begin with she seemed to see no point in praying this constellation because she sensed no hope. However, as she prayed the hope expressed in the constellation it appears to have become more real in her experience. An increasing desire to be honest in prayer emerged over the course of the process. By week three she stated that *I can't pretend I don't care* about distress. Following this she then proceeded to express why she did care, how she had responded to the situation and what she wanted God to do in response.

Locus of control

While Fran's sense of personal empowerment appeared to increase as the process transpired theological challenges about the nature of God's control in the situation became increasingly troubling for her. The first hint of this was the comment in the first week where Fran made the observation that *...divine intervention has seemed slow to come for me.* Accompanying this observation was emerging anger at God because of God's perceived inaction. It seems from this initial observation that, at least theologically, she believed God would intervene. Therefore, the anxiety was produced when this had not occurred. The idea of divine intervention was reinforced in Fran's journaling with perspectives such as *...only God can organize that* and a *...sense of confidence that God will intervene.*

As her journaling continued Fran appeared to gravitate between the poles of anger with God for not acting and a belief which holds to the idea above that God would intervene in our distress. This was never resolved for Fran during the process, though the two perspectives did seem to come to an uneasy coexistence in her mind and her experience as she prayed the psalms. It could be that Fran's lack of control over her distress and her realization that perhaps God did not control her distress was countered by the level of control she felt in the ritual of prayer. To this end she reflected on the idea that *I am helpless* and *only God can help me.*

A further aspect of control emerged as Fran reflected on the words in the psalms about 'enemies'. This again caused her a theological concern. In both her journal and her final interview she expressed the dissonance she felt between words expressing a wish for one's enemy to be destroyed and her perspective on this as a Christian. For Fran these words were taken as literal, not figurative. She appears to believe that if these words of destruction were prayed they might in fact become reality. In this was an embedded angst for her as a Christian person.

Sense of relationship

Fran identified the tripartite relationship between self, God and enemy early in the process. She made insightful observations of the dynamics in the relationships and reflected on these in meaningful ways. Concerning the enemy Fran expressed a strong theological belief that God would deal with them in the end saying God ...*will call us all to accountability*. The psalms of distress seemed to affirm this for her and the view aided her in coping with a lack of resolution. Alongside this was the consistently affirmed belief that God's presence was with her. Again Fran experienced the designated psalms as affirming God's presence. Even Psalm 88 became a helpful experience for her with the absence of an imagining constellation. Though she struggled with the psalm suggesting God caused the distress it at least affirms God's presence with her in the distress.

Through recognizing the tripartite relationship Fran found herself able to appreciate the perspective of her enemy and God more clearly. This appeared to lead to a greater sense of self-acceptance. She also concluded that while a sense of God's presence was significant, her trust that her relationship with God existed was paramount in coping with distress. To this end she displayed an increasing capacity to view the divine-human relationship as a partnership when distress is encountered. She concluded in the sixth week with a prayer that God would provide ...*energy, agility, enthusiasm, sound sleep and good concentration* so that she can cope with distress. Fran also reiterate that praying the psalm provided an opportunity to ...*let the emotions out*. It is interesting that she did not pray for resolution to the distress but, rather, the resources to engage with distressing situations.

Final interview

Fran found the discipline of the process to be a challenge as she did not see this as an area of personal strength. Praying in this way for five days in a row was difficult and she often found herself praying the psalm twice a day following a day's break. She did not find praying aloud unusual and felt that the process helped to *externalize the inside*.

Fran found it difficult to cope with certain psalms in some sections because of the depth of expression of distress. She identified Psalm 88, with no imagining constellation, as being particularly difficult to pray. Fran felt that she did not always *see life like the psalmist* and reflected on how a New Testament perspective might provide a different viewpoint. Fran felt prompted to reflect on significant questions about whether Christians could or should pray some of these words. She did, however, find that it helped her to resonate with other people in distress. As an example of this Fran cited one particular close personal relationship where she discovered empathy with one she felt was *the enemy*. In dealing with the content Fran added that she emended the psalms to her own situation. She also added in the exact issue of distress being experienced and changed language which she felt did not reflect what she wanted to say.

Fran found the rigidity of the ritual comfortable but had to remind herself of specific aspects involved. She said the ritual was easy to follow and the colour-coding was very helpful. She also found the movements from one constellation to another *abrupt* and the hand movements were *at times distracting* rather than helpful. Physically she found lifting her hands up above the shoulder, sometimes for long periods, very difficult to do. The opening prayer was great in setting the scene by reinforcing safety and security. Fran did not find the breathing useful. Despite this she did go on to say that when she cried the breathing came naturally back to her as a way of coping with this expression.

Journaling was not a difficult task for Fran to do and she felt it was useful both generally and specifically. The writing was helpful as a further means of expression and the questions helped focus her reflections. She pointed out that she felt comfortable responding with specific answers to the specific questions and adding general reflections at the end. However, Fran added that after journaling she found that *there is still stuff here* and so sensed that this process was incomplete in and of itself. She did feel the journaling process promoted expressing emotion and that there was great value in *being able to say it and get it out there.*

The matrix of lament and its constellations made sense to Fran and she found it helpful in understanding the content and structure of psalms of distress. She felt that without the matrix framework it would be difficult for her to understand, or engage with, the content. she also concluded that the psalms did reflect personal distress very well and helped in *feeling your feelings.* Some psalms connected very well with her personal experience while others did not. Fran also felt that *words in the psalms and words out of the psalms* connected strongly. She explained this idea by saying the words of someone else could be reworked or reworded to one's own words.

Fran pointed out that she would not use the psalms of distress as a continuing way of engaging with her personal distress as she uses other methods. However, she added that she felt the use of psalms of distress would be useful for those who did not have a process for engaging with distress. She also noted that while she *expected* the psalms of distress to have a high note (that is, an imagining constellation) she now realized that this constellation was not always present. Fran indicated that she did not seek support from others but discussed the process with one friend.

Psychometric testing

Below are the collated results of Fran's pre- and post-psychometric testing in table form:

Depression Anxiety Stress Scale - Fran

	Before	After	Change
Depression	Mild	Normal	-ve
Anxiety	Mild	Normal	-ve
Stress	Mild	Normal	-ve

Table 32

Locus of Control – Fran

	Before	After	Change
Type of control	Internal	Internal	-
Level of control	Very Low	High	+ve

Table 33

Spiritual Assessment Inventory (Relationship) - Fran

	Before	After	Change
Awareness	Very true	Very true	-
Acceptance	Very true	Very true	+ve
Disappointment	Moderately true	Substantially true	+ve
Grandiosity	Not at all	Not at all	-
Instability	Slightly true	Slightly true	-

Table 34

The decrease in depression, anxiety and stress on the DASS test are congruent with Fran's experience as she expressed it in both her journal reflections and her final interview. It was evident at both points that the process of engaging with her distress through praying psalms of distress was viewed by her as helpful in this way.

The rise in internal locus of control was significant for Fran. Again the LOC result is a reflection of Fran's reflections and responses to interview questions. It appears that while Fran did not find resolution to her situations of distress she did find the process offered a sense of control over her situation and the way she responded to it. Finally, the rise in realistic acceptance suggests that she became more realistic in her assessment of the effects of her distress on her and the rôle her relationship with God played in her dealing with distress. It was not surprising to observe the rise in her disappointment with God. It seems that, as the process unfolded, Fran came to a greater awareness that God had not responded to her distress as she had desired and perhaps not at all. This appears to have caused her to reassess the concept of divine activity in the individual's situation and move to a position of viewing the relationship as the pre-eminent factor in facing personal distress.

Participant 12 – Donna

Journal reflections

Given the limited amount of information from Donna it is impossible to draw any conclusions about the effect praying psalms of distress had on her in the two days she participated. However, it does seem possible that the short time of involvement may have exacerbated her feelings of distress to the point where she felt withdrawal was her best option.

Final interview

Donna agreed to an informal interview following the designated period for the process. While she did not give any specific reasons for her withdrawal she did indicate that personal experiences of distress leading up to the beginning of the process made it difficult for her to continue.

Psychometric testing

Donna did not complete the post-psychometric testing. However, her initial results are recorded below in table form:

Depression Anxiety Stress Scale - Fran

	Before	After	Change
Depression	Normal	NR	NR
Anxiety	Normal	NR	NR
Stress	Normal	NR	NR

Table 35

Locus of Control – Fran

	Before	After	Change
Type of control	Internal	NR	NR
Level of control	High	NR	NR

Table 36

Spiritual Assessment Inventory (Relationship) - Fran

	Before	After	Change
Awareness	Very true	NR	NR
Acceptance	Very true	NR	NR
Disappointment	Very true	NR	NR
Grandiosity	Slightly true	NR	NR
Instability	Not at all	NR	NR

Table 37

As Donna withdrew from the process at a very early stage and did not submit a journal or complete the post-psychometric testing there is no way of making any informed observations about her experience of thesis psalms.

We have now completed a detailed examination of participants' reflections and responses to each of the three psychodynamic foci identified at the beginning of this chapter. The final perspective on the results of this study consists of a summary of the group's responses to the experience.

Final group session

A final meeting of the group was convened one week after completing the process. Eight of the participants attended while the four who withdrew from the process did not. It should be noted that of the four who withdrew, three indicated that they would have attended the final group meeting if they had been available. One original participant indicated that she did not wish to attend the meeting.

The first part of the group meeting consisted of completing the post-psychometric testing including the *Depression, Anxiety and Stress Scale* (DASS), *Locus of Control* (LOC), and the *Spiritual Assessment Inventory* (SAI). Following the testing the group engaged in a discussion of their experiences during the project. This discussion concentrated on the three psychodynamic aspects of the participant's experience during the process identified in chapter 5:

- Level of distress
- Locus of control
- Sense of relationship

Level of distress

The majority agreed that praying these psalms had helped them to feel more *real* and more *human*. The consensus of the group affirmed that both the matrix of lament with its constellations and the content of psalms of distress reflected the experience of distress for them in their own situation. All the participants also agreed that praying these psalms did not resolve distress. In fact some observed that it made them more aware of the continuous presence of distress in their daily lives. However, the majority found a greater sense of calm following voicing their distress through praying a psalm. In contrast to this some noted that they experienced a deeper level of a particular distress than previously encountered. This sometimes resulted in a reaction of crying, deep sobbing or silent contemplation.

The group felt that rather than move people away from the distress it actually provided a doorway to engage with it and access it more deeply. From this deepening experience the majority found an opportunity to reflect on their distress and their reactions to it. For most of the group this in turn led to new levels of personal meaning-making as they gained new perspectives on their experiences of distress.

Locus of control

A very strong sense was expressed by the whole group that they felt more empowered by the process to face personal distress in very specific ways. They all agreed that this sense of empowerment came from the experience of God *amid the distress* with them rather than a sense of God being detached from personal distress. Praying psalms of distress often highlighted this insight. So for all the participants in this group session the nature of the distress and the presence of the distress became subordinate to the sense of divine presence. This sense of divine presence led to a feeling of empowerment where the distressed individual felt they could continue despite a lack of resolution. John, reflecting on his sense of empowerment from an awareness of divine presence, suggested that we cannot realistically look for a time where distress is absent because life is made up of these experiences. However, he went on to argue that our experience of distress can be markedly different if we have a sense of divine presence with us.

All the participants indicated that they felt empowered by this sense of divine presence because they were aware of it. The sense of divine presence also reinforced the idea that there was a greater force ultimately in control of their lives and their world. They did not feel alone amid distress but had a sense of facing the distress with God. Fran and Joan commented that the structure of psalms of distress and the ritual of regularly praying them provided a sense of safety and security for all the participants which in turn facilitated an added sense of personal empowerment.

Understanding the matrix of lament combined with the prescribed ritual also provided a sense of self-control for some participants. This is reinforced by the increase in internal locus of control for eight participants. Some also reported a deeper sense of God being in control. For others it caused them to reflect on God's control and the theological concept of omnipotence. The emphasis for most of the group here was focused on managing the emotions and thoughts rather than focusing exclusively on the distress itself. Most of the group reported a sense of feeling more in control *with* God in a partnership when facing distress.

Sense of relationship with God

The group's general feeling suggested that the words of the psalms enabled them to express their deepest feelings *in* relationship with God rather than outside such a relationship. They saw this as a significant aspect of the practice. Despite the value placed on the relationship some tension emerged for the majority between the intimacy of the relationship with God and expressing anger.[10] For most this became a theological conundrum which struggled with how honest one can be with God. In contrast to this Charles and Joan argued for the necessity of this kind of expression saying that anger is often expressed to those closest to us. As a result they believed that expression to God avoided the potentially destructive effects of expressing anger to those closest to us.

The group then explored the nature of the divine-human relationship obvious in psalms of distress. Despite the reservations about expressing anger highlighted above, most agreed that the whole raft of emotions could be vented in a divine-human relationship which is characterized as one of deep trust. As a response to this idea several participants expressed concern at the graphic nature of some wording found in psalms of distress. However, they added that they felt the words often resonated with feelings they had experienced in response to their personal distress.[11] In this sense they felt both uncomfortable at expressing these feelings and yet the permission to be able to express them. Samuel observed that praying these psalms had put the nature of the divine-human relationship in clearer focus. The potential intimacy offered to us in our relationship with God remained a significant feature of this focus for all the participants.

Interestingly Jim and Charles noticed that in praying these psalms they found themselves identifying with the oppressor in the psalm and this concerned them.

---

[10] This was particularly noticeable for Sandra but others in the group also expressed similar sentiments.

[11] This was particularly so with imprecatory expressions of prayer sometimes found in psalms of distress.

However, they went on to reflect that because of this identification they felt *safe* to admit their oppressive behaviour and ponder a course of action in dealing with the issue their reflection had raised.

The consensus of the group remained that praying these psalms engendered a deeper trust and intimacy between themselves and God even though some found the mode of expression a more confronting form of prayer than they were used to. The concept that emotions associated with distress could be expressed *to God* rather than *apart from God* seemed to be a new discovery for some and significant for all.

In light of the responses to questions and reflections by the group on their experience we will now briefly survey the pre- and post-psychometric testing to see what, if any, congruence is evident from the results.

Whole group psychometric comparison

P	D	A	S	LOC	A	RA	D	G	I
1	-	-ve	-ve	+ve	-	-	-ve	-	-
2	-ve	-ve	-ve	+ve	+ve	+ve	-	-	-
3	-ve	-	+ve	-	-	-ve	+ve	+ve	-
4	-	-	-	-	+ve	+ve	-	-	-ve
5	-	-	-	+ve	+ve	-	-	-	-
6	-	-	-	+ve	-	+ve	+ve	-	+ve
7	-	-	-	+ve	+ve	+ve	-	+ve	-
8	NR	NR	NR	NR	NR	NR	NR	NR	NR
9	-	-	-	-	+ve	-ve	+ve	-ve	+ve
10	-ve	-	-ve	-	-	-ve	-ve	+ve	-ve
11	-	+ve	-ve	+ve	-ve	-	-ve	-	-ve
12	-ve	-ve	-ve	+ve	-	+ve	+ve	-	-

P = Participant; D = Depression; A= Anxiety; S = Stress; LOC = Locus of Control (note that +ve indicates increased internal locus of control); A = Awareness; RA = Realistic acceptance; D = Disappointment; G = Grandiosity; I = Instability

Table 38

In light of the individual reflections and the group discussion several congruent themes can be observed in the table above. Again these will be summarized under the umbrella of each of the three psychodynamic foci identified at the beginning of this chapter.

Summary

The summary above indicates that, for those participants who registered changes in levels of depression, anxiety and stress, the overwhelming majority showed signs of a decrease in those three factors. Only two participants over the three categories of the DASS registered an increase. This is congruent with the reflections of the individual participants and the discussion within the final group session. Within this indication of overall decrease of depression, anxiety and stress it is significant to note that participants indicated anecdotally in their journals that the process initially exacerbated their sense of stress and anxiety. It seems that the levels began to decrease after the first two weeks for those who persisted in the process.

The results for the whole group in the LOC testing show that over half showed an increase in internal locus of control. Again this is congruent with the journal reflections, final interviews and group discussion. In each setting the sense of an increased feeling of the 'self' being in control is evident. The ritual aspect of the process and the lens of the matrix of lament appear to have played a significant part in this increase for most who registered a change in locus of control. Ordering the process in a specific and intentional way and the view of the psalms through the matrix of lament led the majority to attend to their experiences of distress in a more controlled and thoughtful manner. This approach in turn appears to have led to a greater sense of emotional stability in the face of distress.

Of those participants who registered a change the majority showed an increased awareness of God. This again was congruent with the reflections of most individual's and the results of the group discussion. The realistic awareness showed mixed results with more registering an increased awareness than those with reduced awareness. It is unclear how the process impacted this aspect of the participants' experiences. The case was similar with the category of disappointment with God where about the same number registered an increase as those who registered a decrease. The category of instability was also quite evenly spread between those who showed an increase and those who showed a decrease. The individual's results in these categories were congruent with their journal reflections and final interview. However, themes across the group were not so evident.

It seems from the individual journal reflections that theological presuppositions may have played a significant rôle in the responses to the SAI questions. This may be because the SAI focuses particularly on theological themes associated with the individual's relationship with God. It was evident in the journal reflections of most participants that they struggled with issues such as God's presence or absence in their distress, God's action in response to distress and the appropriateness of imprecation. Most reflected on these theological difficulties resolving them sufficiently enough to continue in the process. However, those who withdrew displayed an inability to continue to grapple with or resolve the presenting theological difficulties. These difficulties appeared to exert stress on those who withdrew causing both cognitive dissonance and emotional strain which ultimately led to them discontinuing. So, the variety of presuppositions, and participants' reflections on them, may have resulted in the mixed results in the SAI summarized in the table above.

This chapter has focused on describing and summarizing the variety of data collated from the participants praying psalms of distress. The journaling feedback of each participant has been compared and contrasted with the results from the pre- and post-psychometric testing. The first aim was to observe whether the content of the participant's journal reflections and interviews were congruent with the psychometric testing or not. The second aim was to build a picture of what the experience involved for each person as they took in part in the process. The final section of this chapter summarized the responses of the group as a whole as they met and reflected on their experiences of the process. This discussion was then compared and contrasted with the whole group's psychometric test results. The overall goal here was to identify any particular themes which reflected or contrasted with the individual's experiences.

In the following chapter we will revisit the theoretical basis for this study. The revisiting will take place in the light of the results examined above. In doing this I will seek to discover links between the various aspects of the theoretical basis and the action research carried out as part of this study.

Chapter 8

Discussion

Having completed the action research component of the study this chapter will explore links between the results discovered and the various aspects of the theoretical background to the study examined in the first four chapters. First, general observations will be made in relation to the signposts identified in chapter two. The purpose of such a focus is to examine whether these signposts had any relevance to the use of the selected psalms of distress by participants in this study or not. Second, the efficacy for the participants of viewing psalms of distress through the lens of the matrix of lament with its constellations, presented in chapter three, will be examined. Third, the efficacy of using these particular psalms as a way of engaging practically with experiences of personal distress will be highlighted by reflecting on the foci of psychodynamic changes presented in chapter four.

As with the results chapter the following discussion will be interspersed with vignettes from the journals and interviews with individual participants to illustrate the concepts being revisited.[1] So first we turn to an examination of the results in connection with the signposts in psalms' research presented in chapter two. These signposts are:

Signpost 1	-	Lament: What's in a name?
Signpost 2	-	Cultic function and ritual
Signpost 3	-	Discourse and dialectic
Signpost 4	-	Form and meaning-making
Signpost 5	-	Speech act and prayer

General observations[2]

Lament: What's in a name?

Signpost 1 pointed to the discussion on how best to label what have typically been referred to as lament psalms in both their individual and communal forms. In surveying the territory, the use of 'lament', 'complaint' and 'disorientation' were discussed as alternative descriptors. Despite the value of using any of the descriptors discussed, and recognizing that the features of lament, complaint and disorientation are obviously inherent within the text, I proposed that 'psalms of

---

[1] Note that all vignettes can be identified by the usage of italics.

[2] Note that where the description 'all participants' is used this excludes Donna because of her very early withdrawal from the process.

distress' is a more comprehensive descriptor for these particular psalms.

In discussing the term 'lament,' during the first group meeting, it quickly became obvious that participants had little or no understanding of what this term suggested about content or process when used to describe particular psalms. Describing the psalms to be used as psalms of 'complaint' elicited a more understanding response from the group and the idea of disorientation also resonated somewhat. However, suggesting my preferred descriptor, 'psalms of distress,' proved to be helpful for the participants in initially trying to understand the psalms' content and the potential of a process using these psalms.

The resulting journal entries self-evidently showed that by connecting the text of the psalms with their experiences of distress they were able to grasp both the content and the process perhaps more easily that if another descriptor was used. Interestingly though, once the connection between the ideas of distress, as an experience, and lament, as a process, had been explained most participants used the term 'lament' to identify *both* the particular type of psalm and the process they were involved in rather than 'psalms of distress.' John, for example stated that he *woke with a **desire** (emphasis his) to pray a lament psalm!* He continued to use this term in preference to the word 'distress.' Joan, referring to her experience in the final interview used the term to describe the process saying that at one point she found it *odd to be lamenting* in this way (a prescribed way). Both these comments suggest the participant's identification of lament as both a **form** of psalm and a **process** in which they were engaged.

It seems fair to conclude, from participant feedback, that the nomenclature 'psalms of distress' is an effective way of referring to this type of psalms for those who have not encountered the type previously. Initially it aided the participants to grasp the content of the psalms and then to understand lament as a process of voicing and engaging with personal distress. Having said this, the participants in this study seemed to find the use of the term 'psalms of distress' as more explanatory than utilitarian. As a result the majority preferred to use the term lament to describe both the psalm's content and the process.

While the summary above has highlighted the usefulness of my preferred descriptor for the psalms for the participants in this study but, at the same time, recognized that most reverted to the term 'lament.' We now turn to the participants' reflections on the ritual as they took in part in its various aspects and how they perceived its efficacy for themselves.

Cultic function and ritual

The second signpost pointed to the historical use of the psalms of distress by individuals as a ritual activity. It also highlighted the potential function of ritual as a pathway to expression, the possibility of it being transformative and the function it has in recognizing divine involvement in a situation. Because of the discussion I suggested that we needed to go beyond any historical use of ritual involving psalms of distress to explore what might take place when they are connected with ritual as a form or prayer.

Discussion

Before their involvement in this study participants' experiences varied from those who had been involved in formal or ritualized approaches to prayer to those who were more used to extemporary forms of prayer. None of the participants was experienced in using the Psalms as a form of prayer although all had read the Psalms at various times in the past. As a result the responses to the ritual were varied but with some common strands of reflection. None reacted negatively to the requirements of the ritual, in a general sense. However, different aspects of the ritual appeared to be more significant for different participants.

The preparation phase of breathing was an aspect of the ritual which a few participants noted as helpful. Tanya's comment that after doing this she ... *felt calm* is indicative of comments by other participants about its efficacy for them. It is also significant that Anton reported in his final interview a greater sense of *focus* following the breathing and Tanya felt that it *slowed her down* in preparation for praying. It appears from these reflections that the breathing was helpful as a preparatory action and at times a physical way of settling the participant's emotions in response to distress.

Most affirmed the use of the 'I am ready to begin...' prayer as a significant starting point for the process each day. For Anton it was *central to the experience* while Sandra found that it gave her a stronger *sense of God*. Sandra's observation was reinforced by her feeling that the prayer also provided a sense of *safety and security*. These sentiments were also expressed by others in the group. Of all the aspects of ritual in this study this prayer contributed most positively to most of the participants. It appears to have helped them to focus on their thoughts, feelings and experience while, at the same time, providing the foundation of a safe environment for such focus. John's reflection on the prayer that by using it *I started the ritual off on the right footing* captures the sentiments expressed in various ways by other participants.

The body movements met with a mixed reaction when used with praying the designated psalms. Charles began using the movements with *some trepidation* but found eventually that they actually influenced how he thought and felt in positive ways describing them as *moving me into a different sphere*. Both Joan and Sandra indicated that the movements *reinforced* the ideas of each constellation while Peter went even further in saying that the body movement actually *enhanced meaning* for him. Anton and Fran took a different view noting that the movements were *distracting* rather than helpful. Two participants also noticed that the use of movement with the longer psalms was *physically taxing* although still of value.

Few comments were made in the journals about praying each psalm repeatedly over five days. However, a question regarding the practice in the final interviews prompted many thoughtful reflections. John observed that the repetition helped him to *get into it more* which he clarified as sensing a greater connection with the content as the week continued. Joan also noted that in the psalms where the constellations were less sequential in formation it helped her to experience the *ebb and flow* of the psalm and how this can reflect the real life struggle with distress. A number expressed the value of the discipline of repetition especially when they did not feel like praying the psalm again. Both Jim and Sandra pointed out that because of the repetition they were able to see things *from a different perspective (Jim)* and *slow down and connect with the words (Sandra)*. This in turn enabled them to reflect more deeply on the content of the particular psalm and their personal connection with the words. None found it taxing to repeat the psalm although, as pointed out earlier, some found the focus on distress over the whole process difficult to cope with.

In summary then, the responses in both journal reflections and interviews indicate that the various aspects of the prescribed ritual mostly contributed in positive ways to the use of psalms of distress. The positive contribution reflects quite closely the potential functions of ritual examined in signpost two. The ritual aspects of the process provided a pathway, or *framework* as some described it, to voice their experiences. Various aspects of the ritual discussed above appeared to promote a greater level of expression of thoughts and feelings around experiences of personal distress. The body movements and praying the words of the psalms aloud reportedly helped several participants to feel that they were more involved in the process. In addition, the ritual aspects of the process appear to have been a significant part of any transformation which took place in participant's thinking and feelings about distress.

Based on the observations of the participants, the ritual achieved these functions in two ways. First, by developing a familiar pattern which gave a sense of safety and security to the participant and second, by offering tools which helped in preparing the individual to engage with the designated psalm in a focused and thoughtful manner. The ritual actions connected with praying the psalms of distress influenced the experience of the participants in various significant ways. However, we will now examine participants' responses to the language of the psalms of distress which emerges from a discussion of discourse and dialectic in chapter two.

Discourse and dialectic

Signpost three pointed to both the narrative and poetic qualities of the text found in psalms of distress and the potential significance of both these forms of discourse for articulating distress. As well as the narrative and poetic features a dialectic was also identified as being played out as a tripartite relationship between the 'self,' God and the enemy in the form of a psalm. Identifying the dialectic led to the suggestion that the impetus for the matrix of lament may come from the dialectic interaction displayed within the tripartite relationship found in psalms of distress. These observations raise the question, 'What dynamics are present when an individual in distress enters the tripartite dialectic in the place of the psalmist?'

In examining the participants' responses it becomes apparent that for most both the poetic imagery and the narrative nature of the psalms of distress resonated with their experiences of distress and seemed to invite them into the dialectic described above. The imagery produced by metaphor and simile, particularly in expressing feelings of powerlessness and isolation, was often referred to as meaningful in most participants' journal entries. It was also interesting to note that often whole verses or parts of them were cited as being significant for the participant as she or he prayed the psalm. An example of this is John's reflection on the language of betrayal used in Psalm 55 and how the story it told and the picture it produced for him resonated with his reflection on personal distress at that time. Sandra noticed the imagery of a bird also found in Psalm 55 as a picture of her situation. These are a couple of examples of how participants found the imagery, and the language used to produce that imagery, both resonated with their sense of self, God and others and became expressions of their own thoughts and feelings.

The narrative character of psalms of distress was prominent in most participant's thinking as they reflected on their praying of the psalms. It appears from journal entries that praying these psalms provided both permission to 'tell the story' of a particular situation of distress and to subsequently find validation of their experience. The journaling revealed many stories, both past and present, being retold because of praying psalms of distress. This aspect of storytelling was so prominent for Joan that she actually reworded a psalm to *include her story* as part of its content. In this way most of the participants felt that their story and the story of the psalmist became one in the form of a psalm prayed to God.

The dialectic nature of psalms of distress was not addressed directly by any of the participants in their reflections. However, an awareness of the tripartite relationship between the 'self,' God and others is threaded through their reflections. Although several participants faced a theological challenge as they embraced the dialectic most continued praying it anyway. A clear example of this is with Sandra who struggled with being angry with God, and wanting to express it, and having been told that *being angry is ungodly*. Despite the struggle the dialectic nature of the psalms of distress appears to provide the framework of dialectic necessary for the psalmist's expression of anger to become her own. This was also the case with Julie and Tanya. Tanya concluded that the language of the psalms *allowed me to express my anger and frustration... it gave me permission.* The dialectic also became obvious in other relationships for other participants. Charles struggled with anger with himself and seemed to create a dialectic between himself and his own beliefs and attitudes. John, Anton and Sandra focus more on the dialectic with their perceived enemies.

In all these cases the participants affirmed in different ways that they felt able to enter the dialectic relationships within the psalms in the place of the psalmist.[3] By doing this they were able to express a broad range of thinking and emotions, some of which had never been expressed before through prayer. This level of expression through *personal participation in the dialectic* seemed to contribute

---

[3] Or, in two cases at times, in the place of the 'enemy.'

to a willingness to explore their distress in some significant ways. First, the dialectic produced a challenge for some participant's theological presuppositions. Second, the style of the discourse using direct quotes from God and the 'enemy' aided some in gaining a perspective of themselves from outside themselves. Third, the poetic narrative quality of the text invited some to develop their own story in the form of a personal psalm and employ imagery which described their specific circumstances of distress.

Given that the language of psalms of distress exists within the form of the matrix of lament, we now turn to examine participant's responses in this regard. How did the framework of the matrix of lament assist them as a way of viewing the content of psalms of distress?

Form and meaning-making

The fourth signpost described the form of psalms of distress as a matrix of lament with four constellations which are related but distinct. It was suggested that viewing the psalms of distress through the matrix of lament may promote a greater level of meaning-making as individuals engage with their distress by using psalms of distress.

Three participants had been engaged in formal study of the psalms before taking part in this study and had an understanding of the form of psalms of distress. The others were mostly aware that they existed but had not examined their form at all. For the whole group, except one,[4] the idea of viewing the psalms of distress through a particular framework such as the matrix of lament was new but helpful. The constellations, each with a description of their content and function, helped the participants to engage with the content through understanding what was happening in the psalm itself.

Most of the participants recognized in their journaling and their final interview that the matrix of lament aided them in understanding both the content and the form of this type of psalms. Anton's journal reflection on the usefulness of the matrix of lament pointed out that while it was not helpful *as he prays the psalm* it did help to understand what formed the psalm. Being aware of the psalm's form before and after praying seemed to provide a framework for reflection. John felt that understanding the matrix of lament *makes praying this psalm so practical.* His observation suggests that, for him, the knowledge of the matrix form had an effect on his attitude towards a psalm of distress and his ability to use it.

In reflecting on the usefulness of being aware of the form of these psalms Sandra noted that the matrix *set a framework* for acknowledging and appreciating the various aspects of her experience of distress. Because of recognizing the framework Sandra realized that she had been *internalizing for so long...* and found it helpful to *see it and deal with it* through using these psalms. Sandra's

---

[4] This participant, Tanya, did however express a greater understanding and appreciation of the matrix of lament after having participated in the study.

observations suggest that the presence of the matrix of lament with its 4 constellations in the mind of the person praying as they approached the psalms provided reference points for the reflections which were subsequently recorded. These reflections then formed the basis for making sense of both the experience of praying the psalm and the experiences of personal distress on which the participant was focusing.

The group expressed a consensus that the matrix of lament and its four constellations helpfully represented the form of psalms of distress. The group also agreed that the differing constellations reflected the variety of facets to the experience of distress. Two further observations are also of interest. Julie expressed a growing understanding of the matrix of lament and described how, because of this, she began to restate the constellations of the matrix. She did this by creating her own psalm of distress to reflect more specifically her own circumstances. Jim noted that in looking at psalms outside the ones selected for this study he could see the presence of the matrix of lament

In summary then, the matrix of lament offered a helpful approach to understanding the form and content of these particular psalms. On that basis the psalms appeared to become more relevant and connected with most participants' experiences as they prayed the psalms with knowledge of the matrix form as a starting point. By viewing the psalms of distress through the lens of the matrix and making the connection between the four constellations and real life personal distress most participants subsequently engaged actively in various levels of meaning-making. There are many examples of meaning-making throughout most participants' journals and interview reflections. One such example is found in John's journal reflection as he reflected on a past event of personal distress and ponders his relationship with God in light of the experience. In his attempts to make meaning out of the event itself and to make sense of his thoughts now John discovered that, for him, *God was actually present during this initial event of distress.*[5] From this new realization John became aware that while his distress was painful it did not mean that God was necessarily absent at the time. This line of reflection ultimately led him to realize that when he experiences personal distress now or in the future he can envisage a god who is present with him *in* and *through* the situation. The fresh realization, in turn, would provide him with a fresh resolve to face distress rather than denying or ignoring it.

To this point we have examined how the participants responded to connecting intentional ritual with praying psalms of distress, the nature of the discourse used to express the prayer and the form in which the language of lament takes shape. However, in this study the psalms of distress were not treated simply as words on the page. Because of the fact that participants were invited to pray the psalms aloud we will now examine participants' responses to the text being speech that actually *does something* when verbalized.

---

[5] These kinds of attempts at meaning-making can be observed in the detailed discussion of the personal journals found in appendix 15

Speech act and prayer

The final signpost identified and discussed in chapter two was that of speech act and prayer. The signpost suggested that the psalms of distress are formed by various speech acts. This being the case, it also suggests that if the words of the psalms are used as prayer and verbalized they may *do something* to the speaker as a result. Both the journal reflections and the interview responses from this study suggested at various points that speaking the psalms as prayer had in fact affected them in various ways.

It is important to note that all the participants indicated that praying these psalms aloud was unique for them. While two pointed out that they were familiar with the practice of praying aloud it was limited for them to use of a prayer book, in one case, and extemporary prayer, in the other case.

In chapter two a distinction was made between speech acts which are 'informing' and those which are 'situating.' The reflections from most of the participants suggest that as they verbalized the psalms of distress both these aspects came into play. Fran reflected on her feelings of anger which *crystallized* for her as she prayed one particular psalm. As she reflected on her anger it appears that the praying aloud of angry words provided an 'informing' function so she became aware of the emotion present in herself in response to her personal distress. In contrast to this Sandra prays words of imprecation in one psalm and reflects on the result that this kind of prayer was *foreign but liberating*.... It appears that Sandra was able to 'situate' herself with the psalmist and her thoughts and feelings towards her 'enemies.' Jim provided an example where the praying aloud of the psalm becomes both 'informing' and 'situating' for him. He reported finding that quoting the words of others in a psalm caused him to realize that *he* felt like the 'enemy' as he found *himself* quoting the words of the enemy against the psalmist. Jim clearly stated that *I found myself on the side of the oppressor*.... In a provocative discovery the verbalizing of the words had revealed something to Jim that he believes he would otherwise have ignored.

The concept explored in chapter two of speech acts in a ritual being able to perform this 'situating' function is particularly evident in those participants who completed the whole process. As a general observation it appears that the verbalizing of the psalms in the first two weeks or so performed a more 'informing' function while later in the process they became more 'situating' for those praying the words aloud. Besides this, chapter 2 also addressed the idea of speech acts *creating* the situation so reflection and meaning-making can take place. Again this appears to be the case for most participants. One result of praying the psalm aloud was to recognize the situation of the psalmist and to find that as the words were verbalized they 'created' the actual distress of the participant as well. An example of this is from John's reflections on Psalm 88 where he observed

> it felt as if the LORD had really left me, that his **wrath** did **lie heavy upon me.** *I have definitely felt something from the asserting sections of the matrix today. I was being truthful about my emotions, and I was so relieved (in my depression??) to*

Discussion

have such words to use. (The emphases here are in the original journal)

John's reflection also highlights a further issue highlighted in chapter two. He displays a high level of self-involvement in the words of the psalm. In fact he voices what was identified in chapter two as the 'voice of self-involvement.' Extended examples of this 'voice' can be observed in Sandra's journal reflections where her reflective responses to the psalms become prayers of her own, sometimes modelled on the psalms of distress.

Speech acts as prayer also focused on the concept of prayer being an expression of relationship. Again this is congruent with the reflections of most participants. None had difficulty viewing their speaking the psalm aloud as words to God. Perhaps the most obvious example of seeing prayer as divine-human relationship is where various participants questioned whether particular attitudes were permissible to be expressed to God or not. One such instance was Sandra wondering whether *being angry is ungodly* as she reflected on praying the angry words of a psalm of distress.

Most of the participants found it insightful to hear themselves pray the psalm aloud. A number made the observation in their journals and interviews that the *words of the psalms became their own* more that if they had prayed them silently or simply read them as a text.[6] Promoting expression of thoughts and feelings aloud to God was viewed as both a freeing and a challenging experience. Half the participants expressed concern to varying degrees about the appropriateness of verbalizing some sentiments, such as anger, aloud to God, or even at all. This presented a theological conundrum for some who felt that expressing emotions, such as anger, is better kept to oneself. Despite this they all prayed the psalms 'as is' and found expressing such emotions ultimately to be a validating experience.

A further aspect to praying aloud was participants' responses to verbalizing God's words and the 'enemies'' words at various points in the designated psalms. The majority noted the sense of reality this brought them as they reflected on their relationships from the different perspectives. For most it reaffirmed God's relationship with them being one of expedience and a feeling, although uneasy for some, that they could sometimes blame their 'enemy,' or even God, for their predicament.[7]

The journal reflections and interviews also suggested that most participants felt that by speaking these words they had a sense of doing something with words rather than simply reciting them. However, congruent with observations about the goal of prayer in chapter two, the participants recognized their desire for resolution of their distress. However, the greatest value of the psalms of distress

---

[6] It is interesting that the terminology used by most participants *'became my own'* is a reflection of the terminology used to describe the experience in chapter two.

[7] The idea of blaming became more problematic for one person in Psalm 88 with idea that God was to blame. One person chose only to blame 'Satan' and one person chose only to blame 'self.'

appeared to be in the participant being offered an entry into a process of engagement. Entry into this process through prayer may or may not lead to resolution but appears to promote transformation of some kind to the one who participates. Joan provides one such example of transformation summing her experience up as the *process of the week has 'drained off' a lot of the intensity*. Sandra also reflects on her praying of a psalm of distress and coming to a fresh realization of the importance of *being true to oneself* and *being true to God.* This ultimately led to a transformation in her attitude towards a particular situation of distress.

Finally, the level of honesty evoked by the psalms of distress appears to have led most participants to a more intimate sense of relationship with God. It seems that *because* they could verbalize their deepest thoughts and feelings about personal distress in prayer their relationship with God was enhanced, not damaged. For example, Samuel described his experience of relationship with God amid distress as being like a *team*. It appears that no matter how significant the sense of isolation from God revealed in the face of personal distress the process facilitated a reconnection between the person praying and God through verbalized prayer.

Having revisited the signposts of chapter two, in the light of the results from the action research, we will now discuss the four constellations of the matrix of lament in connection with participants' observations and reflections.

The matrix of lament

As a point of reference for the following section I have listed below the constellations of the matrix of lament with their constituent elements:

- **Expressing**
    - Invocation
    - Complaint
- **Asserting**
    - Confession of sin
    - Assertion of innocence
    - Plea
- **Investing**
    - Imprecation
    - Affirmation of confidence
    - Acknowledgment of divine response
- **Imagining**
    - Vow
    - Pledge
    - Hymnic blessing
    - Anticipation of thanks

The expressing constellation

Taken together the participants' journals represent the expression of a broad range of emotions in response to various experiences of distress. John's observation that *the prayer, reflection and response process is actually helping me to express myself better* summarizes the sentiments of several participants as they continued to pray the psalms and reflect on the efficacy of the expressing constellation. The expression was not always limited to the struggle with negative affect. Again, John's comments show how expressing hope was also integral to the expressing constellation for participants at times. He stated that *more than I can think of during my life thus far, I have peace that transcends my own understanding.*

Even when a particular participant began with a narrow range of emotional expression the constellation appears to have accessed their deeper feelings and provided a 'languaging' opportunity for them to be voiced. Anton began the process with very little expression of his emotional state. However, the expressing constellation broadened his reflection to the point where he could *express the isolation I feel and the experience of suffering I am feeling.*

The initial articulation of the questions and emotion through the expressing constellation also provided permission for verbalizing thoughts and feelings which had been either ignored or denied in the context of the divine-human relationship. For example both Charles and Sandra found themselves expressing anger towards God. While some found emerging negative affect initially problematic most eventually found it to be helpful.

A strong focus of emotion for most participants appeared to be a sense of isolation from God and feeling doubt that God would or could act. At one point Jim expressed his sense of isolation saying, *I miss you.* The words of the psalms of distress designated for this study resonated very strongly with the emotions being experienced by the participants. It is apparent from the journal reflections that once they grasped the idea of invocation and the freedom to complain about their situation an increasing freedom to express emerged. Expressing emotion did not seem to end with invocation and complaint. For some it led to an ability to express a sense of *how empowered I am as a son of God* (Samuel) and for Joan to express *faith in God's control/provision/care....*

In summary then it could be noted that, in terms of negative affect, the expressing constellation performed a 'permission-giving' rôle. It also functioned as a beginning point for expressing positive affirmations about self, God, and hope for the future.

The asserting constellation

The majority reported that they found the asserting aspects of the psalms to be eye-opening and empowering. Of the three elements forming this constellation (confession of sin, assertion of innocence and plea) confession of sin was prominent among the reflections of three participants. Anton provides a clear example of this kind of reflection when he perceived *the need of forgiveness in this area of my life.* While there were no obvious examples of assertions of innocence several participants reflected on the issue of blame for distress. Two participants in particular resolved the issue of placing blame by asserting a belief in a *satanic figure* who caused distress.

Although the 'plea/petition' was identified as a significant and deeply evocative feature of the asserting constellation, very rarely did any of the participants identify the ability to ask God for intervention as being important. It seems that most participants viewed the act of bringing the whole psalm before God as forming a plea. In preference to requesting resolution there appeared to be an increasing desire for resources to sustain the participant *through* distress. This is clearly shown as Sandra appeals directly to God to *sustain* and *help*. She also continued from this plea to employ several verbs asserting **her** action, such as *asked, gave* and *fulfil*. Because of asserting her expectations of God Sandra then signaled that she felt some sense of hope emerging for her.

Many appeared surprised at times about what the psalmist saw fit to assert about themselves, God and their 'enemies.' However, on entering these assertions but praying the words themselves many participants reflected on the discovery of a resonance with the issues asserted. Because of this kind of reflection some such as Julie were encouraged to be more self-assertive. Faced with a particular experience, Julie responded with assertive statements such as *I talk..., I look for..., I will continue et al* to express her taking of personal responsibility in response to distress.

Despite the observation above that the plea was not as prominent in reflection as might have been expected it appears the opportunity for the participants to asserting themselves often led to an increased investing in God. Tanya noted that the shift from the asserting constellation to the investing constellation *is striking for me*. Despite expressing a deeply painful experience of distress and asserting herself before God through praying the psalm she was then able to be expressed at length her sense of God's love and presence. Finally, Tanya affirmed that she could *trust Him with everything ... even my heart* and concluded that she *refuse[s] to become a victim*.

The way in which the asserting constellation led many of the participants towards investing in God and in themselves and to face distress is congruent with the movement towards a higher internal locus of control.[8] It is interesting to note, however, that this increase in internal locus of control did not lead the participants to discount God's rôle *with* the individual in facing distress.

The investing constellation

As highlighted above the imprecatory aspects of the investing constellation caused some angst for about a third of the participants. They struggled to reconcile the idea of wishing evil on 'enemies' with their understanding of their faith in the light of the New Testament. None of those troubled by imprecation resolved the issue although most eventually viewed it as an expression of emotion,

---

[8] This increase can be observed in the group psychometric testing summary in chapter 7.

as opposed to actually doing the evil themselves. Fran reflected at length on imprecation stressing strongly and consistently her belief that God alone would do the avenging. She stated at one point that God *will call... to account...*, and appeared to take a very literal view of imprecatory words in the psalms. This conclusion appeared to bring a certain comfort to her even though expressing it troubled her deeply.

The opportunity to affirm confidence in God and acknowledge divine response evoked strongly positive responses from most participants. Joan noted that this aspect of the psalm was *life-giving* and understood as *affirmations of what I know to be true; that God does see and know, and there will be justice.* Because of the investing constellation Joan also stated that *I seem to be less acutely aware of pain in the memory.*[9] It seems that the movement from asserting to investing provided an impetus to continue to pray. In this regard John noticed that the investing constellation of the psalm *brought on a compelling passion* as he prayed. The affect shift from a more negative view of the distressing experience to more positive one appears to find a catalyst in the investing constellation. However, a balanced view which accepts continuing personal distress is still present. Sandra reflected on this shift and observed that *I am amazed at how hopeful I feel when reflecting on something which could be perceived as gloomy and hopeless.*

The idea of investing in God's presence *within* the situation of distress and affirming a confidence in God formed a significant foundation for most participants as they reflected on facing distress with God. Despite a frequently expressed ambivalence about God's presence and God's omnipotence investing in God appears to have been easily forthcoming from all participants. The sense from many journal reflections was one of 'Who else can I rely on?' Because of investing the participants found movement to the imagining constellation a welcome transition.

The imagining constellation

The sense of hope formed by the imagining constellation was consistently evident for most participants. A number described their sense of anticipation of this constellation once they were familiar with a particular psalm. Samuel pointed out that his anticipation of the imagining constellation was helpful in encouraging him to pray through the psalm to the end. It appears that participants could 'express,' 'assert,' and 'invest' *because* they knew that the 'imagining' was present. All the participants found expressions which pledged loyalty to God comforting and encouraging. Jim found the imagining in Psalm 22 to be an affirmation that *I imagine my world not empty of God.* The capacity to imagine God's presence is significant given that he also pointed out that he did not necessarily *sense any*

---

[9] Joan also noted at this point that the hand movement associated together with the investing constellation was particularly strong in reinforcing the shift in affect she had experienced.

response from God but that he did *sense [God's] presence* as he prayed.

The imagining constellation seemed to reinforce the shift which took place for some between the asserting and investing constellations. John indicated that it was in the imagining constellation that he expressed his praise to God and found *new meaning in [his] distress.* Fran concluded her reflection on the imagining constellation seeing *a movement between yesterday and today — emotions much calmer today even though the situation remains unchanged.*

As with the investing constellation several participants noted the significance of raising their hands as they prayed this constellation. John noticed at one point that his hands were *more emphatically raised, higher, straighter; that straight in fact I could feel my eyes drawn to them... a noticeably different pose.* He went on to point out that for him the physical movement was an expression of his emotional state at the time in response to his personal distress. As well as this John also noted that he had actually experienced the 'imagining' described in Psalm 10 at the time of past distress without realizing it at the time. He observed that he was able *to relive it now* through praying this psalm. John's observation is congruent with three concepts discussed earlier. First, it suggests that ritualizing of the imagining constellation performed a 'situating' function for John and second, that speaking the words in prayer actually appeared to re-create the situation in John's mind. The third concept John's experience supports is that the imagining constellation is a reflection of normative response to distress.

It is significant that Psalm 88, which did not contain the imagining constellation, proved problematic to most of the participants. As well as absence of imagining the concept of blaming God for personal distress emerged. Both these caused great consternation and obviously a challenge to some theological presuppositions about God's providence and God's omnipotence. Julie found the psalm *difficult to relate to* and *draining and dismal* and was unwilling to blame God saying *God has not caused my distress.* Yet Fran noted the psalm at times *touched something deep.*

John reflected on Psalm 88 to the point of recognizing there may be some situations like this in life where no hope will ever be present in the immediate circumstances. He was able to connect the sentiment of the psalm and the absence of an imagining constellation with his life experience. Because of the connection John remarked, *how good it would have been to be able to pray this psalm in those days.* He felt that this psalm also helped express his desire to rely on God and that *God is so good to allow this sort of darkness in His Word.* The rest of the group attempted to reconcile the words of this psalm and their personal experiences with little success.

From the discussion above it can be observed that the constellations and most of their forming elements were prominent in the participants' reflections as they prayed each psalm. It cannot be concluded that participants *became aware* of the matrix of lament and its constellations purely through participation, as they were introduced to the concepts before commencing the study. However, it is apparent that their participation in praying the psalms of distress heightened their awareness of both the discrete constellations and the overall matrix framework.

The matrix of lament, formed by the coexistence of the constellations, appears to have functioned in two ways. First, it provided a basis for understanding the content of the psalms of distress. Second, it provided indicators of where an individual praying such a psalm may have come from and where they might be going to in reflection on their engagement with personal distress.

The characters within lament

As well as the constellations discussed above, chapter three also explored the three relationship evident within psalms of distress. In chapter three they were described as follows:

- The 'psychological' relationship
- The 'theological' relationship
- The 'social' relationship

It can be observed in the discussion above, about the constellations, that the process of praying psalms of distress in an intentional ritual manner provided a pathway for the participants to engage with their thoughts, feelings. This process also promoted a greater self-understanding. In this sense the process was 'psychological.' The reflections of all participants suggested that they were able to become more acutely mindful of themselves and their responses to their personal distress as they prayed the psalms of distress. What each participant did with this mindfulness varied enormously from moving to a deeper level of self-reflection to recoiling from the process altogether and ceasing to reflect, at least formally. For example, John at one point indicated that *it has been safe to just go and check* on past experiences and led him to deeper reflection on the issues for him as a person. In contrast Jim withdrew from the process saying *I just don't think it is healthy to keep on reflecting on (particularly if you aren't experiencing it)*.

The 'theological' relationship within psalms of distress is also prominent throughout the participants' reflections. The person's sense of relationship with God is paramount for most as they engage with their experiences of personal distress. In a paradoxical way, the personal reflections discussed above suggest that God's presence, while sought after by all, was both comforting and problematic to the individual. One positive response to the paradox can be observed as Anton resolves to seek for God's presence *even in debilitating circumstances*. His resolve came directly in response to a situation of distress where he fails to see God. In contrast to this Fran experienced a lack of God's presence in caring for her through distress. This resulted in *huge anger* for Fran. At this point she concluded that recognizing anger is *unbeneficial* and continued to move on from it rather than reflect more deeply on it.

Again the 'social' relationship aspect of the psalms was evident in the reflections of most participants. However, the focus was firmly placed on perceived 'enemies' rather than those how might support the participant. Because of the focus on 'enemies' some found that their own distress could be more clearly understood in terms of who their 'enemies' were and what they were doing. An example of this is Sandra's observation that *people spoke ill of me to others*.... While she admits that viewing anyone as an 'enemy' is difficult, recognizing the nature of the relationship actually seems to help her in reflecting on her reactions and redefining her response to the situation. So, in a sense, defining the 'enemy' appears to have aided some in becoming more mindful of their responses and sharpening the definition of themselves.

Having examined the matrix of lament in the light of the action research we will now reflect on lament in practice, as discussed in chapter 4, and how the responses of the participants relate to that discussion.

Lament in practice

In chapter four it was observed that a process of lament could be valuable for any person, whether he or she was currently experiencing specific distress or not. The reflections of the participants in the action research provide some responses to the observation.

First, it was obvious from the journal reflections and the final interview that each participant was able to identify specific distress that they were currently experiencing. Although the level of the identified distress varied from quite minor experiences through to quite traumatic experiences the process promoted an awareness of the distress and an opportunity for it to be named. The awareness and the naming came as a direct result of using the psalms of distress as prescribed in the action research. A second aspect of participants' reflections was the way in which engagement in the process promoted a connection with past distress for all those involved. It was noted earlier that some began with current distress and moved to reflect on past distress while others moved in the opposite direction. However, either way, personal distress was not difficult to identify.

Based on the observations it could be inferred that the *process* of lamenting in this study was helpful, in various ways, for most of the participants. The helpfulness did not depend on the individual having any particular current or past experience of personal distress. It seems that the *process* itself helped to reveal personal distress which could then be engaged with reflectively if the participant chooses to do so.

If a process of lament can promote the emergence of personal distress it is then important to ask what such a process might ultimately offer. Again chapter four highlighted several potential benefits from a process of lament. The idea of praying about distress away from the experience as a pathway to praying about distress in the experience appears to be borne out in the reflections of some participants. For those who began the process by focusing on past distress, while praying the psalms, a shift is evident to them praying the psalms in relation to current distress.[10] Such a movement from past to present is consistent with the concept of *praying away* from distress leading to the ability to *pray in* the distress.

A second observation in chapter four was the way in which a process of lament might 'limit' the experience within certain parameters. Again this is plainly reflected in the observations of several participants who indicated that the process provided them with a sense of *safety and security* for engaging with their distress. It also appears that the limit of praying each psalm for a week also offered an obvious point of closure to each part of the process, by it, offering an artificial limit to the experience. It should be noted that although the process appears to have in fact been helpful in limiting some participants' expressions of distress there were others who seemed to find that the process moved outside their own boundaries of lament. Most obvious here are those who withdrew from the process. It may be that the process was not limiting enough for them and, therefore, did *not* provide the safety and security found by others.

A further aspect highlighted in chapter four was the way in which a process of lament may in fact encourage connection with God. The participants' reflections are congruent with this observation at many points. As pointed out earlier, rather than grappling with distress and the perceived lack in God's responsive action the participants felt a deepening of their connection with God as they engaged with their experiences of distress. Sandra provides an extended reflection which perhaps best shows the idea of connection with God saying:

I felt a real connection with myself, God and others and how I related to people. God helped expose deep hidden hurts and needs that were unmet and co-dependent coping habits that had formed and there was a beginning of healing and release.

The final observation about a process of lament in chapter 4 was its ability to provide articulation for experiences which are often 'language shattering.' The reflections provided suggest that in praying the psalms all the participants discovered, at some point, language in the psalms of distress to voice their own thoughts and feelings which would otherwise have been difficult to put into words. This is not to suggest that the words were the epitome of the process for all. There are various points where the 'language shattering' nature of distress and resulting attempts to pray about that distress by using a psalm of distress led the person beyond words to *crying* or *silence*, among other reactions. So in this sense, some found that the process provided language for experiences which shattered language. This 'new' language in turn opened a pathway for other forms of expression.

A further consideration was to ask how a lament process can be engaged with effectively. The image of a 'divine dance' was introduced in connection with ritual as a way of visualizing the relationship between God and the person within

---

[10] Although it was noted earlier that the reverse was also true for some participants.

such a process. The reflections of most participants again displayed a deepening connection with God through both the ritual and the words of the psalms at various points. It appears that praying the psalms in an intentional ritual manner was a significant factor in helping the participants both to discover and express the divine-human relationship in fresh ways.

A second consideration was the effect of an intentional introduction of a lament process into the experience of an individual regardless of what distress they were or were not experiencing at the time. The action research in this study was able to do this most effectively. Most participants embraced the responses that such an introduction provoked for them. For some introducing a lament process simply uncovered distress which was close to the surface. For others the process seemed to expose deeply hidden distress, often from the past, which was not enthusiastically embraced. Either way, the process seemed to introduce varying levels of disorientation which presented an opportunity for reflection.

Finally, the process of lament was identified as an opportunity for a 'restorative retelling' of distress. The reflections, particularly from those participants who completed the whole process, indicate that this was a benefit. The process seemed to provide an opportunity to revisit past distress safely for most participants. John, for example, stated that it was an *enormous comfort to me to reflect back.* However, it was more than simply reflecting, or going back. Most participants who engaged in this level of reflection showed varying degrees of being able to move on from the experience. Because of the retelling through prayer they had a sense of feeling restored and hopeful for the future. To this end Joan reflected at the end of the last week of the process that *I feel like I am 'done.'* She then observed that *the issues of lament have been drained of the urgency and power.*

Lament and meaning-making

From exploring lament in practice in the light of this study's action research component it becomes clear that a significant aspect to any process of lament is its inherent function in meaning-making. In chapter four the idea of meaning-making was examined in the following categories:

- What the lament process and psalms of distress suggest about the nature of God;
- What the lament process and psalms of distress suggest about the nature of humankind;
- What the lament process and psalms of distress suggest about the relationship between God and humankind.

Two major issues were highlighted about the nature of God in psalms of distress. The first was a belief on the psalmist's part that the prayer of distress could in fact affect the way in which God acted towards a person in distress and towards those who were sensed as 'enemies.' A belief that God could be affected by such a prayer is regularly present throughout the reflections of all participants in the process. Anton provided an example of this thinking as he reflected on a god *who reaches into the lives of the afflicted.* There is no sense in the journal reflections or interviews that God is passive, either unwilling or unable to act in response to the person's prayer. However, it was noted earlier that most of the participants seemed content to see God's action in providing the resources to endure the distress rather than a solution for the distress. While the plea for resolution is clear in the text of psalms of distress it appears that expressing **the plea** was enough for most participants.

The second issue focused on the rôle of relationship and its potential transformative function as a person engages with distress. This observation is borne out in the reflections of those who completed the whole process. It appears that a sense of praying to a god with whom relationship was assured, regardless of the outcome, provided a resilience for the participant to continue. The ability to continue is even more pronounced when the distress is *not* resolved and yet where the participant continued to pray and reflect on their unresolved distress. In sum then, the idea of praying to a god who is characterized by relationship did appear to provide a basis for the prayer and reflection on distress to continue for some participants. However, we must now examine the idea of meaning-making and the divine-human relationship in the light of the reflections from this study's participants.

Chapter 4 also highlighted coexisting experiences of faith and doubt in psalms of distress. While the reflections of the participants rarely contained these specific words both experiences appeared to be present for all participants. The response to this coexistence is where the participants could be viewed as two distinct groups. Those participants who withdrew provided various reasons. Jim, for example, reflected that he felt that he was *trying to be distressed.* However, a closer examination of participants' journals suggested that the struggle to come to grips with coexisting faith and doubt was one of the root causes. On the other hand those who persisted to the end of the whole process had similar questions about whether to trust God or not and similar experiences to those who withdrew. Yet, they were able to persevere through the paradox of faith and doubt as they continued. The paradox was never resolved for any of the participants. However, those who persisted seemed to find that the process enabled them to accept faith and doubt coexisting as they reflected on their distress.

I also suggested that the way in which praying psalms of distress may highlight paradoxes such as faith and doubt could be characterized as subversive. That is, they might display aspects of our human nature which we might seek to intentionally ignore or conceal. While none of the participants explicitly described their experience of the process in these terms, the journal reflections suggest that at many points various individuals discovered thoughts, feelings and attitudes which, before this, they were either denying or ignoring. An example of the 'subversive' nature of the process may be evident in Samuel's reflections as they unfold. He began with what could be described as either an ignorance of, or denial of, distress in his life experience. However, as he continued to pray the psalms of distress he records many reflections on both present and past distress which he had either attempted to ignore or deny in the past.

Finally, it is important to reflect on the nature of the divine-human relationship as portrayed in psalms of distress and in the light of participants' reflections. Chapter 4 highlighted the context of psalms of distress in terms of an overarching covenant relationship with God. In this sense the covenant appears to provide a kind of protective cover under which questions and challenges can be safely put to God. This seems to be the case for the participants in this study. Whatever they asked or stated to God in prayer, whether it be in the words of the psalmist or in their own words, the underlying belief was one of confidence that their relationship with God remained secure. So, in this sense, the participants found freedom of expression without an accompanying threat of disbarment from relationship with God.

The second observation made earlier was that psalms of distress were about growing in understanding and appreciation of how God works in the world through a process of interaction. In other words perceptions of God and God's work are not confined to *observing* but, rather, helped by an interactive process which not only allows question and challenge but may actually encourage these expressions. Reflections of all the participants suggested that they were willing to enter the questioning and challenging interaction. As a result they were aided in forming a fresh perspective on God's work in their life and the world around them. A helpful example of fresh perspective gained through an interactive process of question and challenge emerged from Psalm 10 for several participants. The focus on the words 'But you do see...' helped create a picture of one aspect of God's rôle in their past and present distress which provided a great sense of comfort as they reflected on this divine action.[11]

So the potential for use of psalms of distress to provide fresh perspectives on the nature of God, humankind, and the relationship between the two appears to have been realized in most participants' experiences. We now move the final aspect of relating the action research results to the foundational concepts explored in earlier chapters.

Implications for processing distress

Chapter five began with a discussion of the implications for the cognition, affect and experience of an individual who engages with personal distress by praying psalms of distress. The experience of all the participants in this study was congruent with the wholistic view of human beings introduced in the chapter. In various ways the participants pointed out that engaging their thoughts, feelings

---

[11] In fact two participants indicated that the whole of verse 14 was significant in providing a new perspective. In full it states, 'But you do see! Indeed you note trouble and grief, that you may take it into your hands; the helpless commit themselves to you; you have been the helper of the orphan.'

and physical body in the process heightened their experience of prayer. An example of the process being valuable as a whole person is Charles' observation at many points that he felt *very bodily immersed in this prayer*. As part of this *bodily immersion* Charles also identified the emotion of anger and his thinking around why this might be present. All three aspects were engaged concurrently.

While the wholistic nature of human beings appeared to be reinforced for the participants by the process the opportunity was present for significant thinking about relationship with God *and* individuation from God. Sandra reflected on her distress at one point which led to thinking about the need for individuation from God. She stated, *I saw God as standing afar off like an overseer* and in response remarking, *I felt like I needed to look after myself, to stand up and do what I could in my... situation.* This theme of holding together relationship *and* individuation emerged quite regularly for several participants in similar ways to Sandra's reflection.

The process also seemed to present opportunities for thinking about the disavowed self. Anton's discovery of himself as the *oppressor* in the psalm he was praying led him to thinking about how he had been *taking advantage of others (sic) powerlessness*. A later reflection on this observation led Anton to think about how to respond to the situation. One response was to recognize thoughts he had about the inappropriateness of his attitudes and actions, subsequently entering a process of confession and seeking forgiveness. This kind of processing also suggested a process which engaged with cognitive dissonance and through the interaction within prayer led to a change in thinking about the situation and some resolution.

In terms of affect it was suggested that the verbalizing and the ritualizing of emotions may provide a pathway for 'subsymbolic' thoughts and feelings to find symbols in words and actions. Again this seemed to be the case for many of the participants. Most participants found a broadened vocabulary of expression as they continued to engage with the process. As well as this, the use of hand movements, as part of the ritual, was not experienced simply as something which marked whole person involvement. It provided physical action which at times tangibly reinforced, and/or actually helped to externalize, the emotions being experienced. John described the experience clearly as he observed that *the hand and arm positions helped greatly to accentuate the actual movement in the prayer from that of desperation to hopefulness.* It is apparent then that for some participants the process engaged the emotions which were brought to prayer and contributed towards a movement in affect at certain points.

The experience of a person in engaging with distress was described as a 'process of knowing' which suggested the experience engendered a deeper sense of mindfulness about thoughts, feelings and felt experience. From the journal reflections, the final interviews and the last group session it became evident that the experience of each participant had been one which initiated a 'process of knowing.' For some, initiation into the 'process of knowing' led to a deeper mindfulness of themselves as individuals while for others the process proved too challenging. We now move to reflect on the psychodynamic aspects of experience identified as potential areas of movement for those involved in praying psalms of distress.

Psychodynamic movements

Chapter five suggested three aspects of potential psychodynamic change for individuals who engage with personal distress by praying psalms of distress. The aspects of levels of distress, locus of control and sense of relationship are embedded within the four constellations of the matrix of lament. In the table below these three psychodynamic aspects are listed and, by summary, the *general* movements suggested by the results presented in chapter seven.[12]

- **Level of distress** - Decreased
- **Locus of control** - Increased
- **Sense of relationship** - Increased

It can be observed in the summary table above and from the detailed results in chapter seven that this study suggests significant movements in all three psychodynamic aspects for most of the participants. The relationship between participants' reflections and responses and these changes need to be examined in turn.

Levels of distress

The journal entries from all participants suggested that they had little or no expectations on entering the process about how it would affect their levels of distress. Only Fran clearly indicated that she had done work on her distress in the past saying *this is not the first time of looking at this topic with God.* Therefore, she felt this was simply another way of approaching her experience of life. Despite Fran's prior experience in processing personal distress, or that of any others, the journaling indicated that initially all participants found the engagement with distress particularly confronting. One example of a response is Tanya's *weeping* as a first reaction to praying about her distress.

Each participant identified various aspects of personal distress in terms of thoughts, feelings and experience. Below some sample responses are provided as illustrations of thinking, feeling and experience:

- **Thoughts**
    - Peter described his sense of relationship with God saying *there is a chasm between me and God.*
    - *For me, this brings thoughts of rejection.* (John)
    - *I thought about my emotions as I had been containing them to a large degree.* (Sandra)

---

[12] It is important to stress that the movements indicated here describe the *general trend* of the whole group and do not reflect specific individuals whose experience was different. The individual differences are explicated in detail in chapter seven.

Discussion

- **Feelings**
    - *How is it I feel spiritually strong and reliant on God, yet there is still the odd nagging thought that busts it[s] way in?* (John)
    - *...like coming down a hill having been on top.* (Charles)
    - *express the isolation I feel.* (Anton)
- **Experiences**
    - *...inability to solve [the situation].* (Julie)
    - *...gave voice to the utter helplessness of the situation back then.* (John)
    - *...felt natural healing.* (Charles)

The upshot of being able to express thoughts, feelings and experiences of distress for most participants was a decreased stress and anxiety about their levels of distress. The reflections from journals, final one-on-one interviews and the final group session are all congruent with this observation. It is also notable that although the non-sequential shape of the matrix's constellations was stressed in chapter three, the group expressed a consensus view that they experienced the psalms of distress as a movement towards decreased levels of distress. This might also be described as moving from a sense of despair or desolation to a sense of hope and consolation. Despite the identified movement very few participants said that they reached points of resolution to their personal distress. This again suggests that the significance of praying these psalms is in the *process* rather than in the *resolution*.

An initial focus on present *or* past distress presented a further perspective on how participants engaged with their levels of distress. Around half began by focusing on past distress and half by focusing on present distress. Those who commenced in the past worked their way, possibly subconsciously, towards a balanced focus on the past and the present distress. Those who began with present distress tended to work towards the same balance by increasingly engaging with past distress. Those who began in the present seemed to find that it 'triggered' events from the past as they reflected on their current experience. Tanya specifically described this 'trigger' effect in both her journal reflections and final interview.

Once participants began to explore past distress it became evident in their journaling that meaning-making increased as a part of their reflection. John's response to one psalm and following reflection on a past distress revealed that *knowing that God was actually **there*** (emphasis John's) *was the life-giving component I experienced today.* John's meaning-making is an example of the process prompting him to reflect on his situation of distress. This led him to express his thinking and emotions around the event and then move into a process of creatively seeking to make sense of some aspect of his experience (in this case the idea of the presence of God). Those who completed praying all the designated psalms of distress all displayed these kinds of increasing attempts to make meaning. Decreased levels of distress appear to be one worthwhile result of this kind of process.

A significant factor in the decrease of levels of distress seemed to be the way in which praying the psalms facilitated the participants' ability to retell the story of their distress. The retelling occurred through the person expressing the words of the psalm as prayer and within the context of the divine-human relationship. Joan provided an example of this retelling when she noted that *I see this as God's intervention and blessing* (emphasis Joan's) — *that he truly has rescued me from the horns*. The observation came about as Joan revisited a distress but was able to tell the story from a different perspective through the language of the psalm. As a result, Joan signaled a decrease in her level of distress at that point.

While the retelling appeared to be a productive way of engaging with distress it was also problematic within a faith context for some participants. Most expressed some consternation when thinking about what was, and what was not, an appropriate way to express distress to God. Sandra expressed her consternation by observing that she had been told that *being angry was ungodly*. This, in turn, seemed to create increased levels of anxiety for some as they struggled with the appropriateness of the language in the designated psalms. Although no one expressed a resolution to this difficulty it was clear from the journaling that a raw honesty and authenticity became increasingly evident in all participants' reflections. Fran's expression of anger is one example of such honesty observing at one point that *huge anger rose up at his [God's] lack of care and protection of me*. As a result it also appears that levels of apprehension about honesty between the person praying and God dissipated or were at least relegated to a position of secondary importance. Again the movement towards greater honesty appears to have contributed to a decrease in levels of distress for most participants.

For those participants who began praying a psalm of distress with no specific experiences of distress as a focus situations seemed to emerge naturally and quite quickly. These situations, which became the participant's focus, were often experiences from the past accompanied by significant pain and anxiety. For example, Joan reflects at one point that *all the pain of those weeks just rose to the surface again, even though I thought I had 'done that.'* Initially these experiences caused an increase in levels of distress. Two-thirds of the group continued to engage in the process from this point and, though painful, found some rewarding opportunities for a greater self-awareness, meaning-making and a subsequent decrease in levels of distress. However, it seems that for the other third remembering the past proved too difficult and, therefore, they either avoided it or withdrew at that point. Peter's memory and his observation that *there is a chasm between me and God* caused his level of distress to increase and he withdrew from the process early. Having observed this, it is interesting to note that those who withdrew did provide various insightful comments about their experiences and a collection of significant questions about their experiences of distress. It remains unclear how these comments and questions may have been processed had these participants continued but they potentially form a basis for valuable continuing reflection.

Discussion

None of the participants appeared to believe, at the outset, that participation in the process would resolve their distress, although some may well have implicitly held this hope. The journaling indicated that none did in fact find resolution to their experience of distress as a whole. However, during the process there were instances where individuals expressed some resolution to a particular distress (for example, Sandra's observation of *a greater sense of peace and quiet confidence*) or a greater understanding which they had not previously grasped (for example, Samuel's observation of how *empowered I felt when I 'survived.'*)

The final group meeting came to a consensus that both generalized and specific distress will always be a significant part of life experience regardless of whether a particular situation is resolved or not. This realization came in part through the intensive and intentional focus on personal distress during the process. Therefore, the group as a whole viewed the engagement with distress in life and honesty about such experiences to be of supreme importance. They placed a high level of value on the opportunity they had to situate these experiences within a faith context through prayer.

In summarizing the experiences of the participants it appears that the *process* was of far greater significance than a *result* or a *resolution*. Most who completed the whole process had a sense that their levels of distress decreased. Besides this, most also indicated that their perceptions of their experience also altered. This afforded them the opportunity to reflect on their experiences from fresh perspectives and begin to find a sense of hope and make meaning of their experiences. Joan asks at one point, *Have I discovered any new sense of meaning in my distress?* She proceeds to reflect on how she has in fact found a new sense of meaning and what this looked like for her.

The DASS testing following completing the process was congruent with a decrease in levels of distress for most participants described above.[13] Having examined the movements in levels of distress we now turn to examine the implications of the results for participants' locus of control.

Locus of control

Chapter five also highlighted a potential psychodynamic movement, for the individual in distress, from experiencing a lack of personal control (or disempowerment) to a greater level of self-control *with* God (or empowerment). It was suggested that this could come about when a person engages with distress through the matrix of lament. A diminution of the 'enemy's' power to control the individual in distress was also noted as an associated dynamic.

Initially most of the participants expressed thinking which affirmed God's control of their situation of distress. Joan's clear statement that *God is in control*

---

[13] Of course, it should be acknowledged that other circumstances surrounding an individual's experience during the period of participation has not been taken into account and may have affected their responses in some way also.

is indicative of most participants' perspective of God, at least to begin with. Despite this kind of sentiment, the increasing reflection on the person's sense of isolation from God brought this sense of divine omnipotence into question. John's expressing *disappointment, isolation and sense of injustice* in his relationship with God is both indicative of his sense of powerlessness in the face of personal distress. They also voice his concerns about whether God is in fact in control of his situation.

Those who discovered a new sense of God *in* their distress found the concept of divine retribution for ones 'enemies' helpful in affirming a belief in God's omnipotence despite a seeming lack of divine response. Fran noted at one point a *sense of confidence that God will change things...* which was later characterized by her as calling her 'enemies' to account. Some participants were able to at least call for divine action. However, the added capacity to affirm God's presence *with* the individual in distress appears to have signaled a shift in perspective to at least the possibility of divine-human cooperation in facing distress. This kind of thinking led Samuel to conclude that ultimately it is about facing distress together as a *team* rather than alone.

So an exacerbated sense of powerlessness appeared to be an initial effect of praying psalms of distress. However, as the matrix of lament suggests, most participants discovered two significant movements in their experience as they pray through the psalms. First, most seemed to gain a greater sense of God's presence *in* their situation and, second, most appeared to experience an emergence of a greater sense of self-empowerment in facing the distress.

The investing constellation's description of elements such as confidence in God, imprecation and acknowledgment of divine response represents both recognition of the divine-human relationship and a burgeoning sense that distress is to be faced *with* God rather than alone. Most of the participants reflected this kind of thinking as they grappled with God's rôle and their own rôle in dealing with distress. Sandra expressed her growing sense of empowerment with God as having *a greater sense of peace and quiet confidence* in God's response to her distress. Fran also often affirmed her sense that God will *call to account...* and the sense of control this provided her over her reactions to distress.

Despite the growing belief for most participants that God was not powerless, rarely in the journaling process did a participant resign themselves simply to be indolent and wait for God to act on his or her behalf. The increase in a sense of personal empowerment is congruent with the increase in internal locus of control registered by most participants over the course of the process. However, this self-empowerment is understood by the participants within the context of the divine-human relationship. That is, they can face distress **with** God. The imagining constellation's concept of empowerment being found **in the relationship between** self and God, with the enemy's power being dissipated, is reflected in the journaling of those who completed the process. Julie described her feeling of empowerment to face distress as *I'm sticking with God...* indicating that it is the partnership which helps engagement with her distress. Sandra expressed the

Discussion

'both and' nature of the divine-human relationship saying I *thought to take charge of my emotions, to cry out to God and depend on God now.* This kind of observation suggests a sense of togetherness and individuation characteristic of the imagining constellation. It is interesting to note that the increase in internal locus of control coupled with an increased sense of the importance of the divine-human relationship is congruent with Jackson and Coursey's research reported in chapter 5.

The ritual aspect of the process was also appeared significant for most of the participants' sense of control. Sandra used the words *security* and *safety* which reflected several participants' responses to the helpfulness of the ritual. It appears that for some enacting the ritual increased the sense of the participant's control over their distress which may not have otherwise been available.

Sense of relationship

The final potential psychodynamic movement identified in chapter 5 is the individual's sense of relationship with the 'self' and God. As with the levels of distress and locus of control the matrix of lament incorporates psychodynamic movement in the individual's perception of these relationships. This potential change was identified using Martin Buber's idea of the 'I-Thou'[14] and expanded to be more descriptive of the nature of the relationship between the 'self' and God as portrayed in the psalms of distress. The constellations and their relational qualities are reiterated below:

- **Expressing**
    - I *to* self
    - I *to* Thou
- **Asserting**
    - I *about* self
    - I *about* Thou
- **Investing**
    - I *in* self
    - I *in* Thou
- **Imagining**
    - I *with* self
    - I *with* Thou

The journaling and interviewing indicated that all participants found a greater level of expression in the context of the divine-human relationship than they had previously experienced. This freedom displayed itself with the articulation of anger with God (for Fran) and general complaint about distress (for Sandra) to name just two of many examples. As already highlighted above, the freedom of expression was, at least initially, problematic. Interestingly for those who persisted to the end of the process what appeared to be theological objections to

---

[14] See chapter two.

expressing some thoughts and feelings became subordinate to an increasing desire to be honest. The clearest but not the only example of this was Fran's *anger* which she identified and expressed despite some theological reservations. So, the participants did not appear to have a lack of desire to express their thinking and feelings about self and God to God but, rather, a theological conundrum. Despite this initial reticence *the process* appears to have affirmed the depth and breadth of the divine-human relationship affirming that such a relationship could bear whatever intensity of expression was necessary. While this describes the experience of those who completed the process it seems that limits in personal perceptions of what could, or ought to, be expressed in the context of the divine-human relationship may have contributed to some withdrawing.

Another feature of the growth in the participant's sense of relationship is displayed in an increasing desire to assert themselves before God by retelling the story of their distress in the form of the designated psalm. As John, for example, focused on praying a psalm while reflecting on a specific experience from his past he asserted that *I felt this way; that I could say it validly, that at times, many times, God does not answer*. Despite this honesty which appears to have surprised even John, there was no sense of reticence in voicing what he felt and believing that the divine-human relationship could still survive.

Those who completed the whole process showed an increasing willingness to 'tell it like it is' rather than resorting to denial or ignorance. While this willingness led to an increased assertiveness it was primarily assertiveness of a particular type. As mentioned above the emphasis seemed mostly to be on asserting the continuing existence of the divine-human relationship rather than on a plea or petition for God to resolve the distress. If anything, any plea that was voiced was one requesting the resources to deal with the distress. An example of the cry for resources to cope with his distress is Anton's recognition of the need for forgiveness and his resulting request that it be granted by God. It was the capacity of the participants to *assert* their thoughts and feelings and the potential for divine action which seemed to offer, in part, a sense of hope.

A growing confidence in the 'self' to be able to endure experiences of personal distress and in God to be present with the 'self' became increasingly evident in participants' journal reflections. While relationship with God is rarely viewed as a rescuing one there is a sense of movement from isolation from God towards intimacy with God in the face of distress. So at one point Anton observed that he was able to *express the isolation I feel and the experience of suffering I am feeling*. Yet later he could express a greater sense of intimacy with God and notes his *growing understanding of the love that God has for people*.

These kinds of observations and experiences could suggest that an engagement with distress actually *presents a pathway* from relational isolation to greater relational intimacy, as in the Anton's case. While doubtless all participants held a high regard for God's potential 'power' for responding to their distress emphasis shifted from a focus on that perceived power to a focus on presence. The notion of divine presence *in* distress cannot be underestimated for all the participants. It seems that this single factor contributed greatly to the participants being able to embrace the experiences of distress, reflect on them and make some sense of them through the process.

All reported that the imagining constellation proved to be of great solace when engaging with their experiences of distress. The matrix identification of the key sense of relationship *with* self and *with* God is reflected often in the journaling. Words such as *partner, partnership* and *team* were often used to characterize the sense of relationship that the imagining constellation brought in the face of personal distress. As well as this, the growing freedom in the journaling suggested the ability for participants to accept their thoughts and feelings *for what they were*, rather than *what they might have thought they should be*.

In summary then it appears, from the journaling and participant interviewing, that an early reticence to completely embrace the honesty of the psalms designated for the process contributed to some withdrawing prematurely. However, those who continued to practice the text as prayer found themselves beginning to engage with the words to the point where the psalms gave them a fresh resolve to voice thoughts and feelings as they were. The psalms *gave voice* as John described it and as a result became their own 'voice.' A further result of this discovery is found in Sandra's journaling where the process led her to begin to express her experience of distress in her own words based on the constellations of the matrix of lament.[15]

As a general observation it can be seen that the results of the psychometric testing were congruent with the journaling and interview feedback from the participants. That is,

- *Depression, Anxiety and Stress Scale* registered several participants' decrease in the three categories. Only those who withdrew early showed increases;
- Journaling and interviews were congruent with these results;
- *Locus of Control* test indicated that most had an increased internal locus of control;
- Journaling and interviews also indicated this for most participants;
- *Spiritual Assessment Inventory* indicated a strengthening of relationship with God in most categories;
- Journaling and interviews were congruent with the SAI results. The exceptions again tended to be those who withdrew from the process early.

It is important to note that, despite the levels of congruence between the journaling, interviews and psychometric testing, the journal reflections provided greater insight into each person's thinking and emotions as they engaged with

---

[15] The creation of personally worded lament is also in evidence in some other participants' journals.

distress throughout the process. At times these reflections were at variance with the results of the psychometric testing.[16]

Having revisited the theoretical framework for this study, in the light of results from the action research component, it remains to draw conclusions based on the research which I have undertaken.

---

[16] For example a participant who tested low in stress, anxiety and depression sometimes exhibited high levels of these characteristics in their journal reflections.

Chapter 9

Conclusions

Final reflections

As stated in the first chapter, the aim of this study was to examine the psychodynamic effects on individuals using individual lament psalms intentionally, in the form of ritual prayer, as a way of engaging with experiences of personal distress. In working towards this aim I have presented a theoretical framework for understanding the nature of psalms of distress and the matrix of lament as a model for understanding their potential function. The method developed for this examination was based on both the theoretical framework and the matrix of lament.

The results of this study are based on a group of participants who displayed a clear willingness to engage with the process and, by definition, with their experiences of personal distress. Although most persisted through the whole process, four participants felt that they were unable to continue for various reasons. The upshot of this observation is that the process itself appeared to provide an effective pathway for most of the participants to recognize, acknowledge, and engage with their distress. However, those who withdrew appear to have found this level of engagement to be overwhelming to the point where they felt that they could not continue.

The experiences of distress engaged with varied from those experienced in the past to current distress. They also included circumstances which could be characterized as generalized distress and of a more superficial nature to more specific distress which, at times, appeared to be deeply traumatic for some. While praying psalms of distress allowed more participants to name specific distress it also appeared to be permissive in allowing the distress to remain anonymous while nonetheless real.

For the participants who did continue through to completing the process the ritual and the model of the matrix of lament appeared to be helpful in both understanding psalms of distress and providing them with an approach to their personal distress. The psychodynamic changes (distress, control and relationship) appear to have become increasingly significant features for those who completed as they engaged with their distress. Despite the fact that the early withdrawals showed some signs in their journaling of these changes beginning to occur for them. Their withdrawal does highlight, on the one hand, the possibility that engagement with distress through praying psalms of distress may be threatening and not ultimately an efficacious intervention for some people. On the other hand, it could also suggest that the process itself *can be* valuable but that some who participate may need additional support through such a process. The identification of those 'at risk' could form the basis for further study. In light of these observations it is interesting to note that some participants endeavoured to engage someone close to themselves as a means of support. This could suggest that the process might be more helpful for an individual who has supportive relationships throughout the process.

Combining ritual and psalms of distress as prescribed in this study suggests that these participants engaged with their experiences of personal distress both past and present in a deeper and more meaningful way through the addition of ritual. The matrix of lament provided a structure through which they could view these particular psalms and a framework for their own thoughts and emotions to be contained. In this sense the matrix of lament performed the function of a 'womb' or 'mold' as a liminal space in which a fresh perspective on distress could be birthed.

Self-evidently this research was conducted with a small group of participants. While the results provide indicators of how others might respond to using these psalms conclusions about this cannot be drawn based on this study. As well as this, the study does not consider other factors at play in participants' lives during their involvement which may have affected their responses to personal distress in positive or negative ways. Finally, it is recognized that selecting psalms of distress from the broader body of the Psalter and the exclusive focus on the issue of distress, is contrived. Therefore, it does not provide an indication of the effectiveness of these psalms if used alongside other psalm types.

This study also points towards at least four significant areas of further exploration. First, the process of journaling personal reflections presented a challenge to some participants.[1] This appears to have been largely because of the fact that some were either not experienced at, or felt that they were not proficient at, a journaling style of reflection. It may be that the process could have been more effective if some training in this format of reflection were offered prior to such a process being undertaken or, alternatively, another form of reflection be found.

Second, the group selected for this study was, by necessity, limited to twelve. It would be of particular interest to assess whether these results could be replicated with a subsequent group of a similar number and then whether the results could be replicated with a larger group of individuals.

Third, a further aspect of research could be to examine any group dynamic which might come into play if the participants were involved in a process of praying the psalms of distress together. The assumption here is that the dynamics of the experience could be, in some ways, quite different if psalms of distress were to be engaged with and reflected on as a group experience rather than by individuals in isolation.

Finally, several participants expressed a desire to continue to pray the psalms

---

[1] This was particularly evident in the case of the males in the group, most of whom struggled with the task of writing down their reflections.

of distress as a part of their continuing personal formation in engaging with distress. However, they also voiced a desire to pray these psalms and reflect on their content *with* the other psalm types within the Psalter. Again, it would be significant to develop a longevity study of a group using the whole Psalter as a form of ritual prayer to observe whether an individual's perspective on psalms of distress changes or not.

Finally it can be concluded that, in light of the original thesis of this study, the results indicate that using psalms of distress, as a way of engaging with personal distress, were efficacious for most participants in this study. Therefore, this observation leads to a significant question for those sections of the Christian church which have abandoned or ignored the use of these psalms. 'Why do psalms of distress rarely, if ever, form a vital and ubiquitous expression of prayer for people of faith?'

Appendices

Appendix 1

The matrix of lament

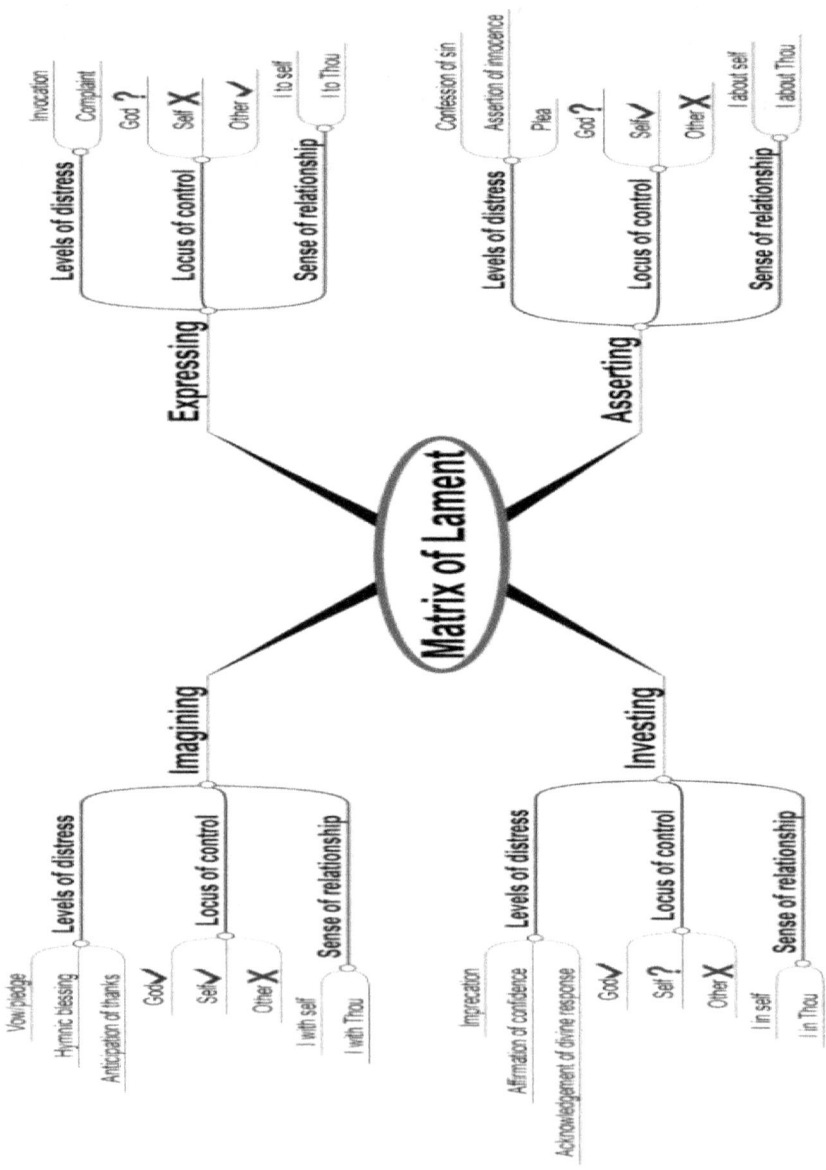

Appendices

Appendix 2

Summary: Matrix of Lament short explanation[1]

Background

A number of years ago I began exploring the biblical psalms and, in particular, a type of psalm usually referred to by scholars as individual lament psalms. These psalms originally emerged from situations of individual distress and demonstrate a prayer response to these kinds of situations. As I examined these psalms I discovered that they reflect and, therefore, suggest a process for engaging with personal distress. To identify this process I have coined the term matrix which will be defined below.

The purpose of this part of the project is twofold. The first part is to assess whether or not the idea of a matrix is a helpful way of looking at these psalms. The second is whether or not the praying of these individual lament psalms in a ritual manner and over a period of time helps people to constructively engage with their distress.

What is the matrix?

A matrix can be defined as a kind of mold into which various constellation are poured, mixed together and produce something new. Another definition is that a matrix is a womb which gives birth to something new. Both these images illustrate what I believe happens when lament psalms are prayed. There are four particular constellations which, when brought together in prayer, ritual, symbol and personal reflection, may help individuals to engage with their personal distress.

So what are the constellations of the matrix?

There are four major constellations in the matrix of lament. They are as follows:

- Expressing
- Asserting
- Investing
- Imagining

All the individual psalms of distress we are using in this project contain these four constellations (with the exception of Psalm 88 which lacks the imagining constellation). In summary these four elements can be described as follows:

1. **Expressing** – The person expressing a range of emotions associated with personal distress.
2. **Asserting** – The person stating how they seem themselves (e.g. innocent/sinful) and what they require of God in the form of a plea.

---

[1] A copy of this explanation was given to each participant at the first group session.

3. **Investing** – Stating confidence in the ability of God to respond and/or act on his/her behalf.
4. **Imagining** – The painting of a future picture which is hope-filled and acknowledges the possibility of personal distress being resolved.

What specific shifts may take place in the process of praying these psalms?
There are three potential areas of psychodynamic movement which I am evaluating in this project. They are as follows:

1. **Levels of Distress**
2. **Locus of Control**
3. **Sense of Relationship**

The psychometric evaluations
You will each be asked to complete three short psychometric evaluations before and after the thirty days of praying these psalms. These are **not** tests. They are simply to allow me some insight into where you are at now in the three areas mentioned immediately above. Doing the evaluations before and after will provide a more objective measure of whether there have been any significant psychodynamic shifts for you as a result of your praying.

The daily process
I will provide you with copies of six individual lament psalms, a schedule for prayer and a description of the ritual you are to follow each time you pray. There will also be a set of reflection questions which I want you to respond to in written form. If there are other thoughts or reflections you have please do not feel limited to the questions asked. They are a guide.

N.B. You do not have to have a particular current or past experience of personal distress in mind when praying these psalms although you may find that it is helpful.

The psalms used
Each of the six psalms used are individual laments. They all contain the four constellations of the matrix, expressed in various ways, except for Psalm 88 which does not have an imagining constellation.

Appendix 3

Description of ritual, reflection/response questions and 'I am ready to begin...' prayer

Ritual:
- Find a comfortable and safe place for prayer.
- Sit with your back straight and your feet on the floor.
- Focus on your lower abdomen breathing in through your nose.
- Hold for 4 seconds and then breathe out through your nose for 6-9 seconds.
- Pause before repeating.

Say the words: I am ready to begin... (see below)

- Think about your point of distress or imagine one from the past before you being to pray.
- Pray slowly and aloud, through the designated psalm pausing or changing pace when and where necessary (phrase by phrase, word by word and repeat words/phrases if you so desire). Use the appropriate bodily movements for each response:
    o Expressing (hands by sides)
    o Asserting (hands with palms facing upwards)
    o Investing (hands lifted with palms pressed upwards)
    o Imagining (hands lifted above head with palms facing up)

Reflection:
Creating a new journal entry for each time the lament psalm is prayed reflect on and respond in your own words to the following questions in the light of your praying:

- What did the psalm enable you to express to yourself and to God about your distress?
- What could you begin to assert about yourself and about God in the midst of your distress?
- In what way did praying the psalm aloud help you to invest in your sense of well-being and in your relationship with God?
- How do you imagine your world differently?
- What was draining about the experience?
- What was life-giving about the experience?

Response:
Record any changes in the following aspects of your experience while praying a lament psalm and re-living your distress:

- Describe any movement in your thinking about self, God or others.
- Describe any movement in your feeling towards self, God or others.
- Describe any effect the bodily movements had on your prayer activity.
- Did you discover any new sense of meaning in your experience of distress as you prayed the lament psalm?

I AM READY TO BEGIN...

I am a creation of God
I have a human face
I laugh
I weep
I wait in hope
I lift my eyes
And stub my toe
I love,
And struggle,
I fail

I stand
And always I stand
On trembling ground

But God is God
And Jesus is the Christ
And the Spirit will lift up my feet.
God is in the centre
God is at my endings.
Nothing lies beyond
The love of God in Christ

Anon.

Appendices

Appendix 4

Coded psalms of distress[2]

> Following is a printout of the six psalms to be used. They are coded (Plain text – Expressing; Italics – Asserting; Underlined – Investing; Italics and underlined – Imagining) to indicate the elements of the matrix and I have included instructions for the appropriate movement alongside each element.

Week One - Psalm 10

(Hands by sides) Why, O LORD, do you stand far off? Why do you hide yourself in times of trouble?

(Hands facing up) *² In arrogance the wicked persecute the poor-- let them be caught in the schemes they have devised.*

³ For the wicked boast of the desires of their heart, those greedy for gain curse and renounce the LORD.

⁴ In the pride of their countenance the wicked say, 'God will not seek it out'; all their thoughts are, 'There is no God.'

⁵ Their ways prosper at all times; your judgments are on high, out of their sight; as for their foes, they scoff at them.

⁶ They think in their heart, 'We shall not be moved; throughout all generations we shall not meet adversity.'

⁷ Their mouths are filled with cursing and deceit and oppression; under their tongues are mischief and iniquity.

⁸ They sit in ambush in the villages; in hiding places they murder the innocent. Their eyes stealthily watch for the helpless;

⁹ they lurk in secret like a lion in its covert; they lurk that they may seize the poor; they seize the poor and drag them off in their net.

¹⁰ They stoop, they crouch, and the helpless fall by their might.

¹¹ They think in their heart, 'God has forgotten, he has hidden his face, he will never see it.'

¹² Rise up, O LORD; O God, lift up your hand; do not forget the oppressed.

¹³ Why do the wicked renounce God, and say in their hearts, 'You will not call us to account'?

(Hands pushing up) ¹⁴ But you do see! Indeed you note trouble and grief, that you may take it into your hands; the helpless commit themselves to you; you have been the helper of the orphan.

¹⁵ Break the arm of the wicked and evildoers; seek out their wickedness until

---

[2] In the original project these were colour-coded.

you find none.
(Hands above head) [16] *The LORD is king forever and ever; the nations shall perish from his land.*
[17] *O LORD, you will hear the desire of the meek; you will strengthen their heart, you will incline your ear*
[18] *to do justice for the orphan and the oppressed, so that those from earth may strike terror no more.*

Week Two - Psalm 22

(Hands by sides) My God, my God, why have you forsaken me? Why are you so far from helping me, from the words of my groaning?

(Hands facing up) [2] *O my God, I cry by day, but you do not answer; and by night, but find no rest.*

(Hands pushing up) [3] Yet you are holy, enthroned on the praises of Israel.
[4] In you our ancestors trusted; they trusted, and you delivered them.
[5] To you they cried, and were saved; in you they trusted, and were not put to shame.

(Hands facing up) [6] *But I am a worm, and not human; scorned by others, and despised by the people.*
[7] *All who see me mock at me; they make mouths at me, they shake their heads;*
[8] *'Commit your cause to the LORD; let him deliver-- let him rescue the one in whom he delights!'*

(Hands pushing up) [9] Yet it was you who took me from the womb; you kept me safe on my mother's breast.
[10] On you I was cast from my birth, and since my mother bore me you have been my God.

(Hands by sides) [11] Do not be far from me, for trouble is near and there is no one to help.
[12] Many bulls encircle me, strong bulls of Bashan surround me;
[13] they open wide their mouths at me, like a ravening and roaring lion.
[14] I am poured out like water, and all my bones are out of joint; my heart is like wax; it is melted within my breast;
[15] my mouth is dried up like a potsherd, and my tongue sticks to my jaws; you lay me in the dust of death.
[16] For dogs are all around me; a company of evildoers encircles me. My hands and feet have shriveled;
[17] I can count all my bones. They stare and gloat over me;
[18] they divide my clothes among themselves, and for my clothing they cast lots.
[19] But you, O LORD, do not be far away! O my help, come quickly to my aid!
[20] Deliver my soul from the sword, my life from the power of the dog!
[21] Save me from the mouth of the lion!

(Hands above head) From the horns of the wild oxen you have rescued me.

²² *I will tell of your name to my brothers and sisters; in the midst of the congregation I will praise you:*
²³ *You who fear the LORD, praise him! All you offspring of Jacob, glorify him; stand in awe of him, all you offspring of Israel!*
²⁴ *For he did not despise or abhor the affliction of the afflicted; he did not hide his face from me, but heard when I cried to him.*
²⁵ *From you comes my praise in the great congregation; my vows I will pay before those who fear him.*
²⁶ *The poor shall eat and be satisfied; those who seek him shall praise the LORD. May your hearts live forever!*
²⁷ *All the ends of the earth shall remember and turn to the LORD; and all the families of the nations shall worship before him.*
²⁸ *For dominion belongs to the LORD, and he rules over the nations.*
²⁹ *To him, indeed, shall all who sleep in the earth bow down; before him shall bow all who go down to the dust, and I shall live for him.*
³⁰ *Posterity will serve him; future generations will be told about the Lord,*
³¹ *and proclaim his deliverance to a people yet unborn, saying that he has done it.*

Week Three - Psalm 35

(Hands by side) Contend, O LORD, with those who contend with me; fight against those who fight against me! ² Take hold of shield and buckler, and rise up to help me!

³ Draw the spear and javelin against my pursuers; say to my soul, 'I am your salvation.'

(Hands pushing up) ⁴ Let them be put to shame and dishonor who seek after my life. Let them be turned back and confounded who devise evil against me.

⁵ Let them be like chaff before the wind, with the angel of the LORD driving them on.

⁶ Let their way be dark and slippery, with the angel of the LORD pursuing them.

⁷ For without cause they hid their net for me; without cause they dug a pit for my life.

⁸ Let ruin come on them unawares. And let the net that they hid ensnare them; let them fall in it— to their ruin.

(Hands above head) ⁹ Then my soul shall rejoice in the LORD, exulting in his deliverance.

¹⁰ All my bones shall say, 'O LORD, who is like you? You deliver the weak from those too strong for them, the weak and needy from those who despoil them.'

(Hands facing up) ¹¹ Malicious witnesses rise up; they ask me about things I do not know.

¹² They repay me evil for good; my soul is forlorn.

¹³ But as for me, when they were sick, I wore sackcloth; I afflicted myself with

fasting. I prayed with head bowed on my bosom,
¹⁴ as though I grieved for a friend or a brother; I went about as one who laments for a mother, bowed down and in mourning.
¹⁵ But at my stumbling they gathered in glee, they gathered together against me; ruffians whom I did not know tore at me without ceasing;
¹⁶ they impiously mocked more and more, gnashing at me with their teeth.
(Hands by side) ¹⁷ How long, O LORD, will you look on?
(Hands facing up) Rescue me from their ravages, my life from the lions!
(Hands above head) ¹⁸ Then I will thank you in the great congregation; in the mighty throng I will praise you.
(Hands facing up) ¹⁹ Do not let my treacherous enemies rejoice over me, or those who hate me without cause wink the eye.
²⁰ For they do not speak peace, but they conceive deceitful words against those who are quiet in the land.
²¹ They open wide their mouths against me; they say, 'Aha, Aha, our eyes have seen it.'
²² You have seen, O LORD; do not be silent! O Lord, do not be far from me!
²³ Wake up! Bestir yourself for my defense, for my cause, my God and my Lord!
²⁴ Vindicate me, O LORD, my God, according to your righteousness, and do not let them rejoice over me.
²⁵ Do not let them say to themselves, 'Aha, we have our heart's desire.' Do not let them say, 'We have swallowed you up.'
(Hands pushing up) ²⁶ Let all those who rejoice at my calamity be put to shame and confusion; let those who exalt themselves against me be clothed with shame and dishonor.
²⁷ Let those who desire my vindication shout for joy and be glad, and say evermore, 'Great is the LORD, who delights in the welfare of his servant.'
(Hands above head) ²⁸ Then my tongue shall tell of your righteousness and of your praise all day long.

Week Four - Psalm 55

(Hands facing up) Give ear to my prayer, O God; do not hide yourself from my supplication.
² Attend to me, and answer me;
(Hands by side) I am troubled in my complaint. I am distraught
³ by the noise of the enemy, because of the clamor of the wicked. For they bring trouble upon me, and in anger they cherish enmity against me.
⁴ My heart is in anguish within me, the terrors of death have fallen upon me.
⁵ Fear and trembling come upon me, and horror overwhelms me.
⁶ And I say, 'O that I had wings like a dove! I would fly away and be at rest;
⁷ truly, I would flee far away; I would lodge in the wilderness; Selah
⁸ I would hurry to find a shelter for myself from the raging wind and tempest.'

(Hands facing up) ⁹ *Confuse, O Lord, confound their speech; for I see violence and strife in the city.*

¹⁰ *Day and night they go around it on its walls, and iniquity and trouble are within it;*

¹¹ *ruin is in its midst; oppression and fraud do not depart from its marketplace.*

¹² *It is not enemies who taunt me-- I could bear that; it is not adversaries who deal insolently with me-- I could hide from them.*

¹³ *But it is you, my equal, my companion, my familiar friend,*

¹⁴ *with whom I kept pleasant company; we walked in the house of God with the throng.*

(Hands pushing up) ¹⁵ Let death come upon them; let them go down alive to Sheol; for evil is in their homes and in their hearts.

(Hands above head) ¹⁶ But I call upon God, and the LORD will save me.

¹⁷ Evening and morning and at noon I utter my complaint and moan, and he will hear my voice.

¹⁸ He will redeem me unharmed from the battle that I wage, for many are arrayed against me.

¹⁹ God, who is enthroned from of old, Selah will hear, and will humble them-- because they do not change, and do not fear God.

(Hands facing up) ²⁰ *My companion laid hands on a friend and violated a covenant with me*

²¹ *with speech smoother than butter, but with a heart set on war; with words that were softer than oil, but in fact were drawn swords.*

(Hands pushing up) ²² Cast your burden on the LORD, and he will sustain you; he will never permit the righteous to be moved.

²³ But you, O God, will cast them down into the lowest pit; the bloodthirsty and treacherous shall not live out half their days.

(Hands above head) But I will trust in you.

Week Five - Psalm 88

(Hands facing up) *O LORD, God of my salvation, when, at night, I cry out in your presence,*

² *let my prayer come before you; incline your ear to my cry.*

(Hands by side) ³ For my soul is full of troubles, and my life draws near to Sheol.

⁴ I am counted among those who go down to the Pit; I am like those who have no help,

⁵ like those forsaken among the dead, like the slain that lie in the grave, like those whom you remember no more, for they are cut off from your hand.

(Hands facing up) ⁶ *You have put me in the depths of the Pit, in the regions dark and deep.*

⁷ *Your wrath lies heavy upon me, and you overwhelm me with all your waves. Selah*

Praying Lament Psalms: The Psychodynamics of Distress

⁸ *You have caused my companions to shun me; you have made me a thing of horror to them. I am shut in so that I cannot escape;*
⁹ *my eye grows dim through sorrow.*
(Hands pushing up) Every day I call on you, O LORD; I spread out my hands to you.
¹⁰ Do you work wonders for the dead? Do the shades rise up to praise you? Selah
¹¹ Is your steadfast love declared in the grave, or your faithfulness in Abaddon?
¹² Are your wonders known in the darkness, or your saving help in the land of forgetfulness?
(Hands facing up) ¹³ But I, O LORD, cry out to you; in the morning my prayer comes before you.
¹⁴ *O LORD, why do you cast me off? Why do you hide your face from me?*
¹⁵ *Wretched and close to death from my youth up, I suffer your terrors; I am desperate.*
¹⁶ *Your wrath has swept over me; your dread assaults destroy me.*
¹⁷ *They surround me like a flood all day long; from all sides they close in on me.*
¹⁸ *You have caused friend and neighbor to shun me; my companions are in darkness.*

Week Six - Psalm 102

(Hands facing up) *Hear my prayer, O LORD; let my cry come to you.*
² *Do not hide your face from me in the day of my distress. Incline your ear to me; answer me speedily in the day when I call.*
(Hands by side) ³ For my days pass away like smoke, and my bones burn like a furnace.
⁴ My heart is stricken and withered like grass; I am too wasted to eat my bread.
⁵ Because of my loud groaning my bones cling to my skin.
⁶ I am like an owl of the wilderness, like a little owl of the waste places.
⁷ I lie awake; I am like a lonely bird on the housetop.
⁸ All day long my enemies taunt me; those who deride me use my name for a curse.
⁹ For I eat ashes like bread, and mingle tears with my drink,
¹⁰ because of your indignation and anger; for you have lifted me up and thrown me aside.
¹¹ My days are like an evening shadow; I wither away like grass.
(Hands pushing up) ¹² But you, O LORD, are enthroned forever; your name endures to all generations.
(Hands above head) ¹³ You will rise up and have compassion on Zion, for it is time to favor it; the appointed time has come.
¹⁴ *For your servants hold its stones dear, and have pity on its dust.*

¹⁵ *The nations will fear the name of the LORD, and all the kings of the earth your glory.*
¹⁶ *For the LORD will build up Zion; he will appear in his glory.*
¹⁷ *He will regard the prayer of the destitute, and will not despise their prayer.*
¹⁸ *Let this be recorded for a generation to come, so that a people yet unborn may praise the LORD:*
¹⁹ *that he looked down from his holy height, from heaven the LORD looked at the earth,*
²⁰ *to hear the groans of the prisoners, to set free those who were doomed to die;*
²¹ *so that the name of the LORD may be declared in Zion, and his praise in Jerusalem,*
²² *when peoples gather together, and kingdoms, to worship the LORD.*

(Hands facing up) ²³ *He has broken my strength in midcourse; he has shortened my days.*
²⁴ *'O my God,' I say, 'do not take me away at the mid-point of my life, you whose years endure throughout all generations.'*

(Hands pushing up) ²⁵ *Long ago you laid the foundation of the earth, and the heavens are the work of your hands.*
²⁶ *They will perish, but you endure; they will all wear out like a garment. You change them like clothing, and they pass away;*
²⁷ *but you are the same, and your years have no end.*

(Hands above head) ²⁸ *The children of your servants shall live secure; their offspring shall be established in your presence.*

Appendix 5

One-on-one interview questions

NAME:

Prayer
1. How did you find the discipline of praying a psalm each day?
2. Can you describe your experience of praying these psalms aloud as opposed to praying silently?
3. Do you think the practice of praying these psalms aloud had any particular effect for you?

Content
4. How did you find the content of the lament psalms?
5. How did you find using psalms as a form of prayer?
6. How did you find lament psalms, specifically, as a form of prayer?

Ritual
7. How did you find the rigidity of the ritual each day?
8. How did you find the content of the ritual?
9. Was it a help or a hindrance?

Reflection
10. How did you find the journaling process?
11. Were the reflection questions helpful?
12. Did you feel that you were able to express particular feelings about your personal distress through the journaling process?

Other issues
13. Did you feel that you understood the nature of the matrix of lament with its four elements?
14. Is this a helpful way of looking at these particular psalms?
15. Is this a helpful way of looking at personal distress?
16. Would you continue to pray the lament psalms as a way of engaging with personal distress?
17. Would you find it useful to pray the lament psalms in context with other psalms (e.g. praise/thanksgiving)?
18. What support for others did you have while participating in this project?

Appendix 6

Final group discussion questions

1. How do you feel your levels of distress were as a result of participating in the process of praying psalms of distress?

2. How do you feel about your sense of control over your distress and your feeling of empowerment to deal distress is now that you have completed the process?

3. How would you describe your sense of relationship with God as you prayed the psalms of distress?

4. Are there any other observations about your experience that you would like to share with the group?

Appendix 7

***Depression, Anxiety and Stress Scale* questions**

DASS   Name: Date:

Please read each statement and circle a number 0, 1, 2 or 3 which indicates how much the statement applied to you over the past week. There are no right or wrong answers. Do not spend too much time on any statement.

The rating scale is as follows:

- Did not apply to me at all
- Applied to me to some degree, or some of the time
- Applied to me to a considerable degree, or a good part of time
- Applied to me very much, or most of the time

1. I found myself getting upset by quite trivial things — 0 1 2 3
2. I was aware of dryness of my mouth — 0 1 2 3
3. I couldn't seem to experience any positive feeling at all — 0 1 2 3
4. I experienced breathing difficulty (e.g., excessively rapid breathing, breathlessness in the absence of physical exertion) — 0 1 2 3
5. I just couldn't seem to get going — 0 1 2 3
6. I tended to over-react to situations — 0 1 2 3
7. I had a feeling of shakiness (e.g., legs going to give way) — 0 1 2 3
8. I found it difficult to relax — 0 1 2 3
9. I found myself in situations that made me so anxious I was most relieved when they ended — 0 1 2 3
10. I felt that I had nothing to look forward to — 0 1 2 3
11. I found myself getting upset rather easily — 0 1 2 3
12. I felt that I was using a lot of nervous energy — 0 1 2 3
13. I felt sad and depressed — 0 1 2 3
14. I found myself getting impatient when I was delayed in any way (e.g., lifts, traffic lights, being kept waiting) — 0 1 2 3
15. I had a feeling of faintness — 0 1 2 3
16. I felt that I had lost interest in just about everything — 0 1 2 3
17. I felt I wasn't worth much as a person — 0 1 2 3
18. I felt that I was rather touchy — 0 1 2 3
19. I perspired noticeably (eg, hands sweaty) in the absence of high temperatures or physical exertion — 0 1 2 3
20. I felt scared without any good reason — 0 1 2 3

21. I felt that life wasn't worthwhile	0 1 2 3
22. I found it hard to wind down	0 1 2 3
23. I had difficulty in swallowing	0 1 2 3
24. I couldn't seem to get any enjoyment out of the things I did	0 1 2 3
25. I was aware of the action of my heart in the absence of physical exertion (e.g., sense of heart rate increase, heart missing a beat)	0 1 2 3
26. I felt down-hearted and blue	0 1 2 3
27. I found that I was very irritable	0 1 2 3
28. I felt I was close to panic	0 1 2 3
29. I found it hard to calm down after something upset me	0 1 2 3
30. I feared that I would be 'thrown' by some trivial but unfamiliar task	0 1 2 3
31. I was unable to become enthusiastic about anything	0 1 2 3
32. I found it difficult to tolerate interruptions to what I was doing	0 1 2 3
33. I was in a state of nervous tension	0 1 2 3
34. I felt I was pretty worthless	0 1 2 3
35. I was intolerant of anything that kept me from getting on with what I was doing	0 1 2 3
36. I felt terrified	0 1 2 3
37. I could see nothing in the future to be hopeful about	0 1 2 3
38. I felt that life was meaningless	0 1 2 3
39. I found myself getting agitated	0 1 2 3
40. I was worried about situations in which I might panic and make a fool of myself	0 1 2 3
41. I experienced trembling (e.g., in the hands)	0 1 2 3
42. I found it difficult to work up the initiative to do things	0 1 2 3

Appendix 8

Locus of Control questions

Based pm J.B. Rotter (1966) Generalized expectations for internal versus external control of reinforcement,
Psychological Monographs, 80, (1, Whole No. 609).

Instructions

Click on the button next to the one statement that best describes how you feel. You can always go back to a question and change your answer.

---

1. Many of the unhappy things in people's lives are partly due to bad luck
   People's misfortunes result from the mistakes they make.
2. One of the major reason why we have wars is because people don't take enough interest in politics
   There will always be wars, no matter how hard people try to prevent them
3. In the long run, people get the respect they deserve in this world
   Unfortunately, an individual's worth often passes unrecognized no matter how hard he tries
4. The idea that teachers are unfair to students is nonsense
   Most students don't realize the extent to which their grades are influenced by accidental happenings
5. Without the right breaks, one cannot be an effective leader
   Capable people who fail to become leaders have not taken advantage of their opportunities
6. No matter how hard you try, some people just don't like you.
   People who can't get others to like them don't understand how to get along with others
7. I have often found that what is going to happen will happen
   Trusting to fate has never turned out as well for me as making a decision to take a definite course of action
8. In the case of the well prepared student, there is rarely, if ever, such a thing as an unfair test
   Many times exam questions tend to be so unrelated to course work that studying seems useless
9. Becoming a success is a matter of hard work; luck has little or nothing to do with it
   Getting a good job depends mainly on being in the right place at the right time

10. The average citizen can have an influence in government decisions
    This world is run by the few people in power, and there is not much a little guy can do about it
11. When I make plans, I am almost certain that I can make them work
    It is not always wise to make a plan too far ahead because many things turn out to be a matter of luck anyway
12. In my case, getting what I want has little or nothing to do with luck
    Many times we might just as well decide what to by flipping a coin
13. What happens to me is my own doing
    Sometimes I feel that I don't have enough control over the direction in my life

Appendix 9

Spiritual Assessment Inventory

Todd W. Hall, Ph.D.
Keith J. Edwards, Ph.D.

Instructions:

1. Please respond to each statement below by writing the number that best represents your experience in the empty box to the right of the statement.

2. It is best to answer according to what <u>really reflects</u> your experience rather than what you think your experience should be.

3. Give the answer that comes to mind first. Don't spend too much time thinking about an item.

4. Give the best possible response to each statement even if it does not provide all the information you would like.

5. Try your best to respond to all statements. Your answers will be completely confidential.

6. Some of the statements consist of two parts as shown here:

2.1	There are times when I feel disappointed with God.
2.2	When this happens, I still want our relationship to continue.

Your response to the second statement (2.2) tells how true this second statement (2.2) is for you when you have the experience (e.g. feeling disappointed with God) described in the first statement (2.1).

---

1 - Not at all true
2 - Slightly true
3 - Moderately true
4 - Substantially true

5 - Very true

1	I have a sense of how God is working in my life.	
2.1	There are times when I feel disappointed with God.	
2.2	When this happens, I still want our relationship to continue.	
3	God's presence feels very real to me.	
4	I am afraid that God will give up on me.	
5	I seem to have a unique ability to influence God through my prayers.	
6	Listening to God is an essential part of my life.	
7	I am always in a worshipful mood when I go to church.	
8.1	There are times when I feel frustrated with God.	
8.2	When I feel this way, I still desire to put effort into our relationship.	
9	I am aware of God prompting me to do things.	
10	My emotional connection with God is unstable.	
11	My experiences of God's responses to me impact me greatly.	
12.1	There are times when I feel irritated at God.	
12.2	When I feel this way, I am able to come to some sense of resolution in our relationship.	
13	God recognizes that I am more spiritual than most people.	
14	I always seek God's guidance for every decision I make.	
15	I am aware of God's presence in my interactions with other people.	
16	There are times when I feel that God is punishing me.	
17	I am aware of God responding to me in a variety of ways.	
18.1	There are times when I feel angry at God.	
18.2	When this happens, I still have the sense that god will always be with me.	
19	I am aware of God attending to me in times of need.	
20	God understands that my needs are more important than most people's.	
21	I am aware of God telling me to do something.	
22	I worry that I will be left out of God's plans.	
23	My experiences of God's presence impact me greatly.	
24	I am always as kind at home as I am at church.	
25	I have a sense of the direction in which God is guiding me.	

26	My relationship with God is an extraordinary one that most people would not understand.
27.1	There are times when I feel betrayed by God.
27.2	When I feel this way, I put effort into restoring our relationship.
28	I am aware of God communicating to me in a variety of ways.
29	Manipulating God seems to be the best way to get what I want.
30	I am aware of God's presence in times of need.
31	From day to day, I sense God being with me.
32	There are times when I feel frustrated by God for not responding to my prayers.
33.1	When I feel this way, I am able to talk it through with God.
33.2	I have a sense of God communicating guidance to me.
34	When I sin, I tend to withdraw from God.
35	I experience an awareness of God speaking to me personally.
36	I find my prayers to God are more effective than other people's.
37	I am always in the mood to pray.
38	I feel I have to please God or he might reject me.
39	I have a strong impression of God's presence.
40	There are times when I feel that God is angry at me.
41	I am aware of God being very near to me.
42	When I sin, I am afraid of what God will do to me.
43	When I consult God about decisions in my life, I am aware of His direction and help.
44	I seem to be more gifted than most people in discerning God's will.
45	When I feel God is not protecting me, I tend to feel worthless.
46	There are times when I feel like God has let me down.
47.1	When this happens, my trust in God is not completely broken.
47.2	I find my prayers to God are more effective than other people's.

SAI v7.1r ♥ 1996 Todd W. Hall and Keith J. Edwards (Used by permission)

Appendices

Appendix 10

Depression, Anxiety and Stress Scale and *Locus of control scale* results

1. **John**
   - **DASS**
     - Depression: no change
     - Anxiety: moved from mild to moderate
     - Stress: moved from mild to moderate
   - **LOC**
     - Increased internal locus of control by two points (medium to high)

2. **Charles**
   - **DASS**
     - Depression: moved from moderate normal
     - Anxiety: moved from extremely severe to mild
     - Stress: moved from severe to normal
   - **LOC**
     - Moved from balanced internal/external to moderate internal

3. **Anton**
   - **DASS**
     - Depression: moved from mild to normal
     - Anxiety: no change normal
     - Stress: moved from normal to mild
   - **LOC**
     - No change in high internal locus of control

4. **Jim**
   - **DASS**
     - Depression: no change normal
     - Anxiety: no change normal
     - Stress: no change normal
   - **LOC**
     - No change in high internal locus of control

5. **Peter**
   - **DASS**
     - Depression: no change low/normal
     - Anxiety: no change low/normal
     - Stress: no change low/normal
   - **LOC**
     - Slight rise in moderate internal locus of control

6. **Samuel**
   - **DASS**
     - Depression: normal no change
     - Anxiety: normal no change
     - Stress: normal no change
   - **LOC**
     - Increased from low internal locus of control to high internal locus of control

7. **Joan**
   - **DASS**
     - Depression: normal no change
     - Anxiety: normal no change
     - Stress: normal no change
   - **LOC**
     - Increased from low to medium internal locus of control

8. **Sandra**
   - **DASS**
     - Depression: normal no change
     - Anxiety: normal no change
     - Stress: normal no change
   - **LOC**
     - No change: medium internal locus of control

9. **Julie**
   - **DASS**
     - Depression: decreased from mild to normal
     - Anxiety: mild no change
     - Stress: decreased from mild to normal
   - **LOC**
     - Slight decrease (1 point) in high internal locus of control

10. **Tanya**
    - **DASS**
        - Depression: normal no change
        - Anxiety: moved from mild to severe
        - Stress: moved from moderate to mild
    - **LOC**
        - Increased from low internal locus of control to high internal locus of control

11. **Fran**
    - **DASS**
        - Depression: decreased from mild to normal
        - Anxiety: decreased from mild to normal
        - Stress: decreased from mild to normal
    - **LOC**
        - Increased internal locus of control from very low to high

12. **Donna**[3]
    - **DASS**
        - Depression: normal
        - Anxiety: normal
        - Stress: normal
    - **LOC**
        - High internal locus of control

---

[3] Donna did not complete the post-psychometric testing.

Appendix 11

Spiritual Assessment Inventory results - John

	A	RA	D	G	I	IM
First score	4.88	4.8	2.14	2.86	1.78	2.8
Final score	4.42	4.8	1.71	2.71	2	3
Change	-0.26	0	-0.42	-0.15	0.22	.2

A = Awareness; RA = Realistic Acceptance; D = Disappointment;
G = Grandiosity; I = Instability; IM = Impression Management

Spiritual Assessment Inventory results - Charles

	A	RA	D	G	I	IM
First score	3	3.67	0	1.28	1.56	1.6
Final score	3.68	5	3.43	1.29	1.67	2.6
Change	0.68	1.33	0	0.01	0.11	1

Spiritual Assessment Inventory results - Anton

	A	RA	D	G	I	IM
First score	2.68	4.6	3.57	1.57	1.89	1.8
Final score	2.58	3.67	4.43	2	1.78	1.4
Change	0.1	-0.93	0.86	0.43	-0.11	-0.4

Appendices

Spiritual Assessment Inventory results - Jim

	A	RA	D	G	I	IM
First score	2.95	2.83	2.43	1.29	3	2.6
Final score	3.95	4	2.29	1.43	1.89	1.6
Change	1	1.17	-0.14	0.14	-1.11	-1

Spiritual Assessment Inventory results - Peter

	A	RA	D	G	I	IM
First score	3.68	4.75	2.14	0.78	2.78	1.4
Final score	4.11	4.4	2.29	1	2.56	1.6
Change	0.43	-0.35	0.15	0.22	-0.22	0.2

Spiritual Assessment Inventory results - Samuel

	A	RA	D	G	I	IM
First score	3.47	4.5	2.86	1	1.78	2.8
Final score	3.21	5	3.43	1	2.22	3
Change	0.26	0.5	0.57	0	0.44	0.2

Spiritual Assessment Inventory results - Joan

	A	RA	D	G	I	IM
First score	4.21	3.6	1.71	1	1	3
Final score	4.84	5	2	1.57	1	3.6
Change	0.63	1.4	0.29	0.57	0	0.6

Spiritual Assessment Inventory results - Sandra

	A	RA	D	G	I	IM
First score	4.42	4.71	3.43	2.57	1.89	3
Final score	4.95	4.29	5	1.29	2.33	2.6
Change	0.53	-0.42	1.57	-1.28	0.44	-0.4

Spiritual Assessment Inventory results - Julie

	A	RA	D	G	I	IM
First score	4.42	4.67	3.29	1.29	2.11	2.2
Final score	4.68	3	1.57	1.71	1.22	3
Change	0.26	-1.67	-1.72	0.42	-0.89	0.8

Spiritual Assessment Inventory results - Fran

	A	RA	D	G	I	IM
First score	2.34	3.86	4.71	1.14	2.39	2.4
Final score	1.58	3.86	3.14	1.14	1.78	3
Change	-0.76	0	0.43	0	-0.61	0.6

Spiritual Assessment Inventory results - Donna

	A	RA	D	G	I	IM
First score	4.11	4.43	4.43	2	1.33	2.8
Final score	n/a	n/a	n/a	n/a	n/a	n/a
Change	n/a	n/a	n/a	n/a	n/a	n/a

Bibliography

Secondary Sources

Ackroyd, Peter R. *Doors of Perception: A Guide to Reading the Psalms.* London: SCM Press, 1978.

Allen, Ronald Barclay. *Praise: A Matter of Life and Breath.* Nashville: Thomas Nelson, 1980.

Alter, Robert. *The Art of Biblical Poetry.* New York: Basic Books, 1985.

Anderson, A. A. *Psalms Vols. 1 and 2*, New Century Bible Commentary. Grand Rapids, Michigan: Eerdmans Publishing Company, 1972.

Anderson, Bernhard W. *Out of the Depths: The Psalms Speak for Us Today.* Philadelphia: The Westminster Press, 1983.

Anderson, E. Byron. "Liturgical Catechesis: Congregational Practice as Formation." *Religious Education* 92 (1997): 349-62.

Anderson, Herbert, and Edward Foley. "Experiences in Need of Ritual." *Christian Century* 114, no. 31 (1997): 1002-08.

———. *Mighty Stories, Dangerous Rituals.* San Francisco: Jossey-Bass Publishers, 1998.

———. "Ritual and Narrative, Worship and Pastoral Care, and the Work of the Pastoral Supervision." *Journal of Supervision and Training in Ministry* 19 (1999): 13-24.

AP-Thomas, D. R. "Some Notes on the Old Testament Attitude to Prayer." *Scottish Journal of Theology* 9, no. 4 (1956): 422-29.

Atkins, Peter. *Memory and Liturgy.* Aldershot: Ashgate Publishing Limited, 2004.

Aune, Michael B. "'But Only Say the Word': Another Look at Christian Worship as Therapeutic." *Pastoral Psychology* 41, no. 3 (1993): 137-44.

Austin, J. L. *How to Do Things with Words.* Edited by J. O. Urmson and Marina Sbisà, 2nd ed. Cambridge, Massachusetts: Harvard University Press, 1975.

Baesler, E. J. *Theoretical Investigations and Empirical Confirmations of Communications and Prayer.* Lewiston, New York: Edwin Mellen Press, 2003.

Bakhtin, Mikhail. "The Problem of Speech Genres." In *The Discourse Reader*, edited by Adam Jaworski and Nikolas Coupland, 121-32. London: Routledge, 1999.

———. *Problems of Dostoevsky's Poetics.* Translated by Caryl Emerson. Edited by Wlad Godzich and Jochen Schulte-Sasse, 8 vols. Vol. 8, Theory and History of Literature. Minneapolis: University of Minnesota Press, 1984.

Bauman, Richard. *Verbal Art as Performance*. Rowley, Massachusetts: Newbury House Publishers, 1977.
Baumeister, Roy F. *Meanings of Life*. New York: Guilford Press, 1991.
Bell, Catherine. *Ritual Theory Ritual Practice*. Oxford: Oxford University Press, 1992.
Bellinger Jr., W. H. *Psalms: Reading and Studying the Book of Praises*. Peabody, Massachusetts: Hendrickson 1990.
Billman, Kathleen D., and Daniel L. Migliore. *Rachel's Cry: Prayer of Lament and the Rebirth of Hope*. Cleveland, Ohio: United Church Press, 1999.
Bjorck, Jeffery P. "Religiousness and Coping: Implications for Clinical Practice." *Journal of Psychology and Christianity* 16, no. 1 (1997): 62-67.
Blackwell, A. L. *The Sacred in Music*. Louisville: Westminster John Knox Press, 1999.
Blommaert, Jan. *Discourse* Cambridge: Cambridge University Press, 2005.
Boivin, Michael J. "The Hebraic Model of the Person: Toward a Unified Psychological Science among Christian Helping Professionals." *Journal of Psychology and Theology* 19, no. 2 (1991): 157-65.
Borditsky, Lera, Lauren A. Schmidt, and Webb Phillips. "Sex, Syntax and Semantics." In *Language in Mind*, edited by Dedre Gentner and Susan Goldin-Meadow, 61-80. Cambridge, Massachusetts: Bradford, 2003.
Boulton, Matthew. "Forsaking God: A Theological Argument for Christian Lamentation." *Scottish Journal of Theology* 55, no. 1 (2002): 58-78.
Briggs, Richard S. *Words in Action*. Edinburgh: T. & T. Clark, 2001.
Brock, Gary. "Ritual and Vulnerability." *Journal of Religion and Health* 29, no. 4 (1990): 285-95.
Brooks, Claire Vonk. "Psalm 51." *Interpretation* 49, no. 1 (1995): 62-66.
Brosschot, Jos F., and Julian F. Thayer. "Worry, Perseverative Thinking and Health." In *Emotional Health and Expression: Advances in Theory, Assessment and Clinical Applications*, edited by Ivan Nyklíček, Lydia Temoshok, and Ad Vingerhoets, 99-114. New York: Brunner-Routledge, 2004.
Brown, William P. *Seeing the Psalms: A Theology of Metaphor*. Louisville: Westminster John Knox Press, 2002.
Broyles, Craig C. *The Conflict of Faith and Experience in the Psalms: A Form-Critical and Theological Study*. Sheffield: JSOT Press, 1989.
Brueggemann, Walter. *Abiding Astonishment: Psalms, Modernity, and the Making of History*. Louisville, Kentucky: Westminster John Knox Press, 1991.
———. "The Formfulness of Grief." *Interpretation* 31, no. 3 (1977): 263-75.
———. *Israel's Praise*. Philadephia: Fortress Press, 1988.
———. *The Message of the Psalms: A Theological Commentary*. Minneapolis: Augsburg Publishing House, 1984.
———. *The Psalms in the Life of Faith*. Minneapolis: Fortress Press, 1995.

———. "Shape for Old Testament Theology, 1." *The Catholic Biblical Quarterly* 47, no. 1 (1985): 28-46.
Buber, Martin. *Between Man and Man*. Translated by Ronald Gregor Smith. New York: MacMillan Publishing Co., 1965.
———. *I and Thou*. Edinburgh: T. & T. Clark, 1970.
Bucci, W. *Psychoanalysis and Cognitive Science: A Multiple Code Theory*. New York: Guilford Press, 1997.
Byrne, Patricia Huff. "'Give Sorrow Words': Lament—Contemporary Need for Job's Old Time Religion." *The Journal of Pastoral Care and Counseling* 56, no. 3 (2002): 255-64.
Calvin, John. *A Commentary on Psalms Vol. 1*. Translated by T. H. L. Parker. London: James Clark and Co., 1965.
Canda, Edward R. "Therapeutic Transformation in Ritual, Therapy, and Human Development." *Journal of Religion and Health* 27, no. 3 (1988): 205-20.
Canfield, John V. *The Looking-Glass Self*. New York: Praeger, 1990.
Capps, Donald. "Nervous Laughter: Lament, Death Anxiety, and Humour." In *Lament: Reclaiming Practices in Pulpit, Pew, and Public Square*, edited by Sally A. Brown, and Patrick D. Miller, Louisville: Westminster John Knox Press, 2005.
———. *Pastoral Care: A Thematic Approach*. Philadelphia: The Westminster Press, 1979.
———. *The Poet's Gift*. Louisville, Kentucky: John Knox Press, 1993.
———. "The Psychology of Petitionary Prayer." *Theology Today* 39, no. 2 (1982): 130-41.
Carlsen, Mary Baird. *Meaning-Making*. New York: W. W. Norton and Co. Inc., 1988.
Carney, Sheila. "God Damn God: A Reflection on Expressing Anger in Prayer." *Biblical Theology Bulletin* 13, no. 4 (1983): 116-20.
Carol, L. Patrick, and Katherine Dychman. *Inviting the Mystic, Supporting the Prophet: An Introduction to Spiritual Direction*. New York: Paulist Press, 1981.
Carroll, David W. *Psychology of Language*. Pacific Grove, California: Brooks/Cole Publishing Company, 1999.
Clinebell, Howard. *Basic Types of Pastoral Care and Counseling*. London: SCM Press, 1984.
———. *Counseling for Spiritually Empowered Wholeness*. New York: Haworth Press, 1995.
Cohen, Cynthia B., Sondra E. Wheeler, David A. Scott, Barbara Springer Edwards, and Patricia Lusk. "Prayer as Therapy." *The Hastings Center Report* 30, no. 3 (2000): 40-47.
Cohen, David J. "Getting to the Heart of the Matter." In *Text and Task: Scripture and Mission*, edited by Michael Parsons. Carlisle: Paternoster, 2005.
———. "The Potential Function of the Lament Psalms and the Relevance of This

to the Practice of Spiritual Direction with Both Individuals and Communities of Faith." Unpublished Masters dissertation. Murdoch University, 1999.

———. "The Usage of the Psalms During the Post-Exilic Period up to 200 CE." Unpublished Honours dissertation. Murdoch University, 1990.

Cooper-White, Pamela. "The Ritual Reason Why: Explorations of the Unconscious through Enactment and Ritual in Pastoral Psychotherapy." *Journal of Supervision and Training in Ministry* 19 (1999): 68-75.

Craghan, John F. *Psalms for All Seasons*. Collegeville, Minnesota: The Liturgical Press, 1993.

Craigie, P.C. *Psalms Vol. 1*, World Biblical Commentary. Waco, Texas: Word Books, 1983.

Crites, Stephen. "The Narrative Quality of Experience." *Journal of the American Academy of Religion* 39, no. 3 (1971): 291-311.

Crow, Loren D. "The Rhetoric of Psalm 44." *Zeitschrift für die Alttestmentiche Wissenschaft* 104, no. 3 (1992): 394-401.

D'Aquili, Eugene G. "The Myth-Ritual Complex: A Biogenetic Structural Analysis." *Zygon* 18, no. 3 (1983): 247-82.

David, J.P., B. Spilka, and Kevin L. Ladd. "The Multidimensionality of Prayer and Its Role as a Source of Secondary Control." In *American Psychological Association*. Washington DC: American Psychological Association, 1991.

Davis, Ellen F. "Exploding the Limits." *Journal for the Study of the Old Testament* 53 (1992): 93-105.

Day, John. *Psalms*. Sheffield: Sheffield Academic Press, 1990.

Day, James M. "Speaking of Belief: Language, Performance, and Narrative in the Psychology of Religion." *The International Journal for the Psychology of Religion* 3, no. 4 (1993): 213-29.

Dombeck, Mary T. "Learning through Symbol, Myth, Model and Ritual." *Journal of Religion and Health* 28, no. 2 (1989): 152-62.

Driver, Tom F. *Liberating Rites: Understanding the Transformative Power of Ritual*. Boulder, Colorado: Westview Press, 1998.

Duff, Nancy J. "Recovering Lamentation as a Practice in the Church." In *Lament: Reclaiming Practices in Pulpit, Pew, and Public Square*, edited by Sally A. Brown, and Patrick D.Miller, Louisville: Westminster John Knox Press, 2005.

Duffy, Mervyn. *How Language, Ritual and Sacraments Work*. Rome: Gregorian University Press, 2005.

Eaton, John. *Psalms and the Way of the Kingdom: A Conference with Commentators*. Sheffield: Sheffield Academic Press, 1995.

Ellens, J. Howard. "Communication Theory and Petitionary Prayer." *Journal of Psychology and Theology* 15, no. 1 (1977): 48-54.

Endres, John C., and Elizabeth Liebert. *A Retreat with the Psalms*. New York: Paulist Press, 2001.

Epperly, Bruce G. "To Pray or Not to Pray: Reflections on the Intersection of Prayer and Medicine." *Journal of Religion and Health* 34, no. 2 (1995): 141-48.

Erickson, Richard C. "Psychotherapy and the Locus of Control." *Journal of Religion and Health* 22, no. 1 (1983): 74-81.

Faber, Heije. "The Meaning of Ritual in the Liturgy." In *Current Studies on Rituals: Perspectives for the Psychology of Religion*, edited by Hans-Günter Heimbrock and H. Barbara Boudewijnse, 43-56. Amsterdam: Rodopi, 1990.

Farmer, Kathleen A. "Psalms." In *The Women's Bible Commentary*, edited by Carol A. Newsom and Sharon H. Ringe, 137-44. London: SPCK, 1992.

Fink, Peter E. "Liturgical Prayer and Spiritual Growth." *Worship* 55, no. 5 (1981): 386-98.

Finney, John R., and H. Newton Maloney Jr. "Empirical Studies of Christian Prayer: A Review of Literature." *Journal of Psychology and Theology* 13, no. 2 (1985): 104-15.

Fløysvik, Ingvar. *When God Becomes My Enemy: The Theology of the Complaint Psalms*. Saint Louis: Concordia Academic Press, 1997.

Friedman, Maurice. *Religion and Psychology: A Dialogical Approach*. New York: Paragon House Publishers, 1992.

Fulghum, Robert. *From Beginning to End: The Rituals of Our Lives*. Sydney: Bantam Books, 1995.

Furnham, Adrian F. "Locus of Control and Theological Beliefs." *Journal of Psychology and Theology* 10, no. 2 (1982): 130-36.

Galindo, Israel. "Addressing the Needs of the Spirit." *Journal of Pastoral Care* 51, no. 4 (1997): 395-402.

Gass, Carlton S. "Orthodox Christian Values Related to Psychotherapy and Mental Health." *Journal of Psychology and Theology* 12, no. 3 (1984): 230-37.

Gay, Volney P. "Public Rituals Versus Private Treatment: Psychodynamics of Prayer." *Journal of Religion and Health* 17, no. 4 (1978): 244-60.

Georgakopoulou, Alexandra, and Dionysis Goutsos. *Discourse Analysis*. Edinburgh: Edinburgh University Press, 1997.

Gerstenberger, Erhard S. *Psalms Part I*. Vol. 14, The Forms of Old Testament Literature. Grand Rapids, Michigan: Eerdmans, 1988.

Goldingay, John. "The Dynamic Cycle of Praise and Prayer in the Psalms." *Journal for the Study of the Old Testament* 20 (1981): 85-90.

Goldin-Meadow, Susan. "Thought before Language: Do We Think Ergative?" In *Language in Mind*, edited by Dedre Genter and Susan Goldin-Meadow, 493-522. Cambridge, Massachusetts: The MIT Press, 2003.

Grainger, Robert. "Forum: How Deep Is the Water?" *Worship* 76, no. 4 (2002): 360-67.

Greenburg, Melanie A., Camille B. Wortman, and Arthur A. Stone. "Emotional

Expression and Physical Health: Revising Traumatic Memories or Fostering Self-Regulation?" *Journal of Personality and Social Psychology* 71, no. 3 (1996): 588-602.
Gunkel, Hermann. *The Psalms*. Philadelphia: Fortress Press, 1987.
Guthrie, Nancy. "Can I Really Expect God to Protect Me? Divine Promises in the Midst of Suffering." *Christianity Today*, October 2005, 56-59.
Hall, Todd W., Beth Fletcher Brokaw, Keith J. Edwards, and Patricia L. Pike. "An Empirical Exploration of Psychoanalysis and Religion: Spiritual Maturity and Object Relations Development." *Journal for the Scientific Study of Religion* 37, no. 2 (1998): 303-13.
Hall, Todd W., and Margaret Gorman. "Relational Spirituality: Implications of the Convergence of Attachment Theory, Interpersonal Neurobiology, and Emotional Information Processing." In *Annual Convention of the American Psychological Association*. Chicago, Illinois: American Psychological Association, 2003.
Hall, Todd W., and Keith J. Edwards. "The Spiritual Assessment Inventory: A Theistic Model and Measure for Assessing Spiritual Development." *Journal for the Scientific Study of Religion* 41, no. 2 (2002): 341-57.
Hayakawa, S.I., and Alan R. Hayakawa. *Language in Thought and Action*. San Diego: Harcourt Inc., 1990.
Heimbrock, Hans-Günter. "Ritual and Transformation: A Psychoanalytic Perspective." In *Current Studies on Rituals: Perspectives for the Psychology of Religion*, edited by Hans-Günter Heimbrock and H. Barbara Boudewijnse, 33-42. Amsterdam: Rodopi, 1990.
Hill, P.C., K.I. Pargament, R.W. Hood Jnr., M.E. McCullough, J.P. Swyers, D.B. Larson, and B.J. Zinnbauer. "Conceptualizing Religion and Spirituality: Points of Commonality, Points of Departure." *Journal for the Theory of Social Behaviour* 30 (2000): 51-77.
Hine, Virginia H. "Self-Generated Ritual: Trend or Fad?" *Worship* 55, no. 5 (1981): 404-19.
Hogue, David A. "Shelters and Pathways: Ritual and Pastoral Counseling." *Journal of Supervision and Training in Ministry* 19 (1999): 57-67.
Hogue, David A., and Pamela Cooper-White. "Supervision of Ritual, Rituals of Supervision." *Journal of Supervision and Training in Ministry* 19 (1999): 9-12.
Holladay, William L. *The Psalms through Three Thousand Years*. Minneapolis: Fortress Press, 1993.
Holquist, Michael. *Dialogism: Bakhtin and His World*. New York: Routledge, 1990.
Howard Jr., J. Grant. "Interpersonal Communication: Biblical Insights on the Problem and the Solution." *Journal of Psychology and Theology* 3, no. 4 (1975): 243-57.
Hughes, Graham. *Worship as Meaning: A Liturgical Theology for Late Modernity*. Cambridge: Cambridge University Press, 2003.

Hughes, Richard A. *Lament, Death, and Destiny*. Edited by Hemchand Gosai. Vol. 68, Studies in Biblical Literature. New York: Lang, 2004.

Hustad, Donald P. "The Psalms as Worship Expression: Personal and Congregational." *Review and Expositor* 81 (1984): 407-24.

Idelsohn, A. Z. *Jewish Music*. New York: Schoken, 1956.

Inch, Morris A. *The Psychology of the Psalms*. Waco, Texas: Word Books, 1970.

Iser, Wolfgang. *The Act of Reading: A Theory of Aesthetic Response*. London: Routledge and Kegan Paul, 1978.

Jackson, Laurence E., and Robert D. Coursey. "The Relationship of God Control and Internal Locus of Control to Intrinsic Religious Motivation, Coping and Purpose in Life." *Journal for the Scientific Study of Religion* 27, no. 3 (1988): 399-410.

Jacobsen, Rolf. "Burning Our Lamps with Borrowed Oil." In *Psalms and Practice*, edited by Stephen B. Reid, 90-98. Collegeville, Minnesota: The Liturgical Press, 2001.

Jakobson, Roman. "Linguistics and Poetics." In *The Discourse Reader*, edited by Adam Coupland, and Nikolas Jaworski, 54-62. London: Routledge, 1999.

James, Wendy. *The Ceremonial Animal: A New Portrait of Anthropology*. Oxford: Oxford University Press, 2003.

James, W. *The Varieties of Religious Experience*. New York: University Books, 1963.

Janssen, Jacques, Joep de Hart, and Christine den Draak. "Praying as an Individualized Ritual." In *Current Studies on Rituals: Perspectives for the Psychology of Religion*, edited by Hans-Günter Heimbrock and H. Barbara Boudewijnse, 71-85. Amsterdam: Rodopi, 1990.

Jennings, Theodore W. "On Ritual Knowledge." *The Journal of Religion* 62, no. 2 (1982): 111-27.

Jenson, Robert W. "The Praying Animal." *Zygon* 18, no. 3 (1983): 311-25.

Johnson, Ben Campbell, and Andre Dreitcer. *Beyond the Ordinary: Spirituality for Church Leaders*. Grand Rapids, Michigan: Eerdmans, 2001.

Johnson, Elizabeth. *She Who Is: The Mystery of God in Feminist Theological Discourse*. New York: Crossroad, 1992.

Jones, Logan C. "The Psalms of Lament and the Transformation of Sorrow." *Journal of Pastoral Care and Counseling* 61, no. 1-2 (2007): 47-58.

Jumonville, Robert Moore, and Robert Woods. "The Role-Taking Theory of Praying the Psalms: Using the Psalms as Model for Structuring the Life of Prayer." *Journal of Biblical Studies* 3, no. 2 (2003): 22-61.

Kelcourse, Felicity Brock. "Prayer and the Soul: Dialogues That Heal." *Journal of Religion and Health* 40, no. 1 (2001): 231-42.

Kelley, Paige H. "Prayers of Troubled Spirits." *Review and Expositor* 81, no. 3 (1984): 377-83.

Kidner, Derek. *Psalms 1-72*, The Tyndale Old Testament Commentaries. Downers Grove, Illinois: InterVarsity Press, 1973.

———. *Psalms 73-150*, The Tyndale Old Testament Commentaries. Downers Grove, Illinois: InterVarsity Press, 1975.

Klinghardt, Matthias. "Prayer Formularies for Public Recitation: Their Use and Function in Ancient Religion." *Numen* 46, no. 1 (1999): 1-52.

Kraus, Hans-Joachim. *Psalms 1-59*. Trans. by Hilton C. Oswald. Minneapolis: Augsburg, 1988.

———. *Psalms 60-150*. Translated by Hilton C. Oswald. Minneapolis: Augsburg, 1989.

———. *Theology of the Psalms*. Minneapolis: Augsburg Press, 1986.

Kselman, John S. "A Note on Psalm 85:9-10." *The Catholic Biblical Quarterly* 46, no. 1 (1984): 23-27.

Kubicki, Judith Marie. "Using J. L. Austin's Performative Language Theory to Interpret Ritual Music Making." *Worship* 73, no. 4 (1999): 310-30.

Kugel, James. *The Idea of Biblical Poetry: Parallelism and Its History*. New Haven: Yale University Press, 1981.

Kundtz, David. *Stopping: How to Be Still When You Have to Keep Going*. Berkley, California: Conari Press, 1998.

Ladd, Kevin L., and Bernard Spilka. "Inward, Outward, Upward Prayer: Scale Reliability and Validation." *Journal for the Scientific Study of Religion* 45, no. 2 (2006): 233-51.

Ladrière, Jean. *Liturgical Experience of Faith*. Edited by H. Schmidt, and David N. Power, New York: Herder and Herder, 1973.

Lanigan, Richard L. *Speech Act Phenomenology*. The Hague, Netherlands: Martinus Nijhoff, 1977.

le Roux, Jurie H. "Augustine, Gadamer and the Psalms (Or: The Psalms as the Answer to the Questions)." In *Psalms in Liturgy*, edited by Dirk J. Human and Cas J.A. Vos, 123-30. London: T. and T. Clark International, 2004.

Leeming, David A. "Myth and Therapy." *Journal of Religion and Health* 40, no. 1 (2001): 115-19.

Lefcourt, Herbert M. *Locus of Control: Current Trends in Theory and Research*. Hillside, New Jersey: Lawrence Erlbaum Associates, Publishers, 1976.

———. *Locus of Control: Current Trends in Theory and Research*. Hillside, New Jersey: Lawrence Erlbaum Associates, Publishers, 1976.

Lefevere, Patricia. "Poetry Opens a Window to Prayer, Healing." *National Catholic Reporter* 38, no. 6 (2001): 34-36.

Levine, Herbert J. *Sing Unto God a New Song: A Contemporary Reading of the Psalms*. Bloomington: Indiana University Press, 1995.

Lewis, C. S. *Reflections on the Psalms*. Glasgow: William Collins Sons and Co., 1978.

Lewis, Leslie C. "Continuity and Meaning." *Journal of Religion and Health* 37, no. 2 (1998): 143-57.

Lusebrink, Vija Bergs. *Imagery and Visual Expression in Therapy*. Edited by

Carroll E. Izard and Jerome L. Singer, Emotions, Personality and Psychotherapy. New York: Plenum Press, 1990.

Lustig, Andrew. "Prescribing Prayer." *Commonweal* (2004): 32-33.

MacCormac, Earl R. *A Cognitive Theory of Metaphor*. London: Massachusetts Institute of Technology, 1985.

Madden, Kathryn Wood. "From Speechlessness to Presence." *Journal of Religion and Health* 40, no. 1 (2001): 185-204.

Magaletta, Philip R. "Prayer in Psychotherapy: A Model for Its Use, Ethical Considerations, and Guidelines for Practice." *Journal of Psychology and Theology* 26, no. 4 (1998): 322-30.

Martin, Buber. *I and Thou*. Translated by Ronald Gregor Smith. Edinburgh: T. & T. Clark, 1937.

Martz, Louis L. *The Poetry of Meditation*. Yale: Yale University Press, 1962.

May, Gerald G. "The Psychodynamics of Spirituality." *The Journal of Pastoral Care* 31, no. 2 (1977): 84-90.

May, Rollo. *The Meaning of Anxiety*. New York: W. W. Norton and Co., 1977.

Mays, James L. *The Lord Reigns: A Theological Handbook to the Psalms*. Louisville, Kentucky: Westminster John Knox Press, 1994.

Mazza, Nicholas. *Poetry Therapy: Interface of the Arts and Psychology*. Edited by Charles R. Figley, Innovations in Psychology. Baton Rouge: CRC Press, 1999.

McCann, J. Clinton. *A Theological Introduction to the Book of Psalms - Psalms as Torah*. Nashville: Abingdon Press, 1993.

McCann, J. Clinton (ed.). *The Shape and Shaping of the Psalter*, JSOT Dissertation Series No. 159. Sheffield: Sheffield Academic Press, 1993.

McCauley, R. N., and E. T. Lawson. *Bringing Ritual to Mind: Psychological Foundations of Cultural Forms*. Cambridge: Cambridge University Press, 2002.

McCullough, Michael E. "Prayer and Health: Conceptual Issues, Research Review, and Research Agenda." *Journal of Psychology and Theology* 23, no. 1 (1995): 15-29.

McDarrgh, John. "The Life of the Self in Christian Spirituality and Contemporary Psychoanalysis." *Horizons* 11, no. 2 (1984): 344-60.

Meisenhelder, Janice Bell, and John P. Marcum. "Responses of Clergy to 9/11: Posttraumatic Stress, Coping, and Religious Outcomes." *Journal for the Scientific Study of Religion* 43, no. 4 (2004): 547-54.

Merton, Thomas. *Contemplative Prayer*. London: Dartman, Longman and Todd, 1981.

———. *The Signs of Jonas*. New York: Image Books, 1956.

Meserve, Harry C. "The Human Side of Prayer." *Journal of Religion and Health* 30, no. 4 (1991): 271-76.

Metz, Johann Baptist. *A Passion for God: The Mystical-Political Dimension of Christianity*. Translated by J. Matthew Ashley. New York: Paulist Press, 1990.

Miles, Jack. "The Human Zoo: Adversaries and Alliances in the Psalms." www.sbl-site.org/Newsletter/04_2003/Miles.html.
Miller Jr., Patrick D. *Interpreting the Psalms*. Philadelphia: Fortress Press, 1986.
———. "Trouble and Woe." *Interpretation* 37 (1983): 32-45.
Miller, Patrick D. "Heaven's Prisoners: The Lament and Christian Prayer." In *Lament: Reclaiming Practices in Pulpit, Pew, and Public Square*, edited by Sally A. Brown and Patrick D. Miller. Louisville: Westminster John Knox Press, 2005.
———. "The Psalms and Pastoral Care." *Liturgy and Music*, no. 24 (1990): 3.
———. *They Cried Unto the Lord: The Form and Theology of Biblical Prayer*. Minneapolis: Fortress, 1994.
Mitchell, Christina E. "Internal Locus of Control for Expectation, Perception and Management of Answered Prayer." *Journal of Psychology and Theology* 17, no. 1 (1989): 21-26.
Mitchell, Leonel L. *The Meaning of Ritual*. Harrisburg, Pennsylvania: Morehouse, 1977.
Mitchell, Nathan D. "The Amen Corner." *Worship* 76, no. 1 (2002): 67-77.
Moore, Gerald. "Without Lament There Is No Life." *Australian Journal of Liturgy* 10, no. 1 (2005): 29-46.
Moore, R. Kelvin. *The Psalms of Lamentation and the Enigma of Suffering*. Lewiston, New York: The Edwin Mellen Press, 1996.
Moore, Robert L. "Contemporary Psychotherapy as Ritual Process: An Initial Reconnaissance." *Zygon* 18, no. 3 (1983): 283 - 94.
Morris, Pam, ed. *The Bakhtin Reader*. London: Edward Arnold, 1994.
Mowinckel, Sigmund. *The Old Testament as the Word of God*. Translated by Reidar B. Bjornard. New York: Abingdon Press, 1959.
———. *The Psalms in Israel's Worship*. 2 vols. Vol. 1. Oxford: Basil Blackwell, 1962.
Muck, Terry. "Psalm, *Bhajan* and *Kirtan*." In *Psalms and Practice*, edited by Stephen B. Reid, 7-27. Collegeville, Minnesota: The Liturgical Press, 2001.
Myers, Lyn B., and Nazanin Derakshan. "The Repressive Coping Style and Avoidance of Negative Affect." In *Emotional Expression and Health: Advances in Theory, Assessment and Clinical Applications*, edited by Ivan Nyklíček, Lydia Temoshok and Ad Vingerhoets, 169-84. New York: Brunner-Routledge, 2004.
Nasuti, Harry P. "The Sacramental Function of the Psalms in Contemporary Scholarship and Liturgical Practice." In *Psalms and Practice*, edited by Stephen B. Reid, 78-89. Collegeville, Minnesota: The Liturgical Press, 2001.
Neufeld, Vernon H. *Reconceiving Texts as Speech Acts*, Biblical International Series. Leiden: E.J. Brill, 1994.
Neve, Lloyd. "Realized Eschatology in Psalm 51." *The Expository Times* 80, no. 9 (1969): 264-66.

Nunan, David. *Introducting Discourse Analysis*. Edited by Ronald Carter, and David Nunan, Penguin English Applied Linguistics. London: Penguin Books, 1993.
Ogelsby, William B. *Biblical Themes for Pastoral Care*. Nashville: Abingdon Press, 1980.
Ostriker, Alicia. "Psalm and Anti-Psalm: A Personal Essay." www.sbl-site.org/Newsletter/04_2003/Ostriker.html.
Paloma, Margaret M. "The Effects of Prayer on Mental Well-Being." *Second Opinion* (January 1993): 37-51.
Paloma, Margaret M., and Brian F. Pendleton. "The Effects of Prayer Experiences on Measures of General Well-Being." *Journal of Psychology and Theology* 19, no. 1 (1991): 71-83.
Pargament, K. I. *The Psychology of Religion and Coping: Theory and Practice*. New York: Guilford Press, 1997.
Parker, Paul P. "Suffering, Prayer, and Miracles." *Journal of Religion and Health* 36, no. 3 (1997): 205-19.
Patrick, Carol L., and Katherine Dychman. *Inviting the Mystic, Supporting the Prophet: An Introduction to Spiritual Direction*. New Yoke: Paulist Press, 1981.
Patterson, David. "The Religious Aspect of Bakhtin's Aesthetics." *Renascence* 46, no. 1 (1993): 55-70.
Patton, John. "Pastoral Ministry in a Fractured World." *Journal of Pastoral Care* 42, no. 1 (1988): 26-36.
Peterson, Eugene H. *Answering God*. San Francisco: Harper and Row, 1989.
Pleins, J. David. *The Psalms: Songs of Tragedy, Hope, and Justice*. Maryknoll, New York: Orbis Books, 1993.
Polanyi, Michael. *Knowledge and Being*. Chicago: University of Chicago Press, 1969.
———. *Personal Knowledge: Towards a Post-Critical Philosophy*. Chicago: University of Chicago Press, 1958.
Quesnell, Quentin. "Interior Prayer and Ritual Drama." *Dialogue and Alliance* 3, no. 4 (1989-90): 64-70.
Quinn, Kenneth. *How Literature Works: The Nature of the Literary Experience*. Sydney: Australian Broadcasting Corporation, 1982.
Rappaport, Roy A. *Ritual and Religion in the Making of Humanity*. Cambridge: Cambridge University Press, 1999.
Reid, Stephen Breck. *Listening In: A Multicultural Reading of the Psalms*. Nashville: Abingdon, 1997.
———. "Power and Practice: Performative Speech." In *Psalms and Practice*, edited by Stephen B. Reid, 40-58. Collegeville, Minnesota: The Liturgical Press, 2001.
Renkema, Jan. *Discourse Studies*. Amsterdam, The Netherlands: John Benjamins Publishing Company, 1993.
Renner, H. P. V. "The Use of Ritual in Pastoral Care." *Journal of Pastoral Care*

23, no. 3 (1979): 164-74.
Richards, Douglas G. "The Phenomenology and Psychological Correlates of Verbal Prayer." *Journal of Psychology and Theology* 19, no. 4 (1991): 354-63.
Ricoeur, P. *Essays on Biblical Interpretation*. Edited by Lewis S. Mudge. Philadelphia: Fortress Press, 1980.
———. *The Rule of Metaphor, Multidisciplinary Studies in the Creation of Meaning in Language*. London: Routledge & Kegan Paul, 1978.
Ritzema, Robert J. "Attribution to Supernatural Causation: An Important Component of Religious Commitment?" *Journal of Psychology and Theology* 7, no. 4 (1979): 296-93.
Robbins, Martha A. "The Divine Dance: Partners in Remembering, Revisioning, and Reweaving." *The Journal of Pastoral Care* 51, no. 3 (1997): 337-47.
Ross, James F. "Job 33:14-30: The Phenomenology of Lament." *Journal of Biblical Literature* 94, no. 1 (1975): 38-46.
Roth, Andrew. "'Men Wearing Masks': Issues of Description in the Analysis of Ritual." *Social Theory* 13, no. 3 (1995): 301-27.
Russell, D. S. "Body Language in Worship and Prayer." *The Expository Times* 112, no. 4 (2001): 123-25.
Sabourin, L. *Psalms*. New York: Alba, 1974.
Saliers, Don E. *Worship as Theology: Foretaste of Glory Divine*. Nashville: Abingdon, 1994.
Saur, Marilyn S., and William G. Saur. "Transitional Phenomena as Evidenced in Prayer." *Journal of Religion and Health* 32, no. 1 (1993): 55-65.
Savran, George. "How Can We Sing a Song of the Lord?" *Zeitschrift Fur Die Altetestamentliche Wissenschaft* 112, no. 1 (2000): 43-58.
Scarry, Elaine. *The Body in Pain*. Oxford: Oxford University Press, 1985.
Schaller, Joseph J. "Performance Language Theory: An Exercise in the Analysis of Ritual." *Worship* 62 (1988): 415-32.
Searle, John R. *Consciousness and Language*. Cambridge: Cambridge University Press, 2002.
———. *Speech Acts: An Essay in the Philosophy of Language*. Cambridge: Cambridge University Press, 1970.
Shannon, Martin. "'A Certain Psychological Difficulty' Or a Certain Spiritual Challenge: Use of the Integral Psalter in the Liturgy of Hours." *Worship* 73, no. 4 (1999): 290-309.
Sheppard, Gerald T. "Theology in the Book of Psalms." *Interpretation* 46 (1992): 143-55.
Siegel, D.J. *How Relationships and the Brain Interact to Shape Who We Are*. New York: Guilford Press, 1999.
Simpson, John Weiner, Edmund, ed. *Oxford English Dictionary*. Edited by John Simpson and Edmund Weiner. 20 vols, London: Oxford University Press,

1989.

Smith, Barbara Herrnstein. *Poetic Closure*. Chicago: University of Chicago Press, 1968.

Smith, Jonathan Z. "To Take Place." In *Ritual and Religious Belief*, edited by Graham Harvey, 26-50. London: Equinox, 2005.

Soskice, Janet Martin. *Metaphor and Religious Language*. Oxford: Clarendon Press, 1985.

Steere, Douglas V. "Prayer in the Contemporary World." Willington, Pennsylvania: Pendle Hill Publications, 1990.

Stoeber, Michael. "Evelyn Underhill on Magic, Sacrament, and Spiritual Transformation." *Worship* 77, no. 2 (2003): 132-51.

Stucky-Abbott, Curtis. "The Development of the Therapeutic Self within the Pastoral Person." *Journal of Supervision and Training* 13 (1991): 49-62.

Sutherland, Anne V. "Worldframes and God-Talk in Trauma and Suffering." *The Journal of Pastoral Care* 49, no. 3 (1995): 280-92.

Sweetman, Robert. "Thomas of Cantimpré: Performative Reading and Pastoral Care." In *Performance and Transformation*, edited by Mary Suydam and Joanne Ziegler, 133-67. New York: St Martin's Press, 1999.

Swinton, John , and Harriet Mowat. *Practical Theology and Qualitative Research*. London: SCM Press, 2006.

Tam, Ekman P. P. "Faith Development Theory and Spiritual Direction." *Pastoral Psychology* 44, no. 4 (1996): 251-64.

Tanner, Beth LaNeel. "How Long O Lord! Will Your People Suffer in Silence Forever?" In *Psalms and Practice*, edited by Stephen B. Reid, 143-52. Collegeville, Minnesota: The Liturgical Press, 2001.

Texter, Lynne A., and Janine M. Mariscotti. "From Chaos to New Life: Ritual Enactment in the Passage from Illness to Health." *Journal of Religion and Health* 33, no. 4 (1994): 325-32.

Todorov, Tzvetan. *Mikhail Bakhtin: The Dialogical Principle*. Translated by Wlad Godzich. Vol. 13, Theory and History of Literature. Manchester: Manchester University Press, 1984.

Tolson, Chester L., and Harold G. Koenig. *The Healing Power of Prayer*. Grand Rapids, Michigan: Baker Books, 2003.

Tostengard, Sheldon. "Psalm 22." *Interpretation* 46, no. 2 (1992): 167-70.

Townsend, Loren L. "Creative Theological Imagining: A Method for Pastoral Counselling." *The Journal of Pastoral Care* 50, no. 4 (1996): 249-363.

Tracy, David. "The Hidden God: The Divine Other of Liberation." *Cross Currents*, no. Spring (1996): 5-16.

Trueman, Carl R. *The Wages of Spin: Critical Writings on Historic and Contemporary Evangelicalism*. Edinburgh: Christian Focus Publications, 2004.

Tull, Patricia K. "Bakhtin's Confessional Self-Accounting and Psalms of Lament." *Biblical Interpretation* 13, no. 1 (2005): 41-55.

———. "Let Evil Speedily Hunt Down the Violent: Reflections on Troubling

Psalms in Turbulent Times." Louisville, Kentucky: Louisville Seminary, 2004.

Turner, Victor. *The Forest of Symbols: Aspects of Ndembu Ritual*. Ithaca: Cornell University Press, 1967.

Ulanov, Ann, and Barry Ulanov. *Primary Speech: A Psychology of Prayer*. London: SCM Press, 1982.

Vall, Gregory. "Psalm 22:17b: 'the Old Guess'." *The Journal of Biblical Literature* 116, no. 1 (1997): 43-56.

VanKatwyk, Peter, L. "Healing through Differentiation: A Pastoral Care and Counseling Perspective." *The Journal of Pastoral Care* 51, no. 3 (1997): 283-92.

Wallace, Howard Neil. *Words to God, Word from God*. Aldershot: Ashgate, 2005.

Watson, P.J., J. Trevor Milliron, Ronald J. Morris, and Ralph W. Hood Jr. "Locus of Control within a Religious Ideological Surround." *Journal of Psychology and Christianity* 14, no. 3 (1995): 239-49.

Weiser, Artur. *The Psalms*. London: SCM Press, 1962.

Wendland, Ernst R. *Analyzing the Psalms*. Dallas: Summer Institute of Linguistics, 1998.

West, William. *Spiritual Issues in Therapy: Relating Experience to Practice*. Basingstoke: Palgrave Macmillan, 2004.

Westermann, Claus. *Praise and Lament in the Psalms*. Edinburgh: T. and T. Clark Ltd., 1981.

———. *The Praise of God in the Psalms*. Richmond, Virginia: John Knox Press, 1965.

———. *The Psalms: Structure, Content and Message*. Translated by Ralph D. Gehrke. Minneapolis: Augsburg, 1980.

———. "The Role of the Lament in the Theology of the Old Testament." *Interpretation* 28, no. 1 (1974): 20-38.

Wheelock, Wade T. "The Problem of Ritual Language: From Information to Situation." *Journal of the American Academy of Religion* 50, no. 1 (1982): 49-71.

Whitehead, James D., and Evelyn Eaton Whitehead. *Shadows of the Heart: A Spirituality of Negative Emotions*. New York: Crossroad, 1994.

Williamson, H. G. M. "Reading the Lament Psalms Backwards." In *A God So Near: Essays on Old Testament in Honor of Patrick D. Miller*, edited by B. A. Strawn and N. R. Bowen, 3-15. Winona Lake, 2003.

Willimon, William H. *Worship as Pastoral Care*. Nashville: Abingdon, 1979.

Wolterstorff, Nicholas. *Divine Discourse: Philisophical Reflections on the Claim That God Speaks*. Cambridge: Cambridge University Press, 1995.

Woolery, Alison, and Peter Salovey. "Emotional Intelligence and Physical Health." In *Emotional Expression and Health: Advances in Theory, Assessment and Clinical Applications*, edited by Ivan Nyklíček, Lydia Temoshok and Ad Vingerhoets, 154-68. NY: Brunner-Routledge, 2004.

Bibliography

Wren, B. *Praying Twice: The Music and Words of Congregational Song*. Louisville: Westminster John Knox Press, 2000.

Author Index

Alter, Robert, 26
Anderson, Herbert, 14, 17, 18,19, 22, 23, 36
Austin, J.L., 42, 43,44
Bakhtin, Mikhail, 29, 30,31, 76, 77, 93
Billman, Kathleen D., 4, 75, 79, 82, 83, 86, 87, 90
Blommaert, Jan, 24
Boivin, Michael J., 93
Briggs, Richard, S., 42, 45
Brock, Gary 22
Brown, William P., 26, 27, 28, 77
Broyles, Craig C., 10, 34, 58
Brueggemann, Walter 4, 8, 11, 25, 39, 74, 79, 80
Buber, Martin, 25, 29, 58, 77, 78, 93, 94, 199
Byrne, Patricia Huff, 41
Calvin, John, 3
Canda, Edward R., 14, 19
Capps, Donald, 80
Cohen, Cynthia, 47
Cohen, David J., 3, 6, 13
Coursey, Robert D., 100, 101
Craghan, John F., 76, 77
Craigie, P.C., 53
Crites, Stephen, 19, 20
D'Aquili, Eugene G., 95, 96, 97, 98
Davis, Ellen F., 53, 79
Day, James, 42, 44, 45, 46, 73
Driver, Tom F., 14, 15, 16, 17, 20, 21, 23, 29
Epperly, Bruce G., 47
Farmer, Kathleen A., 35, 71
Finney, John R., 46
Foley, Edward, 14, 17, 18, 22, 23, 36
Fulghum, Robert, 85
Furnham, Adrian F., 100
Gay, Volney P., 47, 48

Gerstenberger, Erhard S., 4, 10, 27, 35, 37, 38, 72, 105
Gorman, Margaret, 92, 96, 97, 98, 99
Gunkel, Hermann 4, 5, 9, 12, 37
Hall, Todd W., 92, 96, 97, 98, 99, 102, 103, 118, 224, 226
Hine, Virginia H., 20
Hughes, Graham, 40
Hughes, Richard A., 80, 81, 84, 85, 88, 90
Jackson, Laurence E., 100, 101, 199
Jacobsen, Rolf, 78, 83
Jakobson, Roman, 29
James, W. 46
Jennings, Theodore W., 15, 16, 19
Jenson, Robert W., 23
Jumonville, Robert Moore, 84, 85, 90
Kelcourse, Felicity Brock, 49
Kelley, Paige H., 64
Kraus, Hans-Joachim, 4, 13, 51, 115
Kubicki, Judith Marie, 42, 44, 45
Kübler-Ross, Elizabeth, 80
Kugel, James, 26, 27
Ladd, Kevin, 47, 49
le Roux, Jurie H., 28, 45
Levine, Herbert, 17, 29, 30, 31, 77, 92, 93
Lewis, Leslie C., 26, 32, 39
MacCormac, Earl R., 28
Maloney Jr, H. Newton, 46
Marcum, John P., 99, 100
Mariscotti, Janine, 21
May, Gerald, 95, 103
May, Rollo, 93
Mays, James L., 33, 71, 72, 114
McDarrgh, John, 94
Meisenhelder, Janice Bell 99, 100
Merton, Thomas, 3, 94

Author Index

Meserve, Harry C., 48, 49
Migliore, Daniel L., 4, 76, 78, 79, 81, 82, 83, 86, 87, 90
Miller, Patrick D., 36, 48, 77, 80
Mitchell, Christina E., 102
Mitchell, Leonel L., 18
Mitchell, Nathan D., 39
Moore, R. Kelvin, 115
Mowat, Harriet, 40
Mowinckel, 13
Muck, Terry, 89
Paloma, Margaret, 48
Pendleton, Bruce, 48
Polanyi, Michael, 98
Quesnell, Quentin, 21
Quinn, Kenneth, 29
Rappaport, Roy A., 16, 17
Renner, H.P.V., 10
Reid, Stephen B. 78, 82, 89
Renkema, Jan, 24
Richards, Douglas G., 101
Ricoeur, Paul, 11, 26
Ritzema, Robert J., 96
Robbins, Martha A., 39, 82, 83
Saliers, Don E., 81, 85, 88
Saur, Marylin S., 47
Saur, William G., 47
Searle, John, 42, 43, 46
Simpson, 52, 53
Smith, Jonathan Z., 17
Soskice, Janet Martin, 28
Spilka, Bernard, 47, 49
Sutherland, Anne V., 40
Sweetman, Robert, 21, 22
Swinton, John, 40
Tanner, Beth LaNeel, 78, 82
Texter, Lynne A., 21
Tull, Patricia K., 30
Turner, Victor, 15, 16, 17, 22, 85
VanKatwyk, Peter L., 85
Wallace, Howard Neil, 87
Weiner, Edmund, 52, 53
Weiser, Artur, 4, 12, 13
Westermann, Claus, 8, 9, 11, 12, 25, 26, 32, 37, 38, 57, 64, 67, 70, 77, 99

Wheelock, Wade T., 29, 42, 45
Whitehead, Evelyn Eaton, 97
Whitehead, James D., 97
Woods, Robert 84, 85, 90

Subject Index

Abandonment, 64, 78, 148, 159, 161
Action research, 4, 6, 7-9, 56, 58, 100, 131, 187-188, 198, 204, 206-207, 209, 219
Affective, 30, 104, 105-106
Affirmation of confidence, 70, 72, 109, 126
Alienation, 23, 36, 58, 64-65, 73, 76, 148, 165
Asserting, 6, 37, 41, 44, 54, 57, 65-66, 68-69, 72, 87, 108, 110, 114, 122-124, 161, 196, 199-202, 217
Assertion of innocence, 65, 69, 108, 199
Authenticity, 9, 10, 14, 37, 138, 213
Awareness, 21, 33, 43, 57, 64, 66, 101-102, 105, 111, 133-134, 142, 150, 155, 158, 160, 163, 166, 172, 180, 183, 186, 192, 203-204, 213, 245
Birth, 56, 58, 72-73, 139, 224, 230
Cognitive dissonance, 64, 85, 91, 104, 186, 210
Community, 10-11, 14, 16, 20, 38, 65, 68, 76, 79, 83, 86, 89, 92, 97, 123, 126
Complaint, 11, 13, 26, 54, 60, 63-65, 86, 88, 108, 189, 199, 216, 232-233
Confession of sin, 65, 69, 108, 199
Constellations, 40-41, 44-45, 54, 57, 59, 77, 81, 87, 89, 108-109, 114, 117, 121-125, 127, 136, 141, 145-146, 149, 154, 157, 161, 167, 170-171, 175, 179, 182, 188, 191, 193-194, 198, 202-203, 210, 212, 216, 218, 224-225
Cultic, 11, 14-15, 25

Depression, 87-88, 106, 127, 142, 146, 168, 172, 180, 185, 196, 219
Dialectic, 9, 10, 26-28, 34-36, 38-39, 43, 53, 62, 64-65, 73, 77-81, 84, 87, 114, 188, 191-193
Disappointment, 134, 138, 146, 158, 164, 168, 172, 176, 180, 186, 214
Discourse, 6-7, 26, 28, 30-35, 39-40, 45, 53, 191-193, 195
Discourse analysis, 6-7, 26, 39
Disorientation, 12-13, 28, 68, 91, 189, 206
Divine response, 40-41, 59, 69-70, 73, 92, 95, 109, 152, 169, 172, 198, 201, 215
Efficacy, 4-7, 10, 12, 15-16, 18-19, 21, 29, 50, 53, 55, 84-85, 92, 110, 115, 129, 133, 135, 188, 190, 198
Emotion, 3, 10, 17, 23, 28, 30, 32, 39, 78, 79-80, 106, 122-123, 125, 133, 138, 145, 161, 179, 196, 199, 201, 209
Enemies, 10, 13, 26, 27, 34, 38, 40, 65, 68, 70, 77-78, 80, 101, 123, 134, 136, 139, 144, 161, 166, 169, 178, 193, 196, 197, 200, 204, 207, 215, 232-234
Expressing, 6, 10-12, 15, 23, 27-28, 31, 36, 39, 41, 44, 50, 51-54, 56-57, 59, 63-66, 82, 86-89, 104, 108, 109, 110, 114, 122-125, 133-134, 136, 138-139, 140-144, 153, 157, 161, 163-166, 168, 173, 175, 178-179, 184, 192, 197, 198-201, 207, 212, 214, 217, 225
Forgiveness, 143, 152, 199, 209, 217

Subject Index

Framework, 5, 7, 13, 40, 54, 56-57, 118, 144, 164, 179, 191, 193, 194, 203, 219, 220-221

Generalized distress, 6, 13, 85, 91, 132, 220

Grandiosity, 146, 163, 168, 172

Hymnic blessing, 73-74, 109

Imagining, 6, 27, 42, 44, 54, 57, 73, 74, 76-77, 109-110, 114, 122, 123, 125-126, 136-137, 149, 156-157, 161-162, 170, 173-174, 177-179, 201-202, 215, 218, 224-225

Imprecation, 26, 69-70, 72, 80, 109, 123-125, 135, 164, 186, 196, 200, 215

Individuation, 102, 209, 215

Instability, 150, 159, 168, 172, 176, 186

Internalizing, 151, 167, 194

Interview, 7, 115-116, 119-120, 131-138, 140, 142-144, 147-151, 153, 155, 157, 161, 163-164, 166, 168, 169-170, 172-178, 180-181, 186, 189, 190, 194, 195, 204, 212, 218, 236

Intrapsychic, 13, 51, 77-78, 107, 147, 151

Investing, 6, 41, 44, 54, 57, 69, 71, 72, 87, 108, 110, 114, 122-123, 125, 161, 200-202, 215

Invocation, 59, 62-64, 108, 199

Journal, 7, 121, 132-135, 137-139, 140, 142-144, 146-148, 150-156, 158-165, 168-170, 172-178, 180, 182, 185-187, 189, 191-192, 194-197, 199, 201, 204, 207-208, 210-212, 217, 219, 226

Journaling, 115, 119, 120-122, 130-135, 138, 140, 144-145, 149, 151-152, 154-155, 160, 163-169, 171-172, 174, 176-177, 179, 186, 192, 194, 211-213, 215-216, 218-221, 236

Judeo-Christian, 3-4, 15-16, 41, 43, 82, 85-86, 93-94, 114

Lament, 3-7, 9-14, 22, 24, 27-29, 33, 38, 40-46, 54, 56-59, 62-63, 65, 69-70, 74, 76-102, 108, 110, 112, 114-117, 120, 122, 124, 127-128, 131, 136, 141, 144-145, 147, 154, 157, 161, 164, 170, 172, 179, 182-183, 186, 188-189, 192-195, 198, 203-207, 210, 214-216, 218, 220-221, 223-226, 228, 236

Levels of distress, 100, 108-109, 120, 127, 210-214, 216, 238

Literary form, 6-7, 41

Liturgy, 15-16, 25, 48, 80, 83, 85

Locus of control, 7, 63, 100, 109-110, 113, 120, 127-128, 137, 142, 144, 146-148, 150, 154, 158, 163, 168, 170, 172, 176, 180, 183, 185, 200, 210, 214-216, 218, 246-249

Matrix of lament, 5-7, 9, 41, 54, 57, 76-78, 81, 89, 100, 108, 114-115, 128, 136, 186, 193-194, 220-221

Meaning-making, 9, 20, 24, 39, 40, 42-47, 52-54, 84, 92-96, 98-99, 104, 107, 112, 115, 121, 135, 139, 155, 159, 183, 188, 193, 195-196, 207, 212-213

Meditation, 30, 51, 130

Metaphor, 19, 30, 39, 65, 192

Mimetic, 44

Mythic, 19, 20-21, 39

Narrative, 19-21, 24-26, 28, 30-32, 34-35, 39, 43-44, 53, 73, 92-93, 102, 114-115, 192-193

Orientation, 12, 28, 92

Parabolic, 19-21, 39

Pastoral, 4-6, 82, 89, 90-91, 115

Performative, 29, 45, 48

Personal distress, 4-5, 7, 10-11, 15, 19, 20-23, 25-26, 30, 33, 36-37, 39, 42-44, 49, 52, 54, 56, 76, 80-81, 83, 85-86, 89, 93-94, 96, 98, 100, 105, 108-109, 112-115,

251

119, 122, 124, 126, 135-136,
138-139, 144, 147, 149-151,
154-156, 158, 160, 164, 167,
169, 172, 175, 179, 181, 183,
184, 188-189, 191-192, 194-
196, 198, 201-205, 209-212,
214, 217-218, 220-222, 224-
225, 236
Petition, 40, 50, 65, 68-70, 74, 87,
199, 217
Plea, 12, 26, 37, 47, 52, 62-63, 65,
68-70, 78, 108, 110, 123-126,
147, 199-200, 207, 217, 225
Poetic, 26-32, 34-35, 39, 44, 53,
114, 192-193
Polyphonic, 34, 88
Power, 12, 16, 18, 28, 39, 44, 48,
50, 59, 63, 68-69, 72, 79, 80, 95,
124, 126-127, 147, 161, 206,
214-215, 218, 230, 242
Prayer, 4-7, 9, 11-13, 15, 36, 37,
40, 44-45, 48-54, 56, 62, 68, 79,
81, 87, 90, 92-93, 95-98, 100,
103, 106-107, 109-110, 114,
116-118, 121-122, 124-125,
130-132, 134-136, 139-141,
143-146, 149, 151, 153-154,
156-157, 160-166, 168-172,
174, 176-179, 184, 188, 190,
193, 195-198, 202, 206-210,
212, 214, 218, 220, 222, 224-
226, 228, 232-236
Psalter, 3-6, 9-11, 14-16, 25, 29,
31, 40-41, 44, 53, 82-83, 89, 96-
97, 114, 141, 145, 221-222
Psychodynamic, 5-7, 11, 29, 41,
51, 54, 57, 77, 81, 89, 100, 102,
107, 109, 110-111, 113-115,
117, 120, 127-129, 132, 182,
185, 188, 210, 211, 214, 216,
220, 225
Psychometric testing, 7, 116, 120,
131-132, 137, 145, 149, 154-
155, 162, 171, 175, 180-182,
184, 186, 200, 218-219, 249
Psychometric tests, 7, 117, 120,

132
Realistic acceptance, 142, 146,
158, 163, 172, 180
Re-authoring, 27, 53
Reflection, 7, 20-21, 26-27, 30, 44,
46, 49, 52-53, 57, 79, 84, 89, 91-
94, 96, 98-99, 104, 106-107,
111-112, 115, 120, 122-124,
127, 129, 131-133, 135-138,
143, 145, 147-148, 150-152,
156-157, 159, 161, 163, 165-
166, 168-174, 176-177, 180,
184, 190, 192, 194-200, 202-
203, 205-207, 209, 212-214,
221, 224-226, 236
Reorientation, 12-13, 28
Ritual, 5-7, 9, 11, 14, 16, 17-25,
29-30, 32, 35, 38-39, 41, 44-49,
51-54, 79, 89-93, 98, 100, 103-
108, 110, 112, 114, 115-118,
120-121, 132, 135-136, 139-
140, 144, 149, 153, 157, 160,
162, 164, 171-174, 176-177,
179, 183, 185, 188-191, 195-
196, 203, 206, 210, 216, 220-
222, 224-226, 236
Sacramental, 25
Security, 17, 89, 92, 134, 136, 162,
164, 179, 183, 190-191, 205,
216
Self-control, 36, 110, 134, 139,
160, 165, 183, 214
Self-reflection, 153, 166
Sense of relationship, 23, 50, 62,
64, 101, 111, 113, 120, 128,
139, 152, 161, 167, 197, 203,
210, 211, 216-218, 238
Sitz im Leben, 4, 10, 14
Social, 19, 45, 77, 79, 203, 204
Speech act theory, 6-7, 29, 45, 47-
49
Spiritual Assessment Inventory,
117, 120, 128, 131, 137, 141,
145, 150, 154, 158, 163, 167,
171, 175, 180-182, 219, 243,
250-252

Subject Index

Subsymbolic, 105-106, 210
Transformation, 6, 16, 19, 21-24, 26, 95-96, 104, 106, 114, 191, 197
Tripartite relationship, 35, 37, 39, 65, 72, 81, 84, 85, 127, 135, 178, 192
Validation, 15, 83, 85, 95, 151, 156, 162, 192
Verbalizing, 29, 49, 196, 197, 199, 210
Violence, 36, 72, 92, 233
Vow, 40, 73, 74, 109, 125
Womb, 56, 58, 72, 114, 221, 224, 230
Worship, 4-5, 15, 25, 42, 59, 76, 86, 97, 114, 231, 235

www.ingramcontent.com/pod-product-compliance
Lightning Source LLC
Chambersburg PA
CBHW050437240426
43661CB00055B/2414